MEET ME IN

Paris

A MEMOIR

Juliette Sobanet

Saint Germain
press

Cover design, interior book design,
and eBook design
by Blue Harvest Creative
www.blueharvestcreative.com

Edited by Andrea Hurst

Author photography by Carl Israelsson

Lyrics for "The City of Lights"
written by Juliette Sobanet, sung by Marie So,
Copyright © 2015, Carioca Productions,
Distributed by Coop Breizh

MEET ME IN PARIS
Copyright © 2015, Juliette Sobanet

Published by
Saint Germain Press

ISBN-13: 978-0692582558
ISBN-10: 069258255X

Visit the author at:
Website: *www.juliettesobanet.com*
Blog: *www.confessionsofaromancenovelist.wordpress.com*
Facebook: *www.facebook.com/AuthorJulietteSobanet*
Twitter: *www.twitter.com/JulietteSobanet*
Also on: *www.bhcauthors.com*

 Visit Juliette's website by scanning the QR code.

ALSO BY JULIETTE SOBANET

PARIS ROMANCES
Sleeping with Paris
Honeymoon in Paris
Kissed in Paris

PARIS TIME TRAVEL ROMANCES
Midnight Train to Paris
Dancing with Paris
One Night in Paris

CONFESSIONS NOVELLAS
Confessions of a City Girl: Los Angeles
Confessions of a City Girl: San Diego
Confessions of a City Girl Boxed Set (Books 1-2)

For Karen, my writing angel.
You are the brightest star in my sky, and I love you.

~ And ~

For James Shea, who, when I began writing this book,
reminded me: "Speed over Safety."

TABLE OF CONTENTS

UN PETIT MOT DE L'AUTEUR ~ A NOTE FROM THE AUTHOR

This is a work of creative nonfiction. I have detailed the events that take place in this book to the best of my memory. I have also consulted with many of the individuals who appear in the book, and I have referred to information kept in my own journals, letters, and e-mails. It is possible that individuals portrayed in this book may remember these experiences differently. I have crafted the dialogues in the book to convey the essence of what I remember being said and what I remember feeling. I have changed the names of some of the individuals in this book, and I have also altered various identifying details, such as physical appearance, profession, and place of residence, in order to preserve anonymity of those involved. A few select locations in the book have been changed as well, with the exception, of course, of Paris and every other city in France that is mentioned. I have occasionally omitted people and events, and in the interest of the narrative, I have created occasional composites. This story is my own, and as such, it is subject to the imperfections of my own memory.

LA PRÉFACE DE L'AUTEUR ~
FOREWORD BY THE AUTHOR

LET IT be known that I originally intended to tell this story under the guise of fiction.

It's so much easier that way, hiding behind my characters' questionable choices, their hidden desires, their passionate love affairs, their sweet triumphs, and most embarrassing catastrophes. Throw in a few murders and some time travel, and no one could possibly think I'm telling the story of my own life...right?

Readers may speculate, but they will never really *know* with total and complete certainty that the heroine is based on—*gasp*—me! Will they?

Up until the day when I finally decided to take the memoir plunge, I'd been infusing my romance novels with bits and pieces of my own life stories. I know many other authors who have hidden behind their fiction as well, weaving tiny pieces, or perhaps big sweeping moments of their lives into their novels.

I give my journeys to my characters, let them face my battles. If I can't tie up my own love stories into neat little bows of happily ever after, at least I know my characters can.

So, I started writing the novel, the story that would loosely—*ahem*—be based on the most intense, heartbreaking, passionate years of my life. I wrote the prologue and the first fifty pages, and I pitched the book to my agent and my publisher as fiction. I went so far as to put my protagonist in a coma so that even *she* wouldn't have to face her demons.

Talk about hiding behind my art.

But each time I opened the document, I couldn't write past the first few chapters.

Something essential was missing. Something monumental...

Ahh, that pesky little thing I have been going to such lengths to avoid: *The Truth.*

I've always admired women who have the courage to write their true stories on the page and release them to the world: Elizabeth Gilbert in *Eat, Pray, Love* and *Committed*; Jeannette Walls in *The Glass Castle*; Susanna Sonnenberg in *Her Last Death*; Cheryl Strayed in *Wild*; Jewel in *Never Broken*; and Anaïs Nin in all of her diaries, but especially the one that has touched me the most—her tragically beautiful love affairs in *Henry and June.*

Their stories have been my bible for the past few turbulent years of my own life.

What a powerful gift these writers have given us. The gift of truth. The gift of knowing that we are not alone in the grand, epic chaos of our lives. Of knowing that we all share in the universal experiences of loving deeply, facing tragic loss, failing miserably, and somehow, with or without grace, peeling ourselves up off the floor, and trying again.

Until recently, I had no interest in sharing my own imperfections with the world. Nor did I care to share the story of my own personal heartbreaks, my irrational loves, my tragic losses...and the questionable choices that led to those major impasses in my life.

But these days, this is the *only* story that pours from me. It surges through my veins, keeps me up at night, begging to bleed its ink onto these pages and fill up the empty space with the only thing that matters to me anymore: being purely, unabashedly, unapologetically *me.*

As a writer, I must honor this creative intuition. This artistic passion that bursts forth from some invisible line between reality and imagination.

Otherwise, what am I doing here?

And so, for better or for worse, wedded as I am to my craft, I have decided to write the story in my heart.

The story that is mine.

The story that is ours.

The Truth.

Le Prologue

NO MATTER the season, no matter the weather, love is *always* in the air in Paris.

And tonight is no different.

The autumn sun has been swept away by a splattering of gray clouds, blanketing the city's cobblestone streets in one of those inky, mysterious Parisian nights where lovers' secrets will be swept away by the choppy waters of the Seine, or captured whole by the Gothic towers of Notre Dame, or better yet, swallowed up by the bottle of red wine my own lover and I are sharing in a charming little bar near Châtelet.

Yes, I've taken a lover.

In Paris.

A Paris lover.

Oh, how I adore the taste of those delicious words.

The Merlot slips past my lips, smooth and rich, as I smile at this most disarming man I have by my side. I give him a look that is both coy and inviting, in lust and falling—well, more like plummeting—headfirst and harder than ever before.

It is only the third time we've been together, and already, this lover of mine has hopped on a plane from Chicago to spend a few days with me in Paris.

I'm not sure if he understands how much his presence by my side, in my beloved city, means to me. Or how each touch of his strong hands, each adoring smile, each endearing tilt of his head is healing this broken heart of mine.

Divorce has a way of shattering hearts like nothing else. And mine is no exception. It has only been a few months since I left my husband—the man I have loved for twelve years, the man I still love, despite my choice to leave our dying marriage—and I know these days in Paris with my lover will be my only happy ones for some time.

We've spent this crisp fall day strolling hand in hand along the hilly streets of Montmartre, devouring *croissants aux amandes* and *pains au chocolat*, stealing kisses in abandoned courtyards, sipping espresso at hilltop cafés, flirting with every word, every breath, and falling ever so hopelessly in love.

Although neither of us wants to admit it yet.

As my lover drinks his wine, he gives me a sly look that says, *Get up, go to the bathroom, let me slip off your jeans, and I'll take you right here, right now.*

I haven't known him that long, but I know what his looks mean.

"We're only a few blocks from our flat in the Marais," I say to this insatiable man. "And besides, French bathrooms are *so* tiny."

"That's a few blocks too far," he replies, sliding his hand up my thigh. "And *you're* so tiny. I think we'll be just fine."

"*Lover.* You'll just have to wait." I smack his hand, loving the way he wants me so.

The truth is, in the days since I left my marriage, I've been ravenous for affection, for sex, for love. A lioness let out of her cage. Raw, powerful, and in need.

I would let my lover take me anytime, anywhere. And he knows it.

But I *so* enjoy teasing him.

Suddenly my older, playful lover becomes all serious, taking my hand.

A long silence stretches between us as he holds my gaze. I have a feeling that whatever is coming will probably make me cry.

Finally, he speaks.

"No matter what happens with us in the future, whether you're finished with me after Paris or we can't stay away from each other for the rest of our lives, promise me...*promise me*...that at some point in the next five years, we'll meet again in Paris."

I glance down at my lover's silver wedding band, not meaning to, not wanting to, but my eyes go there, if only to remind myself of the reality of our situation. That I am falling in love with a man who is mine and who isn't mine. A man who is healing my heart and ripping it apart, all at the same time.

I can't stop the tears from rimming my eyes as I look up into his intense green gaze, the gaze that unhinges me completely, unravels my heart, makes me do all sorts of things I never would have dreamt of doing before he stormed into my life.

Or before *I* stormed into *his*.

It is here, lost in his eyes, where I forget all about my wounded heart.

"Hmm. Me, you, Paris, in the next five years..." I hesitate, pretending to consider my options.

"Promise me," he demands as he squeezes my waist and pulls me close so he can run those deadly lips of his along my neck.

He can't get enough of me; since the day I met him, he never could.

"Yes. I promise," I whisper, once I've caught my breath.

And then his lips find mine in this bar in Paris, where no one knows us, where no one recognizes the romance writer and her lover, holding on to each other, making promises we aren't sure we can keep, but making them all the same.

When we dash out of the bar moments later, I wonder how many secrets the wind is carrying as it whips past, waltzing over cobblestones, rustling through trees.

Quite a lot, I imagine, in a city this grand, a city this thrilling, a city so gloriously full of love.

Partie I

La Liaison ~ The Affair

"And yet, to say
the truth, reason
and love keep little company
together nowadays."

~William Shakespeare,
A Midsummer Night's Dream

Chapitre 1

THREE MONTHS EARLIER

I AM standing—no, *drowning*—in a sea of romance writers, and I'm lost. Totally, devastatingly lost. Not because I am an outsider; I've been writing romance novels since I was twenty-four years old, and I was pouring through bridal magazines with my mom—an eternal lover of fairy tales—for the ten years before that. I grew up watching Patrick Swayze woo Jennifer Gray on the dirty dance floor, wishing I could step into her sexy silver heels for just one night.

I've been in love with falling in love since I was a little girl.

But today, at this writers' conference where I am surrounded by over two thousand bubbly, bouncing, excited female novelists—okay, yes, one or two male romance writers have braved this conference, but in this moment, as I'm about to lose my shit, I see and hear only estrogen—I am lost because my own happily ever after, *my marriage*, is over.

No, I haven't actually made the move yet. I haven't told the man I fell in love with at nineteen, the man with whom I have built a life and all the sorrow and joy that entails—I haven't told this man that I want a divorce.

Yes, he knows I'm unhappy. Our exhausting fights over brunch and late at night in our bed and early in the morning at sunrise when everyone else in San Diego is riding a surf board or doing down dog by the ocean or sipping their kale smoothies are proof of this extreme unhappiness I am lugging around like a tattered fifteen-year-old suitcase with one wheel and a broken zipper.

But what my husband *doesn't* know is that every night, as he falls asleep, I've been reading titles on my Kindle such as: *Should I Stay or Should I Go?* by Lundy Bancroft and Jac Patrissi, *Deal Breakers* by Bethany Marshall, *Contemplating Divorce* by Susan Gadoua, and more.

Half of the time, after I turn off my inconspicuous e-reader at night, I slither to the other side of the bed, as far away from my husband as I can get, imagining a life free of all the mini prisons and marital hells we've created in our sunny San Diego apartment that overlooks an expansive canyon and sits only a few miles from the Pacific Ocean. I'm amazed that our love, which was once as sure as the sunrise that floats over our canyon each morning, could become this tarnished in a place so breathtakingly beautiful.

The other half of the time, I wrap myself around my husband, my anchor, almost to the point of smothering him, and I cry, silently, as I try to imagine a life without his love. A life without his kind smile, his warm bear hugs. His innocent, wounded blue eyes that have melted me and protected me since the night we first met in the eighties room of a DC dance club when we were only kids.

He doesn't know I've been waking at 4 a.m. for months now, shooting out of bed with my eyes peeled open, terrified that *this* has become my life. That *this* contemplating whether to stay or to go is really *real*.

That I could actually, truly consider leaving him. My rock. My love.

My husband.

When we stood on a cliff overlooking the Pacific Ocean eight years ago and pledged our eternal vows to one another, I never, *ever*, thought it could come to this.

But here I am, on my third glass of wine, at my annual romance writers conference—which used to be my absolute favorite work event of the year—dying inside and pretending to be happy and successful and *fabulous!* I'm wearing a killer black dress and a sexy pair of heels. I'm thinner than I've been in years, and I'm smiling.

Always smiling!

No one would know that I feel like I may actually be sick right here, right now, on this ugly hotel carpeting. Or that I may pass out. Or burst into tears. Or all three simultaneously.

I am completely gutted because I know, down to the core of my being, that it's over. It's been over for me for a while now, and I've just been too terrified to admit this truth to myself, let alone admit this truth to my husband. I fear that in doing so I will shatter him.

And what about me? I am already a shell of the woman I used to be, and I am certain that if I stay in my marriage much longer, even that thin, eroding shell will crack. Who will I be then?

I'm still staring at that ugly hotel carpeting, willing myself *not* to make it even uglier, when Sarah, a total sweetheart of a woman I met earlier that day at the conference, approaches.

"So, Juliette, what are you working on right now? Another Paris book?"

Not even her motherly Texan drawl can comfort me tonight. If I dare open my mouth to respond, I'm going to start crying.

We're at that point.

"Sarah, I'm so sorry, would you excuse me? I'm supposed to be meeting someone at the bar, and I think I just spotted her." I hope she isn't offended, but I also know full well that I am in no state to keep anyone else comfortable right now when I can barely stand on my own two feet.

I dash off and circle the hotel bar, shielding my bloodshot eyes from all the writers, editors, and agents who are talking a mile a minute, their incessant chatter turning the dull pulsing in my head into a deafening roar.

And it is in this lost, devastated, barely functioning state that I first see him.

A tall stranger with sweeping dark hair and piercing green eyes that shoot through the crowd and land on mine all too quickly.

I have to go to him, I think as I feel my weak hobble turn to a stride, then to a strut. The intensity with which I am drawn to this man reminds me of the way Nicolas Cage's and Meg Ryan's characters are drawn together in the movie, *City of Angels*, a film I've watched at least fifteen times. I've always been enamored with the choice Cage's character, Seth, makes to give up his place as an angel in heaven and dive into a painful human existence just to be with Maggie, the woman he loves, played so perfectly by Meg Ryan.

To feel her skin, to taste her lips, to make love to her, he makes the ultimate sacrifice: he gives up eternity.

The way Seth loves Maggie is the way I've always wanted to be loved. It is the way *I* love. I give and I give and I give, often to the point of losing myself in the process, which is partly why I have arrived at this distressed, reckless point in my life.

I barely know who I am anymore.

Of course, as I approach the mystery man in the hotel bar, I give no indication as to the storm of emotions brewing inside of me. I remain calm, cool, and enticing—once again appearing *fabulous!* when underneath it all, my life is falling apart.

He is chatting with a few authors I know, which provides the perfect opportunity for me to slide right into the conversation.

Soon, my hand is sliding into his, and our lives, for better or for worse, have collided.

As soon as our skin touches, I know that it is more—*much more*—than his striking gaze or sexy physique that is pulling me to him like a magnet.

It is the feeling that everything in my life—the joy and the heartache, the love and the disasters—has led me to this moment. This moment where an alluring stranger's smile lights me up so brightly that for an instant—brief though it may be—I feel something I haven't felt in months: *hope*.

"Juliette's a beautiful name," he says.

"How—?"

He nods down at my name badge.

"Oh, right," I say, feeling a flush creep up my neck. I am about to reveal my real name and tell him that Juliette is my pen name, but something stops me. I've been hiding behind Juliette since my first novel was published two years ago. Why stop now?

"I'm Nick," he says.

"I've always wanted to name one of my characters Nick," I tell him. "Well, Nicholas, but Nick for short."

He lifts a brow, takes a step closer to me. "Will this Nicholas character be the hero or the villain?"

"Hmmm...depends," I say, loving how quickly this turned into flirtatious banter.

"I guess I better behave myself then, huh?"

Judging by the sly grin on his face, I can see that this man has no intention of behaving himself.

I wonder if he can see the fire in my eyes, the way I want him, already, in these first seconds of knowing him.

I wonder if he has any clue how dangerous this will be for me.

Or for him.

Because I sure as hell don't.

IT TURNS out that Nick is in town on business and just happens to be staying at the same hotel that hordes of sex-crazed romance writers have taken over.

How serendipitous.

It also turns out that Nick is married.

In that first moment that my hand slides eagerly into his, I take a quick peek at his left ring finger and notice a silver wedding band glinting beneath the fluorescent hotel lighting. Not more than a few seconds pass when Nick's eyes trace a path down the low V-neck of my dress to my waist and make a brief stop on my left hand, too.

I am still wearing the beautiful platinum diamond engagement ring my husband gave me on a rainy winter night two days before Christmas in Rockefeller Center. A flash of that night storms into my dizzy head, and although it feels like it happened a million years ago to a couple I barely know anymore, I can still see him—my adoring twenty-four-year-old boyfriend, down on one knee in the pouring rain, asking me to marry him.

The girl I see in this long-ago fairy tale is only twenty-two, and although she is far more mature than your average college graduate—having been weathered considerably by multiple parental divorces, a neglectful father, a shattered mother, and most recently the tragic death of her beloved cousin—she is still only a child. A child who has no idea that the love story she is about to embark on is one that will, at times, make her the happiest girl in the world, and at other times, make her lie in bed with silent tears streaming down her cheeks, wishing for a safe and easy escape route from the restricting confines of her marriage.

She has no idea, as she lights up and says *yes* with every fiber in her being, that this love will someday unravel her and transform her into a woman she no longer recognizes. A woman who can stand in front of a man she has only just met and be totally undeterred by the fact that he is married, or by the fact that she is married, and wish instead for something—*anything*—to take away her pain, if only for a night.

Chapitre 2

A FEW hours later, I have joined Nick and a few of his colleagues for drinks at a crowded dive bar down the street. Bon Jovi is blaring over the speakers as the two of us break from the group and squeeze into a corner booth. Once I've downed my second glass of wine, I find the courage to ask the question I've wanted to ask since I spotted the ring on his finger.

"So, how long have you been married?"

"Fifteen years," he replies, breaking eye contact and focusing instead on the large TV screen over the bar.

"Wow...fifteen years," I echo, thinking I should stand up and walk away *right now*, and wondering what the hell is wrong with me when my butt stays planted to the sticky booth.

I still want Nick more than I've wanted anyone or anything in years. His marriage and mine feel like they exist in a different universe—one that I have no desire to live in right now.

"What's your secret to marital bliss?" I ask.

He hesitates, finally lifting his eyes to mine. "The truth?"

"We'll probably never see each other again, so why not?" I say.

He throws back a sip of his gin and tonic before answering. "We both travel a lot for work, so we keep things open."

"Meaning...?"

"When we're home, we're together, and things are great. She's my best friend, and we've built a life together. A life that we both love. But the intimacy piece just isn't there anymore."

"That's normal after being together for so long," I say.

"It is...but I'm a man, and I still need it, you know?"

I nod, a little too vigorously. "*I know.*"

"My wife gets that. And we're not a jealous couple. We've both acknowledged that it's not realistic to think that we're only going to want to have sex with one person for the rest of our lives."

"How progressive," I say, wondering if this is the story he tells to get women into bed when he's away from home, or if he is, in fact, telling the truth.

Regardless, the idea that Nick may actually be in an open marriage *does* make me feel better about the fact that I have no intention of leaving his side tonight.

Nick nods toward my sparkly ring. "What about you? Happily married?"

"We used to be, yes. Really happy." I bite my lower lip. How do I even begin to explain the trajectory that has led to such a tragic, no-turning-back point in my marriage?

Finally, I say the only sentence that will come out of my mouth. "It's nearing the end."

"As in divorce?"

I nod, avoiding his gaze as I take an extra-long sip of my wine.

"Damn...I'm sorry." Nick's voice is tender and empathetic, a stark contrast to the rock music booming in the background, grating on my already frazzled nerves.

Nick's hand lands on my arm, snapping me out of my inevitable worst-case-scenario divorce thoughts.

"Want to get out of here?" he asks.

"I thought you'd never ask."

I'D NEVER done drugs before I met Nick. Never been allured by the rank smell of pot in my college dorm, or by the so-called thrill of seeing trippy hallucinations on acid, and certainly not by the dark, scary circles underneath my late cousin's eyes after the first time he tried heroin.

I didn't have much use for alcohol either after hearing the treacherous stories of my mother's childhood growing up with an abusive, alcoholic father, and experiencing firsthand the way that man destroyed my mom's ability to believe she could ever be worthy of love. I, too, was embarrassed as a young girl watching my own father show up intoxicated at family functions, or hopped up first thing in the morning on what he *said* was a few too many cups of McDonald's coffee, but what I later learned was likely a dose of something much stronger than caffeine.

I'd made it thirty-one years without experiencing the urge to drug myself on any kind of large scale, but on the night I met Nick, I was desperate. I'd been taking the occasional Xanax in my most hysterical moments, just so I could continue functioning in the world, writing my novels, meeting deadlines, and pretending to be okay with the downward spiral of my marriage, but that wasn't cutting it.

I needed more.

My personal heroin arrived on a silver platter in Nick's hotel room later that night. It came in the form of his thirsty lips, when they first pressed into mine. Oh, the relief I felt when he undressed me, when his strong hands wrapped around my waist, when he slipped my underwear down, and when he pushed into me from behind and held me so tightly that I could finally breathe.

Each time his lips traced my collarbone or his solid, forceful body moved over top of me, under me, inside me, all over me, my hungry veins became a bit more satiated, and the unbearable decision to leave my husband was pushed further and further from my mind.

Instead, endorphins swam through my brain, giving me euphoria, relief, and above all: hope.

Hope that there would be life after my marriage. That men would still want me, damaged as I was. That the big black cloud of depression which had been hovering tirelessly over my life for the past year and a half would dissolve one day, leaving sunnier skies in its place.

When we finally settle into bed together, Nick kisses me softly on the forehead and pulls me into his chest. I want to stay here forever, wrapped within him, protected from the harsh realities outside this hotel room.

I lift my face to his. Find his eyes in the darkness.

"I should probably tell you now that Juliette is my pen name," I say. "I'm really Danielle."

He laughs. "That makes so much sense."

"What do you mean?"

His hands roam beneath the sheets, finally resting on the small of my back. "I love the name Juliette, but it doesn't quite fit you. You're totally a Danielle. Beautiful, just like your name," he says, and then he kisses me again before we fall asleep in each other's arms.

That night, Nick's hungry kiss, his sweet words, and the feeling of him inside of me, wanting me, needing more of me, was my first dose of ecstasy, acid, marijuana, cocaine, and heroin all laced into one deadly handsome package.

For my first time on drugs, it was one hell of a ride.

Chapitre 3

IN THE morning, after two more marathon sessions, we are sitting on the fluffy white comforter in our underwear, eating berries, yogurt, eggs, and orange juice.

I am smiling, calm, and happy. I just had the time of my life with this man, and I feel like a completely new person. As we eat, we are chatting and laughing and talking about everything we love to do. I learn that Nick loves watching quirky films, traveling the world, reading everything he can get his hands on, going to the theater, and he even has an affinity for the art of dance. I can hardly believe my ears at this one.

"So, you actually *like* going to the ballet?"

"I do," he says before running his gaze down the length of my body. "You look like a dancer...Have you ever danced?"

"I grew up in the ballet studio," I tell him. "I started dancing when I was seven."

"So, you write novels, you teach French, *and* you're a ballet dancer?" He is shaking his head at me.

"What?" I say.

"Nothing," he says, stuffing a spoonful of berries in his mouth.

"What is it? You were going to say something."

"If I say this, it's going to freak you out."

"No, it won't," I tell him, dying to hear whatever he is thinking, and wondering if he too feels that *this*—whatever we have going on between us—is more than just sex.

Finally, he answers my silent question.

"You're the kind of girl I always *thought* I would marry," he says. "A dancer. An artist. A free spirit."

We are silent for a few moments, Nick's comment weighing heavily between us. I'm not good with awkward silences, so finally, I break ours.

"Well, I stopped dancing after college, when I got married. I've missed it for years, and I only just started dancing again."

Nick's hand slides over my thigh, giving me goose bumps.

"I would love to see you dance someday," he says.

I am momentarily taken aback by his words. Does this mean he wants to see me again?

"I think life is meant to be lived," he says, his lips hovering so close to mine that I can taste him. "I am a constant seeker of happiness, of adventure. I'm kind of addicted to it, I guess. I mean, why not get out there and experience everything the world has to offer, you know? Why limit ourselves?"

"Yes," I say. "*Yes.*"

I think about how *I* am the adventurer, the risk taker in my marriage, and how this quality of mine to constantly seek *more, more, more* out of life makes my husband uncomfortable. It is the source of so many of our arguments, and I know that if I am to stay in my marriage, I will have to stifle, suppress, and even suffocate this spunky, free-spirited side of myself; otherwise our disagreements will never end.

I smile at Nick, loving how everything about him embodies the *you-only-live-once* mentality, and I know that I am finished shutting down that part of myself. The freedom to explore, to travel, to *live* is vital to my existence, to my happiness. I won't let my marriage rob me of that any longer.

As I watch him lick the yogurt off the spoon, I figure that if I only have one life to live, spending one passionate night and one blissful morning wrapped up in the sheets with this beautiful man—when otherwise I'd be curled in a ball in my hotel room in a depressed, hysterical haze—will be worth whatever negative repercussions might come of it.

Of course I decide this while I am still drugged up on the sensual feeling of him and on our mind-blowing night together, so it isn't the soundest decision I've ever made, certainly. But right now, I don't care. I'm just so relieved to feel happy again, even if it is for a mere twelve hours.

"We really don't have *any* chemistry," Nick jokes, before feeding me a spoonful of blackberries.

I laugh, feeling so liberated. So sexy. So *me.*

"I don't think I've ever had *less* chemistry with someone," I poke back, knowing it is just the opposite.

After a few moments pass, Nick is glancing at me with a mixture of curiosity and lust in his big green eyes. He is over ten years older than me, but in this moment, he resembles a young boy who just took a trip to a candy store where topless women are handing out chocolate-covered caramels and French kisses.

"You have this look about you," he says, running his fingers through my long hair. "You're like a seventies beauty—natural, ivory, sexy. Like the models I used to be in love with when I was young..." He trails off, bringing his hand to my chin, examining my eyes with an endearing, sweet softness to his gaze.

Is this guy for real?

I can't even remember the last time a man said things like this to me, or made me feel so beautiful, so adored, so sexy. It's intoxicating.

"God, those eyes," he whispers, shaking his head as if he can't believe that *I* am real, that this is real.

When his lips meet mine, I hear the voice in my head rattling off its stern warnings: *Be careful. He's married. He's going home to his wife later today. Remember, this is a one-night stand and nothing more.*

But everything in my body is screaming *Yes! Yes! Fucking hallelujah yes!*

Our lips part and I smile at him. "Thank you," I say.

"Thank *you*," he says.

We continue feeding each other berries and yogurt until Nick breaks our sweet morning silence with a question.

"So you mentioned last night that you're thinking about divorce." He pauses, letting that sickening word tarnish the air in our little love nest. "Is it imminent?"

"Yes," I respond, knowing that I can be open with this man. After all, we are both married, yet here we are, finding ecstasy in each other's arms. Even though Nick told me he is happy with his marriage, I can only assume that after over fifteen years together and a decision to sleep with other people, he is no stranger to marital dissonance.

"Do you mind if I ask why?" he says.

"Well, there are a lot of reasons, of course," I begin, "but I guess the main problem is that we're simply not growing together. It's gotten to the point where all the things that make me happy and make me who I am—my writing, my passion for France, my free spirit, my love for my friends—all of these things trigger his greatest fears, and so we fight. I have to fight just to be myself. And I'm so tired of living this way."

We are silent for a few moments, and in the silence, I have the distinct feeling that Nick's marriage, for all of its obvious flaws, isn't nearly as weak as my own. And this only makes me feel worse.

"You're a strong woman, you know that?" Nick says.

I nod, not feeling at all strong when I think about what I'll have to do when I go home.

"It has to happen soon," I say firmly, more for myself than for him. "I can't go on much longer like this." My voice quivers, and I can see by the serious look on Nick's face that he understands how grave this is. How the worst is yet to come.

"Shit," he says.

"Yeah...shit," I echo.

I glance at his ring again, and this time, just looking at the silver band makes my stomach churn.

"So, with this open marriage thing you guys have, do you tell each other each time you...?"

"Are you worried I'm going to go home and tell my wife all about you?"

"Well...yeah," I admit. "I mean, she's still a woman. It can't make her feel good to know that you're meeting younger women and—"

"We don't keep each other posted on what happens away from home," he says swiftly.

"So, she never asks? And you don't ask her?"

"There's no point in telling each other what we do on the side. It's understood that it may happen sometimes, but what matters is that we love each other. I really do love her. I want to grow old with her. I hope we're married until we die."

This last sentence is like a knife to my heart.

When I walked down the aisle eight years ago, I hoped my husband and I would be married until we died too. I always used to tell him that we would go down like the two main characters in the movie *The Notebook*.

"One day when we're old," I'd say, "we'll lie in bed together, fall asleep holding hands, and cross over to the other side."

The idea of living even a day on this earth without him was unbearable.

Now the thought of staying in our marriage is unbearable. Yet, so is the idea of leaving him. I have to choose one or the other, though, and as Nick heads to the bathroom to shower, I take a long, hard look at my still glistening body in the mirror, knowing again that the choice I must make, the only choice I *can* make at this point, after this major betrayal, is to leave.

Maybe I jumped into Nick's arms precisely so I wouldn't chicken out. So I wouldn't turn back. Because now, after I've let another man take me to places I haven't been in my marriage for quite some time, how could I go back to my husband with any dignity or integrity and carry on as if nothing has changed?

After Nick showers, he emerges from the bathroom in his towel and jumps into bed with me once more.

"I'm going to be in LA in a month," he says with an enticing lift of his brow. "Any interest in coming to meet me?"

No. This was a one-time thing. My life will be too messy in a month to continue on with this affair.

But as Nick's hands slide over my hips and his ravenous eyes lock on mine, I know I am toast.

Chapitre 4

IT HAS only been six hours since Nick left town to go home to his wife, and I am already experiencing serious, sickening withdrawal. The idea that he is going home to a happy marriage, to his best friend, to the woman he wants to fall asleep next to until death whisks one of them away is making me feel insanely jealous and alone, as if every other married couple in the world has mastered what Nick and his wife have figured out—how to be happy together, stay sexually satisfied, and be honest with each other about the whole damn thing.

Why couldn't my husband and I have this sort of brutal but loving honesty with each other? Why must I constantly stifle my true feelings in order to keep the peace? To keep him comfortable and safe?

Why is it that Nick gets his happily ever after and I am going home to do the unthinkable—to be the deserter, to give up on the last twelve years, to leave the one stable man in my life who still loves me despite all my faults, and tumble headfirst into the unknown?

I wish I could disappear. Become a different person.

I don't want to face what is coming. I honestly don't know if I can.

I remind myself that my marriage isn't stable anymore—it hasn't been for some time. I remind myself that I've spent the past year and a half trying everything I knew how to do to fix us—couples' counseling, although we only made it through three sessions before my husband decided he didn't like the therapist and didn't have time to find a new one with me; seeing my own counselor each week in an effort to work through this extreme marital dissonance on my own; reading fertility books, changing my diet, taking herbs, and going to incessant doctor's visits by myself when my body wouldn't produce a baby for us; reading relationship books when ours seemed to be heading down the tubes; restructuring the way we handled finances so that the years of arguments over money would stop; restructuring *myself* in the hope that perhaps an upheaval of *me* would result in a happier marriage for both of us; learning how to own my personal faults in our disagreements, in the hope that we could, for once, have a productive discussion instead of another one of our exhausting arguments that ended with my head spinning and apologies rolling off my tongue, whether it was me who should have been apologizing or not.

Of course it wasn't only me who was trying—my husband tried to save us too, in his own ways. And yet, it feels as though all of this has been in vain because here we are. Here I am. Shivering in my hotel bed, popping another Xanax, and making frequent trips to the bathroom due to the painful urinary tract infection that has replaced the comfort of Nick's warm body.

I only have one more night left of my conference, and I wish with every fiber in my being that Nick could have stayed this last night, if only so I wouldn't be swallowed up by this ugly abyss of depression, terror, and self-loathing.

I've been through some serious heartache in my life, but *nothing* has prepared me for how badly this feels. And I haven't even told my husband that I want a divorce yet.

When I board the plane the next morning, shaky, exhausted, and sick, I know that the moment is coming.

A complete upheaval of my marriage, of my life, is imminent.

The thought that my husband doesn't know this yet sends tears pouring down my cheeks.

Who have I become? How is *this* my life?

As the plane takes off, I grip the armrests with every ounce of life force inside me, and I know there is nothing left to do except close my eyes and pray.

Partie II

LA LIBERTÉ ~ FREEDOM

"They slipped briskly into
an intimacy from which
they never recovered."

~ F. Scott Fitzgerald,
This Side of Paradise

Chapitre 5

I SPEND the next few weeks quietly planning my escape. Ironically, during this time, my husband and I are actually getting along—not on a deep level, but at least superficially. He takes this to mean that we are doing better, but I know we are only "getting along" because I have given up.

I've stopped asking him to change. I've stopped asking him to be a different person—a person who wants to travel with me, take adventures with me, explore life with me. A person who genuinely likes my friends, faults and all, and who understands that since I have little to no family support, my friends are, and always will be, my family. A person who supports my adoration for France and who understands that there is nothing wrong with my deep love for a place that has always made me feel so at home. A person who respects the compromises I need him to make concerning our complicated family dynamics.

A person who *hears* me.

My husband is a kind, beautiful person, and he loves me. Despite all of our *stuff*, despite the fact that I am constantly asking him to be a person he is not, and despite the fact that I am constantly fighting to be the person that I am, he loves me. But that love doesn't change the fact that he is not the person I need him to be, and I am not the person he needs me to be.

He is only content when I am pretending to be someone I'm not—a girl who fits into this restrictive little bubble we've built together, a girl who doesn't speak up when she's unhappy. And I can't be her any longer. Even though I love him, and even though he loves me, I have reached the point in this relationship where the love that has always bound us, differences and all, isn't enough to keep me here.

Since I've stopped asking him to change or to accept me for who I am, the constant ripples, waves, and tsunamis of arguments have also stopped. Which is why, at the moment, my husband feels like things are sailing along pretty smoothly.

I was already on my way out of the marriage before I met Nick, but finding such unbelievable chemistry and compatibility in his arms has only served to push me out the door not with a subtle shove but with a violent, I-must-have-more-of-*that* kick.

It's not that Nick himself is the *only* drug I am chasing. It is the feeling I had when I was with him—that I can be my free-spirited self, and he was enamored with me! With me being exactly who I am! I didn't have to pretend with Nick. After years of stifling my dreams and passions to keep my husband comfortable, and after this past year and a half of speaking up about who I am and fighting to be me, I now know for a fact that when I leave this marriage, there will be other men—Nick is perhaps only the first—who will embrace me for exactly who I am.

My night with Nick was only a glimpse of what is waiting on the other side, and I want more. I *need* more.

The week I return home from my writers' conference, I get an antibiotic from my doctor for my urinary tract infection, and I schedule an appointment with my counselor. I've been seeing her for the past year, and she has listened patiently, every single week, to my never-ending should-I-stay-or-should-I-go debate.

But today, as I walk into her cozy home office with a purpose, that debate is officially over.

"I'm leaving my husband," I announce. "And I need to prepare for the divorce, legally and financially."

She nods solemnly; she knows I mean business. And being a former attorney who has also gone through a divorce, she is the perfect woman to have in my corner.

"Do you have a paper and pen?" she says.

I pull my notepad from my purse, poise my pen over the paper. "Tell me what I need to know."

Over the next hour, we discuss the details of divorce—the main topic being that of my finances.

"California is a no-fault state," my therapist explains, "meaning that even if your husband finds out about your affair, all assets and debts—with the exception of student loan debt—must be split 50/50 unless a different agreement is reached. Even still, divorce can bring out the worst in people, and there is no way to know how he will react once you tell him you're leaving."

I have watched my own parents go through multiple dramatic, devastating divorces. The idea that our divorce could be even a fraction as difficult as theirs have been is too painful for me to imagine, yet, I know my counselor is right. I must be prepared for the worst.

The problem is, on the financial front anyway, I'm not in the best position to prepare for the worst. I'm not in the best financial position to even be *leaving* in the first place.

Last year, I experienced great success self-publishing my first two novels. In addition to making it possible for me to pay off over half of my massive student loan debt and quit my university teaching position so that I could write full-time, this success garnered the interest of a publisher, who then offered me a four-book deal. The deal included my first two originally self-published Paris books, which they would re-package and re-release; my third Paris novel, which—after two years of pouring my entire heart and soul into—was now complete; and a fourth Paris novel which I had yet to write. Then they offered me a second contract for *another* Paris novel, and finally, a third contract for a short Paris story.

Elated that all of my wildest publishing dreams were coming true, I said *yes!* to all three contracts, signed on the dotted line, and spent a year and a half writing my ass off on deadline and pre-paring for the release of my next books, which I hoped would be even greater successes than my first two had been.

Last week during the writers' conference where I met Nick, my third novel, the book of my heart, *Dancing with Paris,* was released to the world. On that same day, my first two self-pub-lished novels were also re-released.

With three novels all coming out in one day, and with the incredible track record my publisher has to take romance novels straight to the top of the bestseller's list, I was ready for a finan-cial windfall.

In fact, I was planning on that windfall. I was counting on it. I was *sure* of it.

But that windfall didn't come.

My release has not, in any way, compared to that of my peers who write for the same publisher. I know their sales numbers—in this day and age of social media blasts, their outlandish, mirac-ulous numbers are being thrown in my face daily. *50,000 copies sold! 100,000 copies sold! 1,000,000 copies sold!*

My release numbers are pitiful in comparison. To say this is a disappointment would be an understatement. And to say the tim-ing is terrible would be a *gross* understatement.

I am devastated and embarrassed at my low sales numbers. And I desperately need to earn out my book advance as quickly as possible so that I can begin earning royalties, the royalties I'd hoped would get me through this divorce.

But with my subpar sales numbers at release, it's clear I won't be earning out my advance for a long, long time.

This is the reality of being a writer. This is the reality of choosing an artistic career. The reality is that you can spend years—*fucking years*—creating something that is so dear to you, so important to you, something that is the truest reflection of your deepest, most intimate dreams, desires, and self, and this thing of beauty you've created may or *may not* provide you with an income to sustain you. No matter how much blood, sweat, and tears you've poured into your work.

One day you can be at the top of the world, selling thousands and thousands of books. And only a year later, you can be scrounging to pay your rent. Or in my case, planning a departure from my marriage and wondering how in the hell I'll be paying my bills in a few months.

This is the reality of being an artist.

The fulfillment must be found in the creation, and what follows is, oftentimes, largely out of your control.

I know I'm incredibly blessed to have reached the level of success in my writing career that I've already experienced at such a young age. I know this.

But today, as I'm running the numbers with my therapist and trying to figure out how I can pull $15,000 or $5,000 or even $1,000 out of my ass to hide away in the event that things get nasty in my divorce, I wish, with every minute I've spent writing in the last eight years, that my recent release had been more successful.

There is no one to blame, though. Sometimes publishers push your book to the masses, and sometimes they don't. Sometimes books fly off the shelves and sell millions of copies, and sometimes they don't. The publishing business can be fickle, and I can't waste my time blaming my publisher or myself or anyone else.

Here I am. The money I earned last year when my books were topping the charts is gone. And so, I have to work with what I've got. I have to trust that I'm a smart, resourceful woman, and that even though I don't have a safety net in the form of a massive savings account to draw from or a family who will help me financially, or anything at all to fall back on except my own determination, hard will, and talent, I am going to figure this out.

I have to face my bag-lady fears and just *fucking do it.*

"You don't have to rush this," my counselor says, as if she's reading my mind. "Things are calm at home right now, so it would be smart to get everything in order before you tell him."

"I will," I promise her, but I feel the end is storming closer each day, with a force all its own, a force even I cannot control any longer.

"Are you planning to ask for alimony?" she asks.

"No," I say firmly. "Money is such a hot topic for us, and I don't want this divorce to be all about that. If I ask for alimony, I worry that it will ruin any chance we have at staying kind and civil with each other throughout the process, and maybe even being friends down the line. Yes, he was the breadwinner, and I could certainly point out the fact that I followed him around the country for part of our marriage, and in doing so, I gave up the chance to have my own stable career during those years. But at the same time, he could argue that he supported me through all the years when I was teaching and writing, not making a lot of money and not getting a 'real job.' And he did support me. We *both* made sacrifices for each other, and I don't want this to be a war of who did more for whom and who deserves more money. I just want to split everything down the middle and try to keep this divorce as amicable as possible."

Before I leave, my counselor asks, "Are you going to tell your husband about Nick?"

I hesitate.

"What purpose will it serve?" I say. "It will only hurt him, and it's not like Nick is the reason I'm leaving my marriage. Sure, he has been a catalyst—*a big one*—for helping me realize how much I am truly ready to go, but I'm certainly not leaving my husband to *be with* my married-but-in-an-open-relationship lover..."

The lover I may see in only a few short weeks in Los Angeles...the lover I cannot stop thinking about...the lover who is sending me sexy e-mails, giving me butterflies, and making me remember what it feels like to be desired, wanted, and adored.

Okay, *perhaps* having this lover in the wings is playing a bigger role in my urgency to leave than I want to admit, but still, what purpose will it serve to tell my husband all of this? Besides driving a knife through his heart, it is a sure-fire way to make this divorce ugly. And I am still, against all odds, hoping for the best. Hoping he will understand that I am choosing to leave our marriage so that I can be myself and he can be himself without fighting about it any longer, and so that we can both have a chance to be happy again and grow in our own directions, wherever that may lead us. I'm hoping we can be kind to each other throughout the process and still, amid the hurt that leaving him will inevitably cause, part ways with some semblance of the deep love we have shared over the years.

"No," I answer, finally. "I'm not going to tell him."

OVER THE coming days, as I am spending all of my free time crafting a detailed Divorce Spreadsheet, filled with every last to-do item I must complete as I prepare for the end of my marriage, I am corresponding with Nick over e-mail daily.

I have officially agreed to bring my depressed, withering ass— yes, I am still waking up at 4 a.m., I am still crying like a maniac, and I am still barely eating—along with my entire arsenal of French lingerie, on a four-day Hollywood rendezvous with my married-but-in-an-open-relationship lover.

Even though I am not officially split with my husband, I will be soon. I know this is no excuse to betray him again, but this will be the last time. After this trip, once I have things as in order as I can possibly have them, I will leave him.

The week before I am to see Nick, I tell my husband there is a publishing event I must attend in LA. I know he would absolutely despise me if he knew what I was doing right now. But he isn't the type to check up on me or verify my facts. He barely pays attention to what I'm doing anymore. We are already living separate lives under one roof. Business partners who call each other husband and wife. This is a tragedy that happens far too often in marriage, in my opinion.

We have been this way for some time now.

And so, even though it is despicable, I tell the lie. And I hold onto my dream of the four glorious days to come in LA like a life vest.

I'll only go this once, I promise myself. Seeing Nick will be my gift for surviving the last year and a half of hell. For having the courage to both follow and break my heart at the same time. For preparing to take the boldest move of my life and not backing down. For being in the depths of the deepest depression I've ever experienced and still waking up in the morning and managing to function and take care of myself, even if it is only on a small level before I retreat to the shower or to my car or to a deserted path in the canyon to cry and howl and wish I could trade places with the coyotes, the deer, the owls, the birds.

They are free, after all.

In his e-mails, Nick is beside himself with excitement. He is counting down the days until we see each other, and so am I.

One week, six days, five days, four, three, two, one...

And finally, the day arrives.

Chapitre 6

I AM speeding up to LA feeling free as a bird. The windows are rolled down, my hair is flying in the breeze, and I'm blasting the girl power song "Womankind" by Annie Lennox as I sing along at the top of my lungs.

I'm wearing a short black-and-white polka dot dress that I bought in Paris with lacy French lingerie waiting not so patiently beneath, and for the first time in months, *I can breathe.*

As I near LA, the hot air wafting in makes me begin to sweat, but I know this is also nerves. I roll up the windows and blast the air conditioning, thinking about how fun it is to feel so sexy, scandalous, excited, and alive!

I am feeling so comfortable in my own skin right now, and I realize this is because the part of me that loves being a sexy vixen, the part of me that loves adventure and spontaneity and sex— *dear God do I love sex*—has been suffocating in the be-a-good-little-girl-and-follow-all-the-rules box. She has been gasping for air in the grow-up-get-married-then-have-kids box.

She has been dying a slow, painful death in a box she never truly fit into.

And finally, as wretched as it's been to plan my escape, to tell the lie, and to break out of that apartment, *I am free.*

Even if it is only for the next four days, I am free to be as fabulous and crazy and unpredictable as I freaking want to be! I'm free to drive myself to LA and strut into a chic Hollywood hotel and have sex all day and all night with my lover!

And so, that is exactly what I do.

WITHIN MINUTES of arriving in Hollywood, I have been transported to a glamorous new world complete with chandeliers, red carpets, limousines, and tons of twenty-somethings who look famous but probably aren't.

I love it.

Nick greets me at the door with a shit-eating grin on his face. He is wearing shorts that are just a little too short for my taste, and this reminds me of how much older he is than me. I feel just the slightest twinge of hesitation as he lets me into the room, but when his lips meet mine and his hands slither up my short dress and we find our way over to the cushy chaise by the window, I forget all about his shorts.

Our first time back together is certainly a romp to remember. He is mad about me, hungry for me, every inch of me. I can see it in his eyes, feel it in the way he touches me, holds me, kisses me. And I feel the same for him.

The two of us have been starved for passion, for affection, for an extraordinary connection, and so our coming together is nothing short of a dream come true.

While we are in the act, he pulls back for a moment, looks me in the eye. Breathless, he says, "I'm going to have to see you every month."

Even though I've promised myself this LA trip will be my only trip with Nick, in this moment, while he is inside of me, filling me with pleasure, I think this seeing him every month idea is the best one I've ever heard.

LATER THAT afternoon, we are lying naked in the sheets, talking and laughing the way we do so easily. The famous *Hollywood* sign is within view just outside our window, but the glitz and glam waiting beyond our hotel room don't concern me.

We could be in a barn in Oklahoma for all I care.

Simply feeling the warmth of Nick's skin on mine and watching the way his eyes light up when he talks to me is enough to keep me happy for the next decade.

"We must have been lovers in a past life," Nick says.

"What makes you say that?" I ask with a playful grin.

"We're so comfortable together. So natural. I feel like I already know you. I've never felt this with anyone."

"Do you believe in past lives?" I ask.

"I don't know," he says. "But this connection we have, feeling like I've found you again...it makes a strong case for them, don't you think?"

He's right about our connection, about this feeling that we've known each other for much longer than one night, one morning, and one afternoon in a hotel room. This is the kind of romance, the kind of connection I write about in my novels. Over the last several months, though, as the agonizing decision to leave my marriage has consumed my every waking thought, I began to think that the kind of chemistry and passion I was writing about in my books didn't exist outside the pages of a fictitious story. I began to think that the fairytales I'd been writing all these years were all a big load of crap.

It is only in Nick's arms, in his eyes, that I know again, down to the core of my being, that romance is alive in the world. It does exist.

And it is sublime.

"I wrote about past life lovers in one of my novels," I tell him.

"Really?" Nick asks, intrigued. "What's the story about?"

"It's about a woman who travels back in time to her past life where she was a scandalous cabaret club performer in 1950s Paris. She's the main suspect in a murder at the club, and she falls in love with the victim's brother."

"Oooh, ill-advised," he says with a grin. "What happens? Does she stay back in time with her lover, or does she come back to the present?"

"You'll have to read the book to find out..."

"I would love to read it," he says, not skipping a beat.

"Oh, I'm just kidding. My books are really girly. Not usually for the male reader."

"I'm serious," he says. "I would love to read everything you've written. I love how romantic and passionate you are. I'm sure it comes through in your writing."

I am taken aback that this hunk of a man would ever consider reading my romance novels, and so I am momentarily speechless.

"Did your husband read your books?" he asks.

I shake my head. "For years he didn't. I told him how much it would mean to me if he would just read one of them. I know they're not his cup of tea...but they're *me*. And for him to not read even a page of what I'd been working so hard to write all these years was really hurtful. But I'd been asking and asking and asking for so long, that by the time he finally did read one, it was too late. It's like begging someone to tell you they love you, and when they finally do, it doesn't mean as much—or anything, really—because you had to tell them to do it." I don't do a great job at hiding my disappointment over this sore point in my marriage. My writing is the truest reflection of who I am and all that I have experienced, desired, and wanted in life, and for my husband to have never truly shared in that with me—at least of his own volition—has been nothing short of devastating.

Nick takes my hand, squeezes it. "God, my heart hurts just hearing that. If my wife had written a book, I can't imagine not reading it."

"It's okay," I say, but it's not. And Nick knows it's not. But I don't want to waste our short time together discussing the myriad of sad reasons why my marriage is coming to an end.

"You and me," I say, placing a finger on Nick's chest, "we were definitely super-hot, secret lovers in a past life."

Nick laughs and kisses me. "I bet we'll still be hot lovers when we're old. We'll be crazy for each other at sixty, at seventy, at eighty."

I hop on top of him, smile down at his sweet face. "Like Anaïs Nin and Henry Miller. You think we'll be like them, do you?" I run my hand down his chest and try not to think about the complicated logistics of keeping a married-but-in-an-open-relationship lover for the rest of my life.

"I do," he says.

And then, just like they do in the romance novels, Nick envelops me in his strong embrace, paints me in kisses from head to toe, and makes love to me while a breezy hot evening settles over Los Angeles.

Chapitre 7

IT'S DAY two of our illicit Hollywood affair, and we have already turned the hotel room into our own personal love nest. We are lounging on the chaise by the window, wearing only our underwear and typing away on our laptops. It's a Friday, so we both still have work to do. But this doesn't stop our flirtatious banter.

"So, what are you working on now?" Nick asks me.

"I'm starting a new novella series called *Confessions of a City Girl.* They'll take place in different cities: LA, San Diego, DC, and Paris. And in light of this trip, I've decided to write the Los Angeles story first."

"*Confessions*...sounds like it could be scandalous," he says with a mischievous smile. This man clearly loves a good scandal. "What's the LA story about?"

"It's about a DC photographer in a failing marriage who meets an alluring investor at her first exhibit. He gives her an amazing career opportunity in exchange for spending one night with him in Hollywood," I explain. "So, *this* is technically a research trip for me."

Nick lifts a brow. "Ahhh, I see. So you're just using me to get inspiration for your next story."

"If you're lucky," I tease. "Although I might have to start writing erotica to keep up with you."

"I'm not the only one who wants it morning, noon, and night...and every second in between," he points out.

"Okay, scratch that—I'll have to start writing erotica to keep up with *us*."

"That's better," he says, pleased. "This is the most sex I've had in...God, I don't know how long."

"So, you and your wife...you never...?"

"It happens, but it's rare." Nick grows somber for this next part. "When I try to touch her, the way I touch you, she recoils."

"I'm sorry," I say, knowing full well what it's like to be years into a marriage and to watch that exciting, sexy spark you once had die a slow, painful death.

"It's sad," he says. "Because everything else is there. The love, the friendship, the compatibility. It's just that one piece that we've lost."

"It's normal." As I say this, I feel a wave of relief that I am on the verge of freeing myself from such a marriage.

"I know it's normal after this many years together," Nick says. "But it still sucks."

I move my laptop to the bed, and I slide up beside him, kissing his neck and landing on his lips. God, they taste good.

"For what it's worth," I tell him, "I think you are quite possibly the sexiest man I have ever laid eyes upon. You just do it for me."

At this, he lights up, his green eyes bright with that unadulterated joy he carries around everywhere he goes. "Damn, girl. Sometimes I think I'm dreaming you. And it's the best dream I've ever had."

It is lines like this that turn me to mush, that make me melt into a complete love bug right in front of my lover's eyes.

Luckily, he is an even bigger love bug who is melting just as much as I am.

As we spend the rest of the morning ignoring our work, I try to soak up each intimate moment, each sweet laugh, each soft and not-so-soft touch, knowing they are all gifts.

And I tell myself that I will be okay in three days when Nick heads home to his wife. When he is no longer by my side. When I must return home to initiate divorce hell.

I will be okay. I have no other choice.

Chapitre 8

THAT AFTERNOON, I am zooming past palm trees on Wilshire Boulevard, still on a high from my delectable morning with Nick, and even higher because I am on my way to a meeting with a Hollywood producer who wants to turn my first book, *Sleeping with Paris*, into a movie.

As the Southern California sun blazes in through the car window, my excitement turns into a nervous sweat, so I crank up the air conditioning and reach for my cell to dial Karen, my dear friend and critique partner who helped me take *Sleeping with Paris* from an extremely rough first draft and transform it into a publishable manuscript, and eventually, into a bestselling debut novel.

With her fabulous British accent and her witty British humor to match, Karen taught me how to infuse my novels with conflict, romance, and page-turning tension. She taught me how to persevere in the writing world and how to have fun in the process. But most of all, Karen taught me about the kind of woman I wanted to be—the kind of woman who takes joy in all the bits and pieces of life, and who doesn't complain about the parts we don't want to write about in our novels—those moments in life that make us cry ourselves to sleep at night.

And while Karen was one tough cookie, not at all the type to do just that—cry herself to sleep at night the way I have been doing for months now—she had, however, been experiencing far too many of those heartbreaking life moments as of late.

Just before I'd received the news that a producer wanted to read my first novel, Karen had received the news that she had an inoperable brain tumor.

My husband and I were living near Washington, DC, at this time, and just as I learned that Karen was sick, I found out that my husband was in line for a job transfer out to San Diego. We had been dreaming of moving back to California for years, but with Karen's ominous news, the timing was rough. I wanted to spend as much time with her as possible, especially if I would be leaving the East Coast soon.

I was with Karen in the hospital, holding her hand the day of her biopsy. We didn't yet know if it was cancer, but either way, a large tumor sitting right on the brain stem couldn't be anything but life-threatening. Karen didn't cry that day in the hospital, though. She never cursed at the sky, asking *why me?* Instead, she held her head up high, and did her best to talk to me about writing and agent submissions and the new storyline she was already crafting given this drastic change in life circumstances. All of this despite the fact that the tumor's placement on her brain stem was now affecting her speech, her vision, her motor skills—everything.

Karen's biopsy confirmed our worst fears—the tumor was, in fact, cancerous, and the most aggressive chemo and radiation would be necessary to keep her alive.

Within two months of her diagnosis, Karen went from being able to walk and talk like everyone else to being severely disabled. She now needed constant assistance to perform the most basic of tasks such as eating, walking, and using the bathroom. She couldn't type any more, which meant her writing days were officially over, and speaking became increasingly difficult too.

To watch my once vibrant friend—the friend who wore her elegant scarves to every writing meeting, who rocked the most fabulous dangly earrings, and who made being the mother of three boys look like a cake walk—make such a quick transformation to someone who needed care around the clock, was nothing short of agonizing for all of those closest to her, especially her husband of over twenty years and her three sweet boys.

So, when my books were topping the charts and the news arrived about my movie possibility, it was bittersweet. Karen had read, re-read, and read *again* every single scene in my first book too many times to count.

Simply put, that novel would never have been even close to publishable without Karen's guidance and editing expertise, and certainly not without all the love and energy she poured into our friendship and into helping me succeed in my career.

My book would never have hit the bestseller's list or garnered interest from a film producer if Karen had never come into my life.

And just as all of these amazing career happenings were sweeping through my world, Karen couldn't even bring her hands to a keyboard to write a coherent sentence.

It was irony at its worst.

But mostly, it was just sad.

Writing didn't matter. Bestseller lists were awesome, but they weren't going to fix Karen's illness.

I wanted Karen to live longer. I didn't want her to suffer. I wanted her to be able to walk and talk and write and dance again.

She was only forty-nine when the tumor stole all of this from her. It wasn't fair that this could happen to such an incredible person. To someone who was so loved. To someone I drank lattes with every week while we exchanged writing advice and life stories. To someone I depended on so much. To someone who lit up my world and the worlds of so many others.

But then, who ever said life was fair?

One day, I was visiting Karen at her home. We were cuddled up on her couch together, and I was trying to talk to her about things that would lift her spirits—new writing ideas and chocolate and the latest season of *Downton Abbey*—anything that would make her forget about cancer.

But then, in her slow words, she said to me, "I've had an amazing life. I had a wonderful childhood, I married the love of my life, I have three beautiful boys, and nothing bad has ever really happened to me. Everyone has *something*. Well, this is my thing. This cancer—it's the thing I have to endure. I'm lucky, really. I'm lucky that I've made it this far without anything big happening."

Her perspective amazed me. I wanted to wail at the sky and beg for my friend's life back.

But Karen didn't wail. She barely even cried. She was grateful for every moment, and she radiated nothing but love every single day, even on the hardest ones.

Right in the midst of Karen adjusting to life with cancer, my husband's job transfer from DC to San Diego was approved. So, off we went, across the country and three thousand miles away from my dear friend, only two short months after she'd been diagnosed with a terminal illness.

Soon, in that beautiful apartment overlooking the canyon, I was losing my marriage and I was losing Karen, but my career was the one thing that was still on track. So, I held onto it as tightly as I could.

Today, as I am driving into Beverley Hills to meet the producer, I know that I have Karen to thank for this moment. Writing really is a team effort, and without Karen on my team, I wouldn't be where I am.

I wait patiently while her phone rings and rings, hoping to hear her voice on the other line so I can share in this nerve-wracking, thrilling career moment with her. But, as it usually does, her answering machine picks up.

It's Karen's cheery British accent, her beautiful, radiant voice before the cancer ravaged it, telling me to leave a message.

And so, I leave a message to let her know I'm thinking of her and that I miss her. I don't say anything about my meeting with the producer or my imminent divorce or the affair I'm having. None of that matters. What matters is that I miss my friend. I love her. And I want her to know this, above all else.

As I hang up the phone and swallow my tears, I hope, with every fiber in my being, that she will still be here if and when my book—the story she helped me shape and carve into something readers actually want to read—becomes a movie.

She deserves to walk the red carpet. She deserves to shine.

I pull into the parking lot of the producer's posh Beverly Hills office, close my eyes, and swallow the anxiety and the sadness that are threatening to suffocate me, once again. Instead I think of my beautiful, fabulous friend, and I know what she would want me to do. She would want me to hold my head up high and strut into this producer's office and kick some serious *arse*.

So, with one stiletto out the door, I take my first step. And then another. I won't let her down.

Chapitre 9

WHILE I do feel quite glam sitting on the cushy couch in the producer's office wearing a chic new pair of tall pink divorce heels—or what I will soon call my *single and fabulous!* heels, à la *Sex and the City*—our meeting is much more relaxed and chill than I anticipated. The producer is wearing jeans and is just a cool, down-to-earth guy who knows the business like the back of his hand. Not at all the Hollywood experience I was expecting; I'm relieved.

After he read my book, the producer brought a well-known director onto the project, and the two went on the hunt for a screenwriter to complete the film adaptation. They didn't end up finding anyone who was up to the task, though, and while both the producer and director were still excited to make this happen, there wasn't much we could do without a script.

Since I was already in LA "visiting a friend," I set up this meeting in the hope of getting the ball rolling again. But I was nervous as hell that inside this shiny Beverly Hills office, the producer was going to tell me they'd done all they could do, and it was time to let this project go.

We've spent the past half hour discussing my writing career up to this point, and finally, when we reach the topic of the screenwriter search, my heart constricts.

"Without a solid script, we're at a standstill," the producer says.

And just when I think he's about to tell me it's all over, he asks me a question that I absolutely, in a million years, was not expecting.

"We need something to get the project moving again," he says. "So, what do you think about writing the screenplay on spec?"

"Me?" I ask, incredulous. "I...well...you do know I've never written a screenplay before. Only novels and short stories."

"A screenplay is eighty percent dialogue. Do you like writing dialogue?"

"I love it," I tell him.

"Well, your writing is strong and no one knows these characters and this story better than you. Why not give it a shot?"

"Yes," I say. "I'd love to give it a try." Despite my grim financial outlook, I don't, at the moment, worry about the fact that writing this script on spec means I won't get paid a dime for it until and *unless* we actually sell it. Because when everything else in your world is falling apart, and a Hollywood producer asks you to adapt your first novel—a novel he loves—into a screenplay, *you just say yes.*

"I'll help you along the way of course," he adds, "but I think you can do this. What do we have to lose?"

"Nothing," I say. "I'm in."

I'm in and I'm beaming. Positively beaming.

After we discuss logistics and next steps, we shake hands, and I strut down the hallway, willing myself not to start skipping and laughing until I am completely out of sight.

God, this past year has been hell, absolute *hell,* but now *this!* A lover who devours me *and* a chance to write the screenplay for my own book! Is this really happening?

After an emotional cry of victory in my car, I silently send Karen even more love, even more appreciation, for helping me write my first love story—a love story that may actually become a film, written by my own pen.

Next I pull out my phone and text Nick.

> Fabulous news from my meeting.
> Can't wait to share!

He writes back:

> You amaze me.
>
> Champagne will be waiting, you talented sexy vixen you.

Chapitre 10

A BOTTLE of chilled champagne and my lover's hungry lips are waiting when I arrive back at the hotel, but I am too nauseous to taste either of them.

I'm not sure what is going on, but somewhere between Beverly Hills and West Hollywood, cold sweats overtook my entire body and my stomach staged a revolt on the romantic evening I was supposed to be sharing with my lover.

Nick lays me down on the bed and hands me a towel filled with ice, which I press to the back of my neck. I close my eyes and will myself not to throw up in our chic love nest. It is only our second night in LA together, and I really don't want to spend it curled around a cold porcelain toilet. I want to spend it wrapped in Nick's arms.

Nick places a trash can next to the bed just in case, then lies down beside me and runs his hand over my belly.

"Could you be pregnant?" he asks.

I open my eyes, shocked at the softness in his voice. Shouldn't the mere idea of me being pregnant with his child make him want to run for the hills, given his marital situation?

But I don't find panic or fear in his beautiful eyes. Only sweet, genuine compassion.

"No," I say. "God, I hope not at least." I squeeze my eyes closed again as another wave of nausea seizes my insides. Oh, the irony if I were pregnant with this man's baby. After a year of trying to get pregnant with my husband, after being told it would be incredibly difficult for me to conceive without the aid of fertility drugs and test tubes, and then to become pregnant from sleeping with a married man who is never going to leave his wife? When I haven't actually *left* my husband?

Quite the plot twist *that* would make.

As Nick continues to hold me until the nausea subsides, I realize that there is still a part of me that wishes for a baby, or at least for some of those picturesque moments I'd always associated with being pregnant: the love of my life rubbing my belly, just as Nick is doing now.

Or picking out baby names, the way my husband and I did the very first month I went off birth control. I remember sitting on the floor of Barnes & Noble with him, thumbing through baby name books, laughing at all the ridiculous ones and agreeing that we would never name our child something bizarre or trendy.

We liked classic names like Charlotte and Patrick.

But baby Charlotte never came. And neither did baby Patrick.

Will they ever come?

For me?

Or for my husband?

I am a soon-to-be thirty-one-year-old divorcée with serious reproductive challenges. It's realistic that having my own child may never be in the cards for me. Especially if I continue to spend my time with a married man who has no intention of leaving his wife and committing to me.

Unless, of course, this nausea is actually a pregnancy symptom from all the raucous unprotected sex we had during our very first rendezvous.

I feel too sick tonight to even let myself ponder the thought of being pregnant right now, or worse, the thought of *my husband* having a child with another woman. To think about what an amazing, loving father he would have made—or may still make someday—is simply unbearable.

Yes, I am choosing to leave him. But I still love him. Even here, shivering in Nick's arms, I love my husband.

I am simultaneously relieved and devastated to be leaving our marriage.

And I am both thankful and shattered knowing that we are never going to have a child together.

Joy and heartache. Happiness and pain. Ecstasy and sorrow.

My every day, my every waking moment, is a constant mixture of these two extremes.

Perhaps this is why I am feeling so physically ill on one of the most exciting career days of my life. Because I no longer have a grasp on how to function *between* the extremes.

It's a dangerous place to live, constantly tumbling from a high to a low, then soaring back to a high, and plummeting, yet again, to an even lower low.

At least I know I'm alive, though. At least I'm not going to let myself die in the mediocrity and boredom of a life that doesn't fit me any longer.

As I fall asleep on Nick's chest, listening to the sound of his heartbeat, loving the way he has taken care of me so sweetly tonight, I know that beneath the highs and the lows, there is a deeper part of me that is thankful to be exactly where I am.

Without a baby. Preparing to leave my marriage. Exploring what it's like to take a lover.

What will come of me after my weekend with Nick?

I don't know.

But that's the beauty of taking life one moment at a time—it may be a wild success or a devastating disaster—I don't have a clue, and tonight, I don't have to.

THE SUN has just barely risen over the Hollywood hills when Nick wakes me.

"How are you feeling?" he whispers, nuzzling his nose into my neck, our bodies so entwined I don't know where mine ends and his begins.

"Better," I whisper back. "All better."

He takes this as the invitation I meant it to be and slides on top of me, spreads my legs, and finds his way inside.

"I could wake up like this with you every day," he whispers as he envelops me, steals me, makes me his.

I respond by pulling him closer, wrapping my legs tighter, letting him in deeper.

I could wake up like this with him every day too. But I don't tell him that.

After all, *every day* isn't an option for these two star-crossed lovers.

Chapitre 11

OUR FINAL day in Los Angeles unfolds as a series of glossy, beautiful moments that flow effortlessly one into the next. I take a mental snapshot of each one, knowing I never want to forget a single smile, a single touch, a single second with this adoring man.

He is, quite possibly, the best thing that has ever happened to me.

I know this, down to my core, as I lift my arms and let him soap up my satisfied, sweaty body in our steamy hot shower. As he rolls the bar of soap over my every curve, I memorize the striking picture before me: Nick's full head of dark hair as the water soaks him and trickles down his face, past that boyish but manly grin.

God, that grin just *kills* me.

And his wet black lashes, so long and barely blinking, as if he doesn't want to miss even a millisecond of my skin as he continues lathering, touching, feeling me.

I grab his face and kiss him on the lips, wanting him to know—to *feel*—how enamored I am with him. Then I brush my lips over his forehead, his eyelids, his cheeks, neck, and shoulders.

I take the soap from his hand and work my way down his tall, muscular body until I reach the part of him that is ready for me, again. Always.

I take him in my hands and in my mouth, loving the way he feels on my tongue.

He leans back against the wet tiles, lets me take him to a place that exists only for lovers. A place that neither of us ever wants to leave.

WE SPEND the rest of the morning recovering from our intense shower with a dip in the rooftop pool. I wrap my legs around Nick's waist, nestling into his smooth body as he wades through the water, holding me, kissing me, laughing with me.

Perched high above the city, we are weightless in this water.

Weightless but falling.

I wonder when we will hit the ground.

I am so high in his arms that I can't imagine—*don't want to imagine*—what it will feel like to come down. Thankfully, the poolside cabanas and palm trees are keeping us insulated from the harsh realities we don't want to face: from a sleepy, smoggy Los Angeles and a divorce that has yet to begin and a marriage that has seen better days.

A chilly morning breeze ripples over the water, giving me goose bumps. I am certain that even the fog in the air knows it's my last day with Nick.

As my lover pulls me in tighter, his hands melding around my bare thighs, the serious look in his eyes tells me his mind is going there too.

"I just had a really morbid thought," he says. "When I'm ninety and on my death bed, I'm going to think back to this weekend with you and how wonderful it was. I'll never forget it. In case I don't say it again this weekend—*thank you.*"

This is the most beautiful thing anyone has said to me in so long. This is the most passionate weekend I've had in years. And this is the most meaningful relationship to come into my life since I met my husband.

"Thank *you*," I say back, unable to articulate my gratitude in equal eloquence to his for fear of spilling tears and saying too much.

THAT NIGHT, we are strolling the darkened streets of Hollywood hand in hand when we pass by a little house with a neon sign that reads "Psychic" dangling over the door.

"Have you ever seen one?" I ask.

"Once," he responds. "In New Orleans."

"How was it?" I prod. I *love* this stuff.

He stops walking for a moment, and we both glance up at the big yellow full moon, hanging so low in the sky I feel like I could reach out and grab it.

Nick's gaze levels back to mine. "She read my palm and told me I would lead a double life."

A chill ripples down my spine. I know Nick has been having affairs for several years—affairs that he's allowed to have per the "hall pass" arrangement with his wife—but as his eyes burn into mine, I wonder if I—if *we*—are the double life his New Orleans palm reader was referring to.

"Have you ever had anything like this, like us?" I ask.

"No. With the others, it was always out of sight, out of mind. But with you...it's different. I've never wanted to keep seeing anyone more than a time or two. You're already the exception to the rule."

I know this is a compliment, but it's a dangerous one.

Just as we are passing by the psychic's door, I squeeze Nick's hand. "I wonder what she would have to say about us."

"Should we do it?" His voice is so eager that for a moment I have the feeling that he would not only walk through this psychic's door with me, but jump off a cliff, or run to the ends of the earth, as long as I was by his side.

I hesitate, wondering about our fate. Part of me wants to know our future, and the other part of me—the part that is afraid we don't have one—doesn't want to know a thing.

"Do *you* want to?" I say.

He cocks his head to examine the crooked sign, and when he finally turns back to me, I see the fear in his eyes. It's the first time I've seen him look scared since we met.

"I'm not sure I can handle it right now," he says. "But some day, if we're ever in New Orleans together, we have to do it."

"I have a writers' conference in New Orleans next spring." That's nine months away. Nine months too long.

"Spring...that's forever," he says. "What do you have going on next month?"

"Next month?" I've been so intoxicated with our sexy love affair this weekend that I'd completely forgotten. "Next month, I'm going to Paris," I reply with a smile.

It is a trip I'd planned long before the decision to definitively leave my husband. I will be spending the first week traveling through Paris and my other favorite French city, Lyon, with Katie, one of my closest girlfriends who's been dying to do this trip with me ever since motherhood swallowed her whole. After a week of excessive wine and chocolate croissant consumption, she will head back to the States to be with her husband and her little girl, but she won't be taking me with her. Instead, I'll be staying in France for another two and a half glorious weeks, visiting friends in Paris, Lyon, and the South of France.

I didn't invite my husband when I booked the trip because I've been inviting him for years, and with the exception of the one time he visited me in France during my undergrad study abroad over ten years ago, he has never wanted to come. In fact, my yearly trip to France has been the cause of many of our worst fights. It's as if he sees my love for France as a threat, a threat that will one day take me away from him.

The irony is that in not making an effort to share in this passion with me, and instead fighting me on it so fervently, my love for France *is* taking me away from him. My travels to Paris and Lyon have served as the ultimate escape from the prison our marriage has become for me.

But this will be my first trip to France as a free woman.

Nick's voice snaps me back to him, to us, to the big yellow moon sliding higher in the night sky.

"I love Paris," he says. "Want some company?"

Chapitre 12

I DON'T know if it's the possibility of Paris or the fact that it's our last night in LA together or the reality that this relationship has awakened the most sensual parts of me that I buried in a grave called marriage long ago, but whatever *it* is—I am ready to give Nick the night of his life.

Massive Attack's "Teardrop" is playing over Nick's portable speaker as I emerge from our hotel bathroom in a swirl of French lingerie, perfume, and skin. I've slipped into a lacy black and pink bra with a matching thong. A black garter belt wraps around my hips and stretches down to the sheer black thigh highs that span my legs. A sexy strut in my strappy silver heels takes me to my lover, who is sitting on the bed, looking as if he may actually die of pleasure at the sight of me.

"Fuck," he says, shaking his head. "You have got to be kidding me."

I am in full-on sex vixen mode as I straddle him and let him run his hands all the way up my legs, reaching around to grip my bare ass before he turns me around to get a better look.

With a hand on each cheek, he kisses the small of my back, then pulls back again to stare at my butt.

"I'm not a religious guy, but I am a worshipper of your ass. I mean...*fuck*. How is this even real?"

"It's the silver lining of divorce." I spin around to face him, my cleavage meeting his wide eyes. "The divorce body."

The divorce body Nick is raving over is a result of my being so depressed and anxious I can barely eat. Any excess fat I did have on my waist and thighs has melted off along with all the tears I've been crying. While this certainly isn't a healthy way to lose weight, I must agree with Nick—my firm yet still plump butt has never looked better.

Before Nick can say another word, this hungry divorce body of mine is dancing around him, underneath him, and over top of him, releasing years—*fucking years*—of pent up sexual energy, fantasies, dreams, and desire. Desire to be wanted and worshipped and touched the way Nick is doing as I strip him down and rub my lace-trimmed body all over his skin.

I have been a dancer all my life, but they never taught me how to move like this at the ballet barre. These sultry half-stripper-lap-dance/half-sexy-cabaret moves flow naturally from my sex-crazed body, my hips swaying and grinding into Nick, my legs wrapping around him, my hands running over my own curves, appreciating them in a way I never have before.

When the song winds down, Nick is grinning and breathless, his eyes clouded with lust. "That was the best five minutes I've had in years." He looks to the sky, raising his hands in praise. "Thank you, God!"

Next up on the playlist Nick created specifically for this night—specifically for *me*—is Phantogram's "Mouthful of Diamonds." It's the first time I've heard the song, but something about the beat and the lyrics transports me to another world—a world where I feel completely free to be purely, unabashedly me.

And who is this me who is wearing next to nothing as she takes the stage before her admiring lover? She is a woman who loves falling in love. A woman who loves sex and intimacy and romance, who loves music and dancing and writing and creating, and who is basking in the freedom of being able to share and express all of this with a man who totally and completely gets it.

This man gets me.

As I slide a bra strap down my shoulder, letting my breasts spill out for Nick to do as he pleases, I decide that even though he isn't mine, I will give him everything.

I will hold nothing back. I will give him all of me.

And that night, I do.

Partie III

La Rupture ~ The Split

"The course of true love
never did run smooth."

~ William Shakespeare,
A Midsummer Night's Dream

Chapitre 13

MY HOLLYWOOD affair with Nick—brief though it was—
lands me in the hospital.

My body's response to the intense stress I've been experiencing combined with the copious amounts of sex Nick and I shared
in such a short time frame is a continuation of that same raging
urinary tract infection that started during our first forbidden rendezvous, which, two days after I return home from our second,
has turned into a hurricane of pain in my abdomen.

I am doubled over on my bed, trying in vain to write, when
I realize the pain is too intense to even stand up. I call my doctor's office, but they can't see me for another few hours, and this
can't wait.

I still haven't worked up the courage to tell my husband I
want a divorce, but as he rushes home from work to take me to
the hospital, I know that heartbreaking talk will have to wait.

In urgent care, the doctor sooths me with Percocet while he
runs tests to see what is going on.

When I tell him about my urinary tract infection that has been lingering for weeks, he reminds me, "It is imperative to urinate immediately following sexual intercourse."

"I know," I say, wanting to bury my head beneath the sterile pillow, or better yet, descend into the hospital's morgue and never emerge. The urinating-after-sex rule is one I learned long ago, and one I clearly didn't follow in my reckless state over the weekend.

This is karma. Biting me in the ass. And I deserve it; I know that.

But I also know that I don't feel as guilty as I should, after what I've done. My husband is by my side in the hospital, and still I feel like a ghost woman—a hollow, torn-apart, lifeless shell of the woman I used to be with no intention of becoming human again and *just telling him the truth.* Besides my fear that admitting the truth of my recent affair will turn our upcoming divorce into a war—a war that I am not, in any way, prepared to handle—I've been so deeply unhappy in my marriage for so long now, that I am becoming numb to normal human emotions of guilt and remorse. For months, I have been detaching from my husband, from our life together, from the promises we made. Those promises feel null and void after the past few years of fighting, stress, and heartache.

How much more can I take before my body, my heart, my soul, will completely shut down?

As I lay on the hard cot in the urgent care clinic, I can feel that thin shell of a woman I've become cracking even further, shattering the caring, good person I once was.

I am of no use to anyone in this state. Not to my husband, and certainly not to myself.

Maybe the shooting pain in my abdomen is my body's way of waking me up, telling me that I must make a move soon; otherwise I am going to spiral even more out of control than I already have, which will only lead me to cause more damage to both myself and my husband.

After the doctor receives the test results, he explains that it is likely the infection has moved to my kidneys, which would explain the intense abdominal pain—as well as the nausea I was experiencing in the hotel room with Nick—but there is one other possibility that must be ruled out first: an ovarian cyst.

Two years before this foreboding trip to the hospital, I decided I wanted to have a baby with my husband. At this point, we'd been married for several years and although I had spent much of that time debating whether or not I actually wanted to hear the pitter patter of children's feet in our home, something inside me shifted that summer.

Sharon, one of my closest writing friends, had warned me this would happen. She was in her forties and happily married with twins.

"I didn't think I wanted kids either, and then one day, I woke up and I wanted a baby," Sharon told me. "I didn't just *want* a baby—I *had* to have a baby. It's like a switch went off inside me, and there was no turning back. It will happen to you, too. Just wait."

This whole biological-motherhood-switch thing sounded ludicrous to me. I had never been one of those women who knew she *had* to have babies, and I assumed I never would be.

But then, just as Sharon said it would, it happened.

I woke up one day, and I wanted to have a baby with my husband, a family of our own. We had spent so much of our time together catering to dysfunctional family members and trying in vain to keep them all happy, that we'd never had the energy or desire to create our own little family unit.

But I was done with all of that. And I felt it was time. It was *our* time.

It took a bit of convincing to get my husband on board with me—well, to be exact, it took what I called *The Baby Spreadsheet*.

Even though we were financially sound at the time, I knew my husband's main concern would be money. His intentions were pure—he only wanted to save for our future and keep us financially stable. Being the intelligent, talented, motivated man he is, he did just that for our little family of two.

Then, there was me. The dreamy, adventurous, romantic, and at times, highly impractical writer. Despite the fact that I grew up with bill collectors harassing my mom over the phone, cars being repossessed, bankruptcy being filed, and a myriad of other financial disasters constantly in motion while I was too young to have a say in the matter, I still operated in a world of optimism and hope for the best case scenario and a firm belief that things will always work out financially because my husband and I are two competent, resourceful individuals. This optimism didn't always change the cold, hard numbers, though, and that's where my husband's practicality came in.

There were times when I needed him to bring me back down to earth so that I didn't get us into financial trouble, and in turn, he needed me to make him remember that we were always more than *okay,* that we had everything we needed, and that it's perfectly normal to dream and to spend a portion of our hard-earned money on an experience that will enrich our lives and create memories. Which is exactly what I hoped a baby would do for our little family.

Since I knew him so well and didn't want to spend hours arguing over what he might see as my unfounded, unresearched proposal to have a child together, I knew exactly what I'd need to do to convince him we were baby-ready.

Enter: *The Baby Spreadsheet.*

I called all of my friends who'd had babies and asked them to give me estimates of every cost associated with the first year of baby's life—diapers, clothes, doctor's visits, formula in case I couldn't breastfeed, etc. I then compiled all of this information into The Baby Spreadsheet, forming a complete budget of what our finances might look like during our first year with baby. My friends thought this was the most ridiculous thing they had ever heard. When they wanted babies, their husbands did too. Then they had sex and got pregnant. Or paid over $10,000 to do IVF, and *then* they got pregnant.

Either way, there was no spreadsheet involved.

But I loved my husband dearly and after so many years waking up together each morning and going to sleep together each night, I knew what made that man tick. I knew that he needed to *see* the numbers to be sure that we had what it took to bring another human being into this world.

Upon careful examination of The Baby Spreadsheet, and after listening to all of my long-winded arguments about why it would be so wonderful for us to start our own family *now*, my husband finally agreed.

Not exactly the romantic, lying in the sheets, "let's make a baby" conversation I was hoping for, but it still did the job. And I had no doubt my husband was going to be the most loving and attentive father on this earth, so whether that decision came from a spreadsheet analysis or before a romp in the sheets, who cared? We were going to have a baby!

And so, I went off the pill and we decided we wouldn't "try" or worry, we'd just let it happen when it wanted to happen.

Six months after I went off birth control, I missed my period. I was having strange sensations and sharp pains in my lower abdomen, and I thought this meant I was pregnant. All of my pregnancy tests were showing up negative, but I was still certain it had to be a baby.

I dragged my husband to my gynecologist's office to have her run an official pregnancy test. He asked if he really needed to come into the scary room with the metal utensils and feet stirrups, and I insisted that he did. I wanted him to be there, by my side, when the doctor told us we were having a baby.

But the pregnancy test came back negative.

"We're going to have to run some blood work," my doctor said, scribbling notes in my file.

"Do you think something's wrong?" My chest tightened at the notion that I might have reproductive issues. I'd watched a few of my closest girlfriends take devastating trips down Infertility Lane, and I didn't want to move to that neighborhood. I wanted to live on I-only-have-to-look-at-my-husband-to-get-pregnant Avenue.

"Not necessarily," the doctor said. "But a closer look at your hormone levels may provide answers as to why you're missing your period and experiencing pregnancy-like symptoms."

A few weeks later, I was heading into the local community college to teach a French class when a nurse called me. "Your blood work shows signs of polycystic ovarian syndrome, or PCOS," she said.

PCOS is the acronym for the condition that had affected my own mother before she had me, and that had plagued a few of my best friends as well. When a woman has PCOS, she may develop cysts on her ovaries—cysts that can be painful and even burst—and it can be difficult to get pregnant.

I'd watched my college roommate doubled over on the floor one night when one of her cysts had burst, and I wanted no part of this PCOS thing.

But PCOS wanted a part of me, and it only took one ultrasound to reveal what the doctor called "a string of pearls" around my ovaries. That sounded so much lovelier than what it actually was—a string of small cysts surrounding each of my ovaries, wreaking havoc on my hormones and causing the bizarre abdominal sensations and sharp pains I was now experiencing daily.

So, it wasn't a baby, after all.

From that point on, I didn't have another period for over eight months. My skin broke out like a thirteen-year-old with a crush on the wrong boy, and the pain and discomfort only increased. On our cross-country move from DC to San Diego, one of my cysts burst while we were driving through the middle of the Mojave Desert, with no rest stop or hospital in sight. Once we arrived in paradise, during many of our beach walks, I'd have to stop and sit out the unbearable pain that plagued my abdomen on a regular basis.

My doctor advised me to begin taking fertility drugs to force my ovaries to ovulate, and she mentioned that in vitro fertilization may be in my future, if my husband and I chose to take that route.

We didn't end up taking that route, though, or any route that would lead us to a baby.

Instead, my body's inability to produce a baby was the beginning of the end for us. I began to grieve the baby we couldn't have, and my husband detached from the stress of the whole thing. He didn't want to hear about my daily PCOS updates or discuss the myriad of ways I was trying to correct the problem. He didn't want to come with me to my constant doctor's visits or hear about how devastated I was over the possibility that my female body couldn't perform the most basic functions it was supposed to be able to perform—have a period, ovulate, and grow a baby. I honestly don't know for sure why my husband couldn't show up for me during this time, but I know for certain that it wasn't out of lack of love. He loved me and cared for me and never wanted me to hurt, but everyone has their limitations, and perhaps the issue of this baby we couldn't have was simply too stressful for him to be able to jump in, all hands on deck, and support me.

Whatever his reasons were, a wedge developed between us, and soon that wedge grew to the size of the massive canyon outside our window. All of the issues we'd had over the years began to pile into its crevices, one on top of the other, until the divide became so great that neither of us could patch it up.

I refused to stuff hormones down my throat to force my body to do something it clearly wasn't ready to do, especially in the context of our rocky marriage. Instead, I went the natural route. But after months of acupuncture, herbs, yoga, meditation, and counseling, after reading every fertility book under the sun, taking my temperature every morning, testing constantly for ovulation, then throwing those damn sticks in the trash when I realized again, every month, that nothing was happening—nothing except unbearable abdominal pain, bursting cysts, and an eroding marriage—I gave up.

After a year of this hell, I knew that we'd found ourselves in a marriage that I would not want to bring a child into. I was distraught and stressed. I felt trapped and alone. And I knew a baby wouldn't fix that.

So, between too many sleepless nights and oceans of tears cried on the floor of my bathroom, I laid to rest my dream for a baby, for *our* baby, and I talked to my husband about going back on the pill, at least until we'd worked through our marital issues.

This time I didn't need to make a spreadsheet.

He agreed.

Deep in my gut, though, I knew that the tear in our marriage was irreparable.

I knew that a large part of me didn't want to repair it, and that an even larger part of me wanted out.

Back in the hospital, as I am lying in urgent care high on Percocet, I realize it has only been one year since we gave up on having a family, and now, as the doctor performs an ultrasound to be sure I don't have another bursting cyst, a baby is the furthest thing from my mind.

Once the doctor rules definitively that I am suffering from a kidney infection, he sends me home with antibiotics, more painkillers, and a broken marriage.

Chapitre 14

NICK E-MAILS me the night I arrive home from the hospital to give me his potential Paris itinerary and to ensure that I still want him to join me. I don't commit to anything, and instead I write back to tell him that I am high on painkillers from my urinary tract turned kidney infection. He responds with a sincere apology for playing a role in my recent health debacle, and this opens up a dialogue of daily e-mails back and forth.

Nick's e-mails are the only thing that gets me through the next few days, but soon, even his flirtatious, sexy correspondence isn't cutting it. I don't feel sexy anymore, the way I did when we lounged in our underwear and fed each other chocolate and he told me how much he loved my eyes, my hair, my skin. I don't feel flirtatious the way I did when I enticed him with my bold dance moves and my French lingerie which quickly found its way to the floor.

Once the kidney pain subsides, I am now waking all through the night with piercing chest pains. Each time this happens, I shoot out of bed and retreat to the spare bedroom, where I sob in the darkness, often so hysterically that I can't breathe.

I am now the opposite of numb; I am a hurricane of guilt, sadness, and fear, and nothing can calm me down anymore. Not a call from a girlfriend. Not a bottle of wine. Not a trip to my counselor. Not an e-mail from Nick. Not a Xanax. Not a *handful* of Xanax.

There is only one way out, and it is *through*.

LATER THAT week, on the twelve-year anniversary of the night I first met my husband, we receive the news that our close friends have had a baby.

Back to the hospital we go, but this time, to welcome a new life into the world. The baby is as precious as the couple who had her. Our friends are so happy, so proud, so excited about their new little angel. Even the mother who has just given birth that very day is positively glowing.

It takes every ounce of strength within me not to crumble to the floor in a heap of tears as she hands me her newborn child and her family takes photos of me and my husband holding their baby together, a baby we will never have.

It hits me so hard in that moment, that here we are, twelve years after the night we first crashed into each other's lives, and after all this, after everything we've lived through together, after loving each other so deeply for so long, *still*, we are never going to be the couple rushing to the hospital to welcome a child—*our* child—into this world.

All the dreams we had for our life together—they are over.

This will never be our family.

As I give the cooing little babe back to her mom, she squeezes me tightly and whispers in my ear, "*You're next.*"

I didn't think my heart could be any more broken than it already was, but her comment—which is only made out of love and hope, since she knows we've had fertility problems—shatters me.

I'm not going to be next. I'm not going to have a baby with my husband.

The family we once dreamt of, the baby I've already named, is never going to come.

THE NEXT day, I tell my husband I want a divorce.

I tell him I am so unhappy in our marriage that nothing can repair the damage. I tell him that I have to take responsibility for this extreme unhappiness of mine and stop blaming it on him and on our marriage. In order for me to do that, I have to leave. I have to move forward on my own, without him.

I make it clear that I want him to be able to *be himself*, without me constantly asking him to change. It's not fair for me to ask him to be a different person, as if he is not good enough just as he is. And I want to be able to *be myself*, without feeling like the qualities that are most inherent to who I am are ruining us.

And then I say the things I can never take back.

I tell him I don't love him in the same way I used to.

I tell him that the baby we held onto the night of our twelve-year anniversary will never be ours.

I break his heart.

And I break mine.

Chapitre 15

I DIDN'T expect the dismantling of a life, of a marriage, of a love to be easy.

I knew that when I told my husband it was over, it would, of course, get worse—*much worse*—before it would get better.

But my fragile emotional state is not, in any way, equipped for the loss at hand. I am taking Xanax far too frequently to control my hysterical crying episodes, I am barely eating, and I am still waking at 4:00 a.m. every morning, horrified that this is my life. Even more so, I am horrified with myself for being who I am—a woman who could hurt a man who is still, despite all of *this,* doing his very best to stay kind, calm, and rational amid the storm.

"I wish I were a different person," I tell my husband one day, as we are sitting down at our kitchen table to talk divorce logistics. "I wish I were the person who could fit into this life. Into *our* life. But I'm not. I'm just not."

Tears spill down my cheeks as I say this, and as he watches me cry for the millionth time this week, I can see his pain too. It is masked more than mine—after all, he is the stronger one of the two of us, on the outside anyway—but it is there. And it is raw.

He is not only deeply hurt by my decision, he is also confused. He doesn't understand why, when we had been seemingly getting along for the past few months, I would suddenly announce on one random Saturday that I must leave the marriage. He doesn't feel that I have given him enough warning, and perhaps he is right. So much of the storm that has been brewing has been swirling and thrashing *inside of me*, and out of fear of rocking our fragile marital boat any further, perhaps I haven't let the full scope of that storm rise to the surface. There are, perhaps, more steps *we both* could have taken to save us. But the urge to save myself is now stronger than my urge to save the marriage, and since I feel that the *only* way I can save myself at this point *is* to leave the marriage, I am powering ahead whether he gets it or not.

Despite all of this, my husband is still being kind to me. He knows I'm falling apart, and he is trying so hard to keep it all together. So I wipe my tears and nod my head, letting him know I'm ready to get started.

And so, we discuss the big, giant, *how* of ending our marriage.

How and when will we tell our mutual friends? Our families?

Who will file for divorce and when?

Who will move out and when?

Who gets the TV, the couch, the desk, the kitchen table, the car, the truck?

How will we split up our wedding photos and the stacks of photo albums that we've collected over the years, the photos that have recorded all of the beautiful moments of our life together?

What will we do with our wedding rings? Sell them? Keep them as a reminder of what we once had, and what we have now lost?

Who will take our two sweet, fluffy cats, Bella and Charlie?

Will we ever talk again when this is all said and done? Will it ever be possible to be friends?

And the most trivial, but something we still have to discuss: Will we stay friends on Facebook? Will we change our status from *married* to...what? *Single? It's complicated?*

Devastated and wishing for a quick and easy death to stop the unbearable pain this split is causing us both?

My deepest, most pressing concerns aren't about logistics, though. After all, this is the death of us. The death of an era. The death of our dreams, of our life together, of everything we once believed would last forever.

When everything around you is dying, who the fuck cares about Facebook or couches or wedding rings?

What I want to know is what will become of me without him? Of him without me?

Who will we be without each other?

He doesn't have the answers, though, and neither do I. So we split up all the divorce work accordingly, and we go about our days, trying to survive.

My one, shining beacon of light is, of course, *Paris*. If I can just make it to Paris in a few short weeks, everything will be okay, I tell myself.

Paris will patch up my wounded heart.

It is with this wounded heart that I e-mail my lover and tell him, definitively, *"Yes, I would love for you to meet me in Paris."*

Partie IV

LA MAÎTRESSE DE PARIS ~
THE PARIS MISTRESS

"He's more myself than I am.
Whatever our souls are made of,
his and mine are the same."

~ Emily Brontë,
Wuthering Heights

Chapitre 16

IT IS my firm belief that upon leaving one's husband, one should immediately hop on a flight to Paris. There really is no better way to cope with that mess except to abandon it for the land of cheese, croissants, chocolate, wine, and romance.

Ahhh, Paris.

The name of the city alone invokes images of lovers taking refuge amid winding cobblestone *rues*.

Paris.

Couples strolling hand in hand along the banks of the Seine, stopping to kiss on picturesque bridges as street musicians play their accordion renditions of Edith Piaf's "La Vie en Rose."

Paris.

Impossibly sophisticated French women donning elegant scarves and smoking cigarettes as they sip wine, alone, at sidewalk cafés.

Paris.

Ultra-romantic Frenchmen with irresistible expressions like *ma belle, mon amour, mon trésor, mon coeur,* and *ma chérie* rolling off their tongues, making foreign women realize they've never truly experienced romance until they've stripped off a Frenchman's skinny jeans.

Paris.

Artists painting their next masterpiece on the hilltops of Montmartre.

Writers running their fingers over old book spines at Shakespeare & Company, imagining the day when their own book will grace its famous shelves.

Oh, Paris.

It is in this romantic, artistic center of the Universe that wine flows like water, *chocolateries* and lingerie shops speckle nearly every corner, *les fleurs en rouges et violettes* spill over elegant black balconies, and the scent of fresh buttery croissants flows through the city before the sun has even risen.

If I were to sum all of this up in one word, *tout simplement,* Paris says *love.*

Paris stole my young, impressionable heart when I was but a girl of fifteen, growing up in small-town Ohio, kissing boys and running through cornfields. I took a high school trip to Europe with my French teacher and a few of my closest girlfriends, and even though I was already completely boy crazy at this age, for this Ohio girl, Paris really was my first true love.

And now, every time I step foot in this city, every time I breathe in the life that flows through its streets—vibrant and rich and never-ending—I am once again overwhelmed with what a massive space I have reserved in my heart for this place.

To give my husband some credit, it would have been difficult—or damn near impossible—for any man to compete with my love for France. Contrary to the way all men have come and gone in my life, leaving tears and scars and my broken heart in their wake, the ever-adoring city of Paris is always here for me. Always welcoming me with a warm croissant, a glass of wine, and a place where I feel revived, joyful, and fulfilled. Comfortable and at home. Cared for and loved.

Paris has never abandoned me. Paris has never broken my heart.

I never wanted to have to choose between my love for my husband and my love for France, but at times, in those last turbulent years of our marriage, it felt as if that's exactly what I was doing.

Today, as I meander past open-air markets in the Latin Quarter with one of my best girlfriends by my side and our giant American suitcases in tow, I am beaming like a tourist who is seeing all of this magnificence for the first time. And in my jet-lagged state of jubilant delirium, I realize that in the end, as heartbreaking as it has all been, I did make my choice.

And I chose Paris.

IT IS Day Two of our Parisian adventure, and Katie and I have been invited to Vogue Fashion Night Out by Sylvia, one of my fabulous American writer friends who has made Paris her home.

"This is crazy!" Katie says as she tries on her fourth outfit in our adorable Airbnb flat just off the charming rue Mouffetard. "I feel like I'm living in an episode of *Sex and the City.* I'm Miranda the first time she leaves the house without the baby, and you are so obviously Samantha."

"I can't be Samantha—I haven't even had my first Paris romance yet!" I remind her, although in the back of my mind I am thinking of the romance of my life that will be taking place in less than three weeks in this very city.

I haven't found the courage to tell my very married friend about the affair I am having with a married man. She doesn't know about the shopping bag of lingerie that I have stuffed into a hidden compartment in my suitcase. She doesn't know that the reason I was on cloud nine earlier this afternoon wasn't *only* because we were frolicking through *le Quartier Latin, les Tuileries* and down *les Champs-Élysées,* but also and *mainly* because of the beautiful e-mail Nick sent me, telling me how gorgeous and glowing I am in my new Facebook profile picture—a picture Katie took—where I am standing at the entrance of *le Jardin du Luxembourg*, single at last, beaming and gloriously free in the city I adore so much.

I am bursting at the seams to tell her about this man who has swept my shattered divorce heart into a new land of desire, hope, and excitement, but there is one other reason that is holding me back. A big one. While Katie *isn't* judgmental at all—she has been one of the most supportive friends in my decision to leave my husband—she *is* married to one of my husband's closest friends. She is one of those rare girlfriends who does not tell her husband everything, and so I feel ninety-nine percent sure that I can trust her to keep my illicit affair a secret. But what if, after a few glasses of wine, she spills the beans to her husband? I am still friends with him too, and I can't bear the thought of our closest couple friends knowing that I betrayed my husband right before I told him I wanted out of the marriage.

And, what if somehow the story gets back to my husband?

Or I guess, at this point, I should be calling him my soon-to-be *ex-husband*...

Labels aside, he is the man I have loved since I was nineteen, and the man whose heart I have broken into a million pieces as of late. The last thing I need to do is risk hurting him even further. What purpose would it serve?

And so, I keep my mouth shut about the Paris romance that awaits, the romance that will certainly have me romping beneath the sheets and moaning in ecstasy just as Samantha Jones does on nearly every episode of *Sex and the City*.

Instead, my beautiful friend and I take to the rainy streets of Paris wearing tall boots and Parisian scarves and smiles so big and American underneath our umbrellas, I am certain a monsoon could blow through this city and we'd still be deliriously happy just to be existing here, in the lively flow of *Paris*.

KATIE AND I are feeling *quite* glamorous as we strut through Roger Vivier, a designer shoe store situated just down the street from Chanel and Cartier and Prada on Paris's oh-so-fashionable rue du Faubourg Saint-Honoré. A waiter stops and offers us each a flute of champagne from his overflowing tray, which we gratefully accept, jet lag be damned.

"Don't mind if I do!" Katie says, tossing me a wink. I'm amazed at how well my friend, who is normally ensconced in a routine of diaper changes, feedings, baby games, and very little sleep, fits in so very well in this chic Parisian setting. Tonight she is the definition of fabulous. And I love her. I love that she faced her fears of leaving her daughter for the first time to make this long voyage with me to Paris during such a wild, tumultuous time in my life. And I love that she is eating up every second.

As Katie gets caught up in a conversation with a few of my Paris girlfriends, I head out onto the balcony with Sylvia, the friend who so graciously gave us VIP passes to this exciting event.

A light rain continues to drizzle over the bustling street below, but the 5'10" fashion models prancing around in outrageous dresses and the well-to-do Parisians popping in and out of all of the glamorous designer parties aren't fazed in the slightest. Rain is a regular part of life in Paris, as is incredible fashion. I live in San Diego where it almost never rains and where grungy beach gear and flip flops are about as fashionable as it gets.

Why am I not living in Paris?

This is a question I ask myself almost daily when I am home, and about fifty times a day when I'm in France.

I turn to Sylvia and fill her in on the latest big happening in my life—that I left my husband only a few weeks ago and that when I get home from this amazing France trip, I'll be headed into the land of divorce paperwork and splitting belongings and forever leaving behind the only life I've known for the past twelve years.

Sylvia is no stranger to divorce. The first time we met, one year ago at a dinner party she hosted in her beautiful Parisian apartment on the Left Bank, she told me she had discovered that her husband of nineteen years was having an affair with a younger woman. Sylvia's American girlfriends told her to leave the bastard straight away, but her Parisian girlfriends had quite a different opinion on the matter. They advised her, "Don't let him go. You can't let the other woman win."

One Parisian girlfriend told Sylvia that this was *her* fault, that she should have been keeping her own *secret garden* of affairs all these years, which not only would have made her more interesting and irresistible to her French husband, but also would have softened the blow when she found out about his affair.

Which leads me to ask the questions: Are affairs just a way of life for some couples? Should we all be having them so we don't mind as much when our partner does?

Or will the end result be the same either way? If a couple isn't meant to stay together—*if it just isn't working*—will they ultimately find a way to break up the relationship, regardless of who was sleeping with whom or how many secret gardens were kept or unkept throughout the life of their relationship?

In Sylvia's case, she and her unfaithful husband divorced. And it was rough, as divorces always are. But today, as she talks with me on this Paris balcony about my own divorce, which has only just begun, she squeezes my arm, looks me straight in the eye, and says, *"You're going to be okay."*

I smile, almost laughing it off. I mean, I'm in Paris drinking champagne on a balcony on Vogue Fashion Night Out. *I'm totally fine!* I tell her as much.

"Thank you," I say. "But really, I feel fine. I know it was the right decision, and I'm doing pretty well, all things considered."

She squeezes my arm harder this time, looking through my eyes, reaching into the depths of my soul where she knows the hurt, fear, and pain are hiding out while I'm romping around Paris being *fabulous!*—and she says it again.

"You're going to be okay."

There is a wisdom in her voice, a *knowing*, that demands my attention.

What I hear this time is: *The worst is yet to come, my dear, and even so, you will be okay.*

As the night wears on and many more flutes of champagne are consumed and a band dressed in sequined unitards gives a wild, Baz Luhrman movie-worthy performance, I feel light worlds away from that Divorce Land which awaits back home. I feel bright and alive and radiant, the way I always feel when I'm in Paris. But even more so because I am *single* in Paris. Because I am *free* in Paris!

And so, I feel certain that what Sylvia promised me on the balcony tonight is true—I will be okay.

What I don't realize just yet is how drastically my life will plummet into a pool of depression and despair after this trip to France. I don't yet realize that I will go back to her words again and again and again, when I am lying in a heap of tears on my bathroom floor, when I am suffocating in sobs as I drive alone in my car, when I am collapsed in the shower thinking about ways to end my life. I don't yet realize that I will hang onto her words with the desperation of a woman who has lost everything—lost everything at her own will, I might add—and wonder if those words were really true after all.

Tonight, I pluck another flute of champagne off the waiter's tray, eat another French macaron, and laugh with my friends, clueless as to what will come after France.

Looking back, I'm happy I spent those carefree, naïve moments in my favorite city with some of my closest friends.

Sylvia knew it wouldn't be that way for much longer. But I didn't. And I'm glad I didn't.

Chapitre 17

NEXT UP in my prescription for the recently divorced woman is a train ride down to Lyon, a gorgeous, charming city just two hours south of Paris on the TGV—France's high-speed train, or *Le Train à Grande Vitesse* as the French so eloquently say.

During the spring semester of my junior year at Georgetown University, I studied abroad in Lyon and fell *madly* in love with this city. Even more than Paris if that's possible, Lyon makes me come alive, makes me remember who I am, and makes me one of those annoying people you might see strolling through the city by themselves grinning from ear to ear, just because.

That's me in Lyon—a girl who is bouncing on air without a care in the world.

When Katie and I arrive in the city I have gushed about for years now, she says as much.

"You're like a different person here," she remarks as we stroll past the grand Hôtel de Ville in the center of the city. "I don't think I've ever seen you so happy."

"This is my place," I tell her. "My happy place. I don't need a man when I'm in Lyon. I'm in love just being here."

She stops to glance at all of the bustling cafés situated on the Place des Terreaux, then at the blue skies and puffy white clouds floating overhead. Smiling, she says, "I can see why. There's something magical about this city."

Katie and I make our way to my friend Isabella's apartment, which is situated right on the Presqu'île of Lyon. The Presqu'île is the "almost island" that makes up the center of the city and sits between the two lovely rivers that flow to either side—*la Saône* and *le Rhône*.

Isabella greets us at the door, a vision of pure loveliness. Isabella's mother is Italian, her father is French, and she grew up in Australia. Which means she speaks perfect French, Italian, and English, with her beautiful Australian accent. And she's gorgeous—a voluptuous blonde-haired, blue-eyed beauty.

And she's twenty-four—a mature twenty-four—but still a twenty-four-year-old who lives in her very own elegant apartment in the center of Lyon. Oh, and she's a fashion designer too. Could this girl be any more glamorous?

To say that men are falling at her feet every day, every night, and every hour in between would be an understatement.

And yet, despite all of this, she is one of the most down-to-earth, real, honest, and loyal friends I've ever had. She's kind and sweet and understanding, and never judgmental.

I first met Isabella one year ago when I was at a turning point in my marriage. It was the first time in the eleven years I'd spent with my husband that the idea of divorce had become real to me, and our fights had become epic. After the most epic fight of them all, which lasted late into the evening one Friday in August, I awoke at five in the morning the next day and by 9:00 a.m., I had booked a flight to Lyon, booked two different Airbnb flats for my two-week stay, and my close friend Hannah had booked her flight to join me there as well.

When my husband woke up at 9:30 that morning, I told him, "I'm leaving for Lyon in six days. I'll be there for two weeks. I need a break from all of this. I need to feel like myself again."

He wasn't happy about it—as he never was about my trips to France—but I didn't care. I had to hold on to some semblance of myself as things at home were crumbling, and the only way I knew how to do that was to go to the place where I felt most at home—Lyon.

So, six days later, I departed for my beloved city, the tightness in my chest dissipating the minute I stepped on the plane. When I arrived at my first lovely Airbnb flat, I met Isabella and her twenty-eight-year-old boyfriend, a straight-edged architect named Jean-Michel.

I would be staying in their second bedroom for three days until my friend Hannah arrived, at which point we would head to the next adorable Airbnb flat I'd booked.

As soon as I met Isabella, I recognized a bit of myself in her—she had that same flowing, creative energy that I carried around. And as soon as I saw her with Jean-Michel, I recognized the same dynamic from my marriage—the flighty-but-intelligent female artist who has a million brilliant ideas and doesn't see a single reason why she can't make each and every one of her dreams a reality paired up with a straight-edged, practical man who didn't quite *get* her. A man who craved stability and order just as much as she craved freedom and adventure.

This incompatibility in my own marriage had become so exhausting to me that for at least these few weeks, I'd given up on trying to bridge the gap and instead, I hopped on a flight to France.

On my first night at Isabella's apartment, she didn't come home. I asked Jean-Michel where she was, and he replied, *"Chez sa tante,"* which is French for, *"At her aunt's house."*

When Isabella reappeared the next day, her long hair a ruffled-yet-beautiful mess, I spied a mysterious twinkle in those big blue eyes of hers, and I thought, no way in hell was that girl at her aunt's house.

She has a lover.

Later that night, after Jean-Michel went to sleep, Isabella and I had our first heart-to-heart. She confessed to me that she did in fact have a *secret garden*, and growing in her garden was a sexy forty-nine-year-old Frenchman named Jean-François.

"Oh dear God," I said with a giggle. "Jean-Michel and Jean-François? How do you keep them straight?"

She laughed too, and we talked late into the night. She told me how romantic and exciting Jean-François was, how he was the best sex of her life, how he understood her, and how Jean-Michel just didn't get it.

I told her about how stifled I felt in my marriage and how free I felt in France, on my own.

We shared stories about our tumultuous childhoods, and I knew that even though she was only twenty-four, she was an old soul, just like me.

And so it was that Isabella and I became instant friends.

Today, one year after I first met Isabella, Katie and I wheel our heavy suitcases into her stylish apartment where silky fabrics, sewing machines, and drawings of her latest designs are strewn about, and I am so happy to see her again.

After we hug, Isabella shows us to the smaller of her two bedrooms and says, "So, I've accidentally gone and booked up the larger bedroom with Airbnb. So sorry. I mixed up the dates."

Which means there are two other girls staying at the apartment too.

"Oh, it's no problem," I say with a wave of my hand, used to little snafus like this from all of my France travels. Although when I spy the trepidation on Katie's face as she sizes up the teeny-tiny bedroom and the single bed we are supposed to sleep in together, I know we'll have to make other arrangements.

That's the thing with my France friends—they are all so lovely and welcoming and hospitable, but they are also very last minute and sometimes hard to pin down when it comes to plans. They don't have the obsession with planning that we Americans have—the way we plot out our entire lives down to the minute on a Google calendar, send Evites ten weeks in advance to book friends for a simple dinner party, and start planning Thanksgiving and Christmas in July.

In France, my friends don't operate that way. And I love that about them. I love how *laissez-faire* they all are. How easygoing and go-with-the flow they are. And how they simply live life as it comes.

Although, at moments like this, a *bit* of planning ahead would have been helpful.

"This is the first vacation I've had since my daughter was born," Katie reminds me in a whisper. "I need a bed, a *real* bed." She looks frazzled suddenly, like she may cry. "Remember, my daughter didn't sleep for eight months—*eight months, Danielle.*"

"Don't worry, everything always works out in Lyon," I assure her, because it does.

I make a quick phone call to Benoît, my host brother from my six-month study-abroad in Lyon, and within an hour, we are on our way to the gorgeous apartment in the fancy sixth arrondissement of Lyon where I had the privilege of living during my stay here over ten years ago. Benoît is currently living in his own apartment with his girlfriend, and my host mom is staying in the South of France for a while, tending to her family's vineyard and taking care of her father, which means we will have the place all to ourselves.

Benoît greets us at the door with the warmest of smiles and with kisses—or as the French say, *bisous*—on the cheeks. As soon as I see him, as soon as I set foot in this apartment, I am overwhelmed with a sense of place, of peace, of belonging.

I am home.

Katie is gazing up at the chandelier in the foyer and all around at the elegant décor in this five-bedroom beauty of an apartment, and she smiles with relief.

"See," I tell her, "everything always works out in Lyon."

AFTER WE are all settled in our new digs—a grand, old, elegant French apartment filled with antiques and paintings and chandeliers—we set off for a leisurely stroll around the city. I take Katie on a tour through the lovely sixth arrondissement, stopping to show her my favorite fountain at La Place du Maréchal-Lyautey, situated only a few blocks from my host family's apartment. When I was a student in Lyon ten years ago, I used to lie in the grass here and study, watching the water as it flowed below the majestic sculpture of a lady perched high atop the fountain. Sometimes I'd come here to read, to breathe, to simply be.

After that first two-week escape trip to Lyon I took one year ago in an effort to regroup and find myself amid the rubble of a lost marriage, I returned home to San Diego for only a few short weeks before flying right back to France to spend some time in both Paris and Lyon—again, *without* my husband. It was during that second trip to Lyon when I sat at this exact spot, facing the fountain, tears spilling down my face in broad daylight. From my purse, I pulled a piece of French stationary I'd just bought from the *papeterie* down the street, and from some wiser place within me, I wrote a letter to the terrified, lost girl cowering in the crevices of my broken heart, the one who was trying so hard to decide if her place in this world belonged to her marriage, or if it was somewhere else, somewhere free...perhaps right here, at this fountain in Lyon.

Dear Danielle,

You must know above everything, above all else, that I love you. You are unique and beautiful and elegant, and you were made to be exactly as you are. It's okay for you to want to live in France, to be happy, to dance, write, and travel. It wasn't an accident that I made you this way. Your dreams, talents, and desires are there to guide you. Take them by the hand, my sweet girl, embrace them, breathe life into them! You, and only you, can do this! Love and fullness and joy and beauty are waiting for you...in fact, they already surround you. So, don't be afraid. Do you think it was an accident you came to Lyon all those years ago? There are no accidents, my love. Only fate, destiny, and love knocking on your door, showing you the way. Your dreams have arrived. They are coming true.

All you must do is jump.

Love,
Me

As Katie and I pass by the fountain and stroll down the peaceful tree-lined path along the Rhône River, then cross over the most charming pedestrian bridge in Lyon—*la passerelle du Collège*—on our way to have a scrumptious lunch at *Pain et Cie*, my absolute favorite café in a city that is brimming with the most amazing food I've ever eaten, I realize with a sudden startling certainty that—*I did it.*
I jumped.

IT'S OUR first night at my host family's apartment, and while Katie is showering and my host brother, Benoît, is out with his girlfriend, I am walking through this familiar place, running my hands over the kitchen cabinets, remembering how happy I was when I lived here ten years ago. Remembering how my host mom, brother, and sister welcomed me into their family, into their home, with open arms. Like I was one of them. I felt like I belonged when I was here. I was a part of something—part of a functioning, loving family who would be there for me if I needed anything.

I used to have that with my mom. In fact when I was growing up, my mom was much more than a mother to me—she was my best friend, my sister, and my mom all wrapped into one sweet package. And being her only daughter, I was the same for her, but even more so. From the time I was old enough to talk, I became her best friend, her sister, *her* mother, her counselor, her confidant, and oftentimes, her caretaker. This role reversal of mothering my own mother began when I was too young to realize what was going on.

In one of my earliest memories, when I couldn't have been more than four years old, my mom is laid out on the couch in the tiny duplex we lived in together, passed out from one of her ghastly migraines. I remember standing on a kitchen chair, making her a piece of toast because she couldn't stand up without getting dizzy or throwing up. I sat by her side for hours and watched her sleep, poking her in the arm every so often to make sure she was still alive. My parents were already divorced by this time, and my dad was off running with friends, and, according to my mom, doing drugs and God knows what else.

So, my mom was my everything. If she left me, I'd have no one.

Despite the fact that I continued mothering my mom in various ways all through my childhood, my mom did take good care of me, too. She grew up in a warzone of a household with an abusive, alcoholic, gay, bipolar father—try saying *that* three times fast—who hated women, yet had married one and then had three daughters. Considering the hell she was raised in, I still, to this day, think my mom did a damn good job raising me. She didn't have a lot of tools in her toolbox, or support from anyone really, including my own father, and she still gave me everything she could. She paid for my ballet lessons, slippers, and pointe shoes from the time I was seven until I took a break from dancing in high school. She sent me to a private Catholic grade school and worked her ass off as a nurse making next to nothing in the sticks of Ohio to pay my tuition. She sent me on my very first trip to France when I was fifteen, not paying bills on time so that the money could be put toward my trip.

But more important than all of the opportunities she afforded me was the way she loved me. Whenever she would date a man who wasn't too thrilled about the fact that she had a daughter, he was out the door before he could kiss her goodnight. When I was a little girl, we'd curl up on the couch together, me in the crook of her legs, and watch our favorite shows. She would stroke my hair and rub my back until I fell asleep. We even slept in the same bed together for many years, staying up late at night talking like two little girls at a slumber party. She'd tell me sad stories from her childhood, like how the kids used to make fun of her teeth, and how her parents wouldn't pay for braces until she was in high school. She'd tell me about some of the horrors of growing up with her father, like the night he returned home, sickeningly drunk as usual, and she heard him taking a bunch of pills in the bathroom. She knew what he was doing. And instead of getting up to stop him, she lay in bed and prayed as hard as she could that he would die. That the hell of her childhood would end with his last breath.

But her mom found him early the next morning and rushed him to the hospital.

The bastard lived until he was eighty-two.

I remember lying in bed, hearing her stories, and even at six and seven years old, I could feel my little heart breaking for her. She'd had it so rough.

But I would hug her and tell her that she had me now. And everything was going to be okay.

And it *was* okay, or relatively okay at least, until I left for college. Once I was gone, she completely fell apart. She saw my leaving as the ultimate abandonment. It was as if *I* were the mother and *she* were the child, and I'd left my only child to fend for herself. She didn't want to face the cold, hard world without me by her side, counseling her, telling her what to do, assuring her that she would be okay.

Despite the fact that she'd remarried when I was eleven, *I* was still her flagship, her anchor, her rock. And once I was gone, her fragile little boat began to sink.

Thus began the downward spiral of our relationship. She went from being the mom I could tell *everything* to, the mom I could go to with any problem, the mom who was always waiting at home with a hug and a kind word, to the mom that was taking down all of my pictures in the house and sending me late-night e-mails telling me how cruel I was to have left her and telling me never to get in touch with her again.

All because I left Ohio and went to college in DC.

We still spoke on the phone every day while I was in college, sometimes twice a day. I came home for every holiday. She visited me for every parents' weekend.

But that wasn't enough. I'd abandoned her. I'd ruined her life.

While my mother's marriage to my stepfather was strong for several years, by the time I left for college, things were headed downhill for them too. My leaving only exacerbated their marital problems, and during my senior year in college, after a Jerry-Springer-worthy debacle, they divorced.

So, while all of my friends were off drinking cocktails in Cancun, I went home for my senior year spring break and packed up our entire house, the place I called home, all by myself. My mom was walking around the house in a daze, crying and devastated. My stepfather was off in his own little world of denial, trying to pretend that none of this was happening.

And once again, I had to be the mom, the adult, when my mom, it seemed, had lost her capacity to do so. I moved her cross-country to live with family in Arizona, and my stepdad of ten years, who had been like a father to me for many of the years that my own father was mostly absent, left without saying goodbye.

From that point on, I never again had a real "home" to go home to.

The mother I'd grown up with was a different person entirely, a person who blamed me and my stepdad for all of her pain. The father figure I'd had for the past ten years wanted nothing to do with me or the wife he'd loved for the past decade.

So it was that my husband, the only solid person in my life, became my home. Wherever he was, for all the years that we were together, *that* was my home.

It was my husband who held me in his arms when, at twenty-eight-years-old, I finally decided to stop mothering my mother. When I took some time off from my relationship with my mom to heal and to learn who I was when I wasn't constantly tending to her next catastrophe. It was my husband who dried my tears when I grieved the mother I used to have as a child and came to terms with reality—that that woman was gone. And in her place was someone else, someone I had a very hard time even talking to on the phone.

But now, without my husband and without family to rely on, where is my home? Where do I belong? What will I do? Who will pick me up if I simply can't bear the pain of this loss any longer?

It certainly won't be my married-but-in-an-open-relationship lover. Because, after all, as his title states, the man is *married to another woman.*

I am not, and will never be, his priority.

For the first time since I've arrived in France, I break down, crying over my tea at the kitchen table in my host family's apartment, wishing ever-so-fervently that I had my own real family to go home to. To help me through this crisis of divorce. I feel insanely jealous of everyone who has a mother who is there to comfort them when something this horrible happens. A mother who will listen and hug them and *be the mom*, instead of topping my pain with her own enormous, gargantuan, never-ending hurricane of sorrow, so that, once again, it is *I* who am mothering *her*.

This longing for a mother to hold me has got me crying so hard that I have no choice but to sit down and let the sobs rake through my tired body.

It's not long before Katie finds me in the kitchen, wiping the tears from my eyes and sniffling so hard I can hardly catch a breath. She doesn't ask me why I'm crying. She just walks over and hugs me.

And as she listens to me tell her how hard it was to break things off with my husband, how heartbreaking the last few weeks were before I left for France, how terrified I am to go back to California and face the harsh realities of divorce, and how badly I wish I had even the *semblance* of a normal family to support me through this, in the midst of my tears, I realize that I *do* have family.

I have Katie. I have all of my loyal, amazing girlfriends. I have one blessing of a cousin who loves me dearly and calls as much as she can to make sure I'm okay. And I have everyone in Lyon and Paris who has welcomed me back to the cities I love so much with a glass of wine and a chocolate croissant at the ready.

It may not be a mother's hug, but as Katie squeezes me once more and tells me it's perfectly normal for me to be breaking down after everything that has been happening in my life, I know that perhaps, for tonight, it's even better.

Chapitre 18

NICK HAS made me promise to let him take me lingerie shopping in Paris, and while I've agreed to his oh-so-demanding request, I see no qualms about doing a little lingerie shop with Katie before his arrival.

So, here we are at Darjeeling, a beautiful little shop in the center of Lyon that is brimming with silk and satin and lace. I am in heaven perusing these aisles, my mood perking up as I remember again, that I am *single*. I am *free*. And I have a lover who will appreciate every delicate piece of lace and every inch of my skin that the lace doesn't cover.

Katie and I have an absolute ball trying on the entire store, and after our lengthy lingerie fashion show, we both buy two pieces. The bolder, racier one I have chosen is a pink satin bra trimmed in black lace with a matching thong. The other is sweeter and more delicate, while still not leaving much to the imagination. It is a transparent gray bra with little white polka dots trimmed with peach-colored lace that runs all the way up the bra straps, complete with a peach bow in the middle and, of course, a matching skimpy thong.

On our way back to the apartment, as we trot up the banks of the glistening Rhône River, riding on our glorious shopping high, I have an idea.

"So, I know you're trying to build your photography portfolio," I say to Katie. "Any interest in a boudoir photo shoot...*of me?* I mean, I'm still young and I'm newly single. If there were ever a time to take some scandalous but tasteful photos in French lingerie, the time is now."

Katie's eyes light up. "Oh, you are totally becoming Samantha Jones. I'm in."

And so, this is how I find myself posing and laughing and making sultry eyes at Katie's camera while strutting around in my new lingerie and my fabulous pink "divorce heels" on an unsuspecting Thursday afternoon in my host family's apartment.

When I e-mail Nick to tell him about the photo shoot, he responds almost immediately, telling me *not* to send those photos. Focusing on work—and also, I assume, on his wife—will be hopeless, he writes, if photos of me prancing around in French lingerie show up in his inbox.

I oblige, but I am dying to share these pictures with him.

They are a true reflection of the full-on wild mess that I have become: The writer who has left her husband, taken a lover, and jet off to France to bathe her newly single body in tantalizing lingerie and pose for the camera to record this gloriously messy time in her life.

LATER THAT night, Katie and I have joined my host brother and his girlfriend at an outdoor bar in the center of the city where my close writer friend, Dimitri, is bartending for the night.

I first met Dimitri over three years ago when my doctor friend, Hannah, and I took a one-week romp through Paris,

Lyon, and Annecy. Late one night in a pub in Lyon, Dimitri and his friend Serguei were standing next to us, ordering beers. I turned to them and asked, "*Ça va?*" to which they smiled their charming smiles and invited us to their table to have drinks with their friends. We had the best night with all of them, drinking, dancing, and talking about life. Before the sun rose, Dimitri and Serguei walked us back to our hotel, and while Serguei was kissing Hannah outside, Dimitri and I shuffled around awkwardly, giggling like a pair of high schoolers. He knew I was married and was totally respectful of it, so as soon as Serguei and Hannah were finished making out, Hannah and I took the teeny elevator up to our hotel room and thought we'd probably never see those boys again.

But during my escape trip to Lyon one year ago, we reconnected with Dimitri. It had been over two years since we'd last seen him, and in that time, something had changed. He'd become *a man.* I think Hannah and I both had to fan ourselves at the table to keep our libidos under control. Dimitri was suddenly so goddamn sexy that now it was Hannah and I who found ourselves giggling and acting like a pair of high schoolers.

"So, what kind of work are you doing?" Dimitri asked me in his adorable accent.

"I'm a writer," I said. "I write romance novels."

Dimitri's big brown eyes lit up as he proclaimed, "I'm writing a novel too!"

And so, over wine, we talked late into the night about our experiences writing and publishing, and about Dimitri's very first novel, an epic love story centered in the wild nature of Spain where majestic bulls are storming the fields and stunning Spanish women with flowing black locks are the true beauties.

Dimitri had a girlfriend at the time, and I was married, but that didn't stop me and Hannah from staying up into the wee hours of the morning, gossiping about how ridiculously sexy he'd become in the two years since we'd last seen him.

The next day, he took us on a hike into a misty forest and all the way up to one of the highest hilltops near the elegant and majestic Fourvière Basilica that towered over the city. We took pictures up there, the three of us, with the incredible view of Lyon beyond our smiling faces, and then we arrived at what seemed to be a never-ending flight of stairs which led down to the Saône River.

About halfway down this zigzag of stairs, Dimitri said, "You know, when I am riding my bike around the city, I come here, I put the bike on my shoulder like this"—he stopped to demonstrate—"and then I run all the way up these stairs."

I stopped walking, looked down to the bottom and all the way up to the top. "The whole way?" I asked.

He nodded with a grin that was so sexy, I think Hannah almost fainted right there.

"The whole way!" he said.

That night, we stayed up even later talking about how goddamn sexy he was.

"His neck!" Hannah said. "I just want to rip off his shirt and bite his neck."

And since this was during my escape trip last year, when the possibility of divorce was weighing heavily on my mind, I took it one step further. "We could've just jumped him in the woods. I doubt he would have protested."

Again, we postulated and fantasized and giggled late into the night.

The next day, Dimitri took us out to dinner at Le Nord, a Paul Bocuse *brasserie* situated in a prime spot on the Presqu'île. Bocuse is a famous French chef based out of Lyon, and according to Dimitri, Le Nord is one of the best restaurants in the city— which is saying a lot considering Lyon is known to be the gastronomical capital of France.

Inside, the evening dinner crowd had filled the red leather booths to the brim, and servers were rushing around in their crisp black vests and long white aprons, delivering wine and champagne, giving everyone even more of a reason to celebrate another beautiful night in Lyon.

Dimitri brought his girlfriend, and the minute they sat down together, I recognized yet again that same dynamic I'd seen in Isabella and her architect boyfriend Jean-Michel, and the same one that had developed between me and my husband. Except this time, Dimitri was in the role of the creative artist who could barely contain all of his exciting dreams and ideas, and his girlfriend was in the role of the practical, financially minded, rather boring grown-up.

I watched the way Dimitri shut down around her, constantly trying to keep her happy. This was a different man from the one who had described his first novel with such enthusiasm the other night over wine. The man who had so excitedly exclaimed, "The whole way!" when he referred to his jaunt up the never-ending flight of stairs with his bike tossed all nonchalant over his shoulder.

As I sipped my wine and made small talk with his girlfriend, I thought to myself, *their relationship isn't going to work.*

And if that girlfriend only knew what Hannah and I had been imagining the past two nights as we stayed up late talking about Dimitri...it *really* wouldn't work.

Which then led me to think about my marriage, which, at this point in time last year, hadn't yet totally imploded. But I realized that if I was so eager to jump the bones of a Frenchman who had a girlfriend, what did that say about the future of my marriage?

I forgot about all of *that* when dessert arrived.

Le fondant au chocolat. Dimitri insisted that we order it. Never one to turn away chocolate, I responded with a resounding, "*Mais, bien sûr!*"

Le fondant au chocolat is a rich, warm, round piece of chocolate cake filled with hot, overflowing chocolate lava. I took my first bite and immediately had to close my eyes and drown out the sounds around me. All I knew in that moment was *fondant au chocolat.*

"*Oh my God. Oh...God,*" I moaned.

I do believe it was my first ever *food-gasm.*

So, while I wasn't jumping Dimitri's bones that night, I still had an equally sensual experience devouring *le fondant.*

That night, as Hannah and I lay awake giggling, we talked about the chocolate, gossiped about how Dimitri and his girl-friend were a terrible match, and we still couldn't get over the fact that he was *so goddamn sexy.*

"His neck!" Hannah exclaimed again. "I just want to bite it!"

"Maybe one day we'll tell him we wanted to jump him in the woods," I said.

"Yes, we have to. Not this trip, though," she said.

"No, not this one," I agreed.

We didn't tell Dimitri about our fantasies, but we did stay close friends with him.

And so tonight, as I see his endearing, handsome smile for the first time in over a year, I am overjoyed. He grabs me and kisses me on the cheeks.

"My dear Juliette, *ça va?*"

I love how he calls me Juliette as if he recognizes that the writer side of me is more truly *me* than any other aspects of my being.

"*Oui, ça va,*" I coo back before launching into a detailed account in French of everything Katie and I have been up to since we arrived in France and all about how happy I am to finally be *single!* and *free!* and *fabulous!* in a city I am so in love with. The French is rolling off my tongue tonight, so easily, so beautifully. And I am drinking wine outside with my best friends.

And I am in Lyon.

What a gift, I think to myself. Amid every crazy experience and heartbreak life has thrown my way, amid all of the irrational decisions I have made as of late, France has always been such an undeniable, exciting, life-giving *gift*.

Later that night, as we all head to a gay dance club and shake our booties to Beyoncé, I realize that as long as I am here, in the land I love so much, surrounded by the people I adore most, the gifts will keep on flowing.

Chapitre 19

AFTER A few days of experiencing mind-blowing food-gasms in Lyon, the TGV whisks us through the rolling hills of the French countryside back up to Paris. For our brief one-night stay before Katie goes home, we've booked an Airbnb flat near the Palais Garnier, Paris's grand, majestic opera house situated in the 9th arrondissement.

The Palais Garnier is the home of the Paris Opera Ballet, and it is my absolute favorite place in all of Paris. When I was completing my master's degree at New York University in Paris, I was lucky enough to attend a performance of the breathtaking Balanchine ballet, *Jewels*, at the Palais Garnier. From the moment I first nestled into one of the theater's red velvet seats, then gazed up at the colorful Chagall painting and the spectacular chandelier overhead, and watched in awe as the curtain rose and dancers in ruby, emerald, and diamond-colored tutus flittered across that stage, I've been head-over-pointe-shoes in love with the grandiose but intimate beauty inside this magical space. There is nothing like it in all of Paris, and I can't wait to check into our flat so I can show Katie just how lovely the Opéra Garnier is.

Though when we arrive at our flat for the night and discover the seven flights of winding stairs that await and not a single miniscule French elevator in sight—unless it was too small for us to actually *see*, which in France is quite possible—I realize the opera house will have to wait. I'll need a shower and a buttery croissant after I'm finished lugging my ridiculously massive suitcase up all these stairs.

AFTER THE suitcase-staircase debacle and a shower in a bathtub with no curtain, we find a lovely café near the flat, enjoy a quick espresso and a croissant, then set off through the city for one final day of sightseeing together.

The first stop is, of course, the Opéra Garnier—which Katie finds just as spectacular as I have described it to be. Next, we take a brisk autumn stroll down the bustling Avenue de l'Opéra, admiring all of the lovely shops and apartment buildings on our way, until we make it to La Comédie Française, a theater that is much smaller than the Opéra, of course, but regal and stunning in its own right. We stop to listen to the live street musicians playing outside La Comédie, then a quick pass by le Pyramide du Louvre—which is swarming with tourists and cameras and fanny packs, as usual—and finally, we make our way to the River Seine.

After spending a year in Paris completing my master's degree, and after the myriad of trips I've taken back since, I have walked along this river too many times to count. And still, as its dark blue waters come into view and we meander across le Pont du Carousel, I find myself breathless and falling in love with this city all over again, as if I were fifteen, experiencing the magic of Paris for the very first time.

As we cross the bridge, Katie sighs, turning to me. "Danielle, you belong here."

"I know," I tell her, without batting an eye. I *do* know—I've known this for a long time.

Moving to Paris was a dream I gave up on long ago. After I finished my degree in France, I flew back to California and prepared for the arrival of my husband, who had been on deployment with the military for eight months. As soon as he returned and settled back into life at home—a difficult transition in and of itself—it was time for him to prepare for his exit from the service, which meant we didn't have to live in San Diego anymore. Not that I didn't love our beachy little apartment two blocks from the ocean, but the idea of freedom, of not having to live according to the strict confines of the military was so exciting to me, that as my husband began his job search, I began pitching the idea of Paris to him.

We were young, we didn't have children, and with my French skills and my connections in Paris, I could certainly get a good job there, I reasoned. Being a finance guy, he could get a job with an accounting firm that had a Paris office. I came up with a million ideas of how we could make this work, and why it would be such an exciting adventure. I even tried to teach him French in the evenings. But learning French and living abroad simply were not in the program for my husband.

He didn't want to do it. And I couldn't force him.

For all the ways that we were incompatible, there were one hundred more reasons why I loved my husband. And I didn't want to spend any more time arguing over something that he clearly wasn't going to budge on. So, since we were married, till death do us part—or, so I thought—I gave up on moving to France.

My dream to live amongst these cobblestone *rues*, to stop at my local *boulangerie* every morning for a *pain au chocolat*, and to speak the most beautiful language in the world every single day ate away at me over the years, though. Especially as it became clear that not only did my husband never want to *live* in France, he never wanted to *travel* there either. And he didn't want *me* to travel to France because, according to him, it was too extravagant, too expensive. Never mind the fact that I was skilled at living and traveling in Paris on a shoestring budget, he wasn't having it. France simply was not on his agenda, and he didn't want it to be on mine either.

But there was a big problem with that. I'd fallen in love with France when I was fifteen. I'd decided as a freshman in high school that I would major in French in college, study abroad in France, get my master's degree and possibly a PhD in French, and that I would be a French professor. This was my life dream. A dream I'd had long before I met him. A dream he knew about when he came into my life. And a dream he'd supported fully until he was finished with all of his military travels.

At that point, so it seemed, that I, too, would be finished with my travels—well, if it was up to him.

I did realize my dream of finishing my master's degree by choosing to complete my one-year program at New York University in Paris during the same year my husband was on deployment. And shortly thereafter, I realized my dream of becoming a French professor. After my husband got out of the military, we spent several years living just outside of DC in Northern Virginia, and I taught at two local colleges during that time. I adored teaching French every day. But speaking the language and sharing my deep love for the French lifestyle, history, and culture with my students only made me yearn to travel back even more.

So, three years after I completed my master's degree and last inhaled the scent of freshly baked baguettes on the streets of Paris, I told my husband that I wanted to take a one-week trip to France for my spring break. I asked him to come with me, of course, but I made it clear that it was also okay if he didn't want to go. I was more than happy to spend a week in France on my own. The three years I'd been away were three years too long, and I needed this. I needed it for my soul.

The marital version of World War III ensued over the coming weeks after my request for my one-week France trip. I'd budgeted out the whole trip to be extremely cost-effective: I'd be staying with my host family in Lyon, which meant free lodging for half of the week, and I'd saved all the money I'd need for the trip from the many extra hours of tutoring I'd taken on. This wouldn't affect our ability to pay our bills on time, not in the least, and it was dearly important to me.

Still, he argued, *no.*

Brokenhearted, defeated, and furious, I called my close friend Deirdre, with whom I'd studied abroad in Lyon. She'd seen firsthand how happy I became when I was gallivanting around France; I knew she would understand how important this was to me.

"Danielle," she said sternly, "he's not going to divorce you if you go. Yeah, he's going to be angry, but it's not like your marriage is going to end if you spend one week in France. This has always been your dream, and he knew that. You're a French professor, for God's sake. Did he really think you'd never want to go to France again?"

"It appears that way," I said.

"If you don't go now, you're never going to go," Deirdre said. "And you'll resent him forever."

"So you think I should just book the flight? No matter what he says?" My hands were trembling. The thought of defying my husband made me feel empowered and terrified at the same time.

"Yes, book the damn flight. He doesn't own you."

Nothing beats the sage advice of my girlfriends. Nothing.

And so, I booked the ticket.

I spent a glorious week in France on my own, visiting my dear friends and my host family, and while my husband was angry as all hell, Deirdre was right—he didn't divorce me over it.

The next year, I headed back to France for my spring break, this time with my doctor friend, Hannah, in tow. It was during this trip when we first met Dimitri, our friend with the sexy neck who runs up five million flights of stairs with a bike tossed over his shoulder like it's no big thang.

That year, my husband didn't get quite as upset. He knew that I'd go no matter what he said, so while he didn't like it, he bit his tongue. And I, of course, had the time of my life.

Initially, I wished for my husband to join me on these trips. But his negative attitude toward traveling, toward adventure and the *living of life*, and specifically toward something that was so intrinsic to who *I* was, changed my mind. If he didn't want to share in France with me, if no amount of pleading, prodding, or bargaining would convince him to take a week off work and travel to an amazing country with his wife, well, then he could stay home and make spreadsheets.

But France was—and still is—in my bones, and I wouldn't stifle my dreams to keep him comfortable any longer.

Now, years later, here I am—husbandless, with Katie by my side telling me I belong here.

"I have to go home and get a divorce," I remind her, not wanting to think about the big, bad, ugly world of divorce that awaits while I am having such a lovely afternoon squeezing down the skinny sidewalks of rue des Saints-Pères, on my way to sip espresso at the famous Café de Flore.

"Yes, but after that, you're a free woman," Katie says.

"I just have to get through it," I say, swallowing the knot in my throat.

"And you will, Danielle. You always do."

THAT NIGHT, Katie and I take another stroll along the Seine, stopping to gaze up at the giant full moon that is hanging low in the sky, just beyond the Gothic towers of Notre Dame Cathedral.

And instead of thinking of the husband I have left behind, I think of Nick.

In less than two weeks, he'll be here, holding my hand as we wind through these streets together, stopping to steal kisses along the Seine, and running back to our flat as often as we want to make love.

As a cool autumn wind brushes my cheeks, I fix my gaze on that looming full moon as it keeps watch over this grand, mysterious city, and I wonder if Paris will ever be the same after Nick and I have explored its bustling cafés together, after we've tasted its delectable chocolate on each other's lips, after we've made love underneath its twinkling stars.

Right now, Paris is still mine.

Will Nick steal it from me? Will I ever be able to think of anything but him when I return on my own? Will our affair tarnish these streets forever?

Or will Paris become ever more glorious, ever more magical once I've experienced the *City of Love* with my own adoring lover by my side?

Either way, the idea that a man I've only known for a few months and who I absolutely adore is going to fly halfway across the world to meet me in Paris, warms my heart with such love, that for tonight, I don't care what the outcome will be.

I simply cannot wait for my lover to get here.

Chapitre 20

THE NEXT day, Katie and I are back at the Charles de Gaulle Airport, preparing for her departure to the States. I hug my friend goodbye and board the train by myself, en route, once again, to Lyon.

I put on my headphones and smile as Yann Tierson's melodic, oh-so-French compositions from the *Amélie* soundtrack dance through my head, the perfect accompaniment to the rolling pastures and green hills and lush vineyards that zoom by the train window. And it is here, immersed in the peaceful French countryside, that I think back to how this whole love affair with France truly began.

It was in a cold, dark movie theater in Cincinnati, Ohio, that I first laid eyes on *la Tour Eiffel*, the swanky George V Hotel in Paris, the lush French countryside, the vineyards of Provence, and the sandy white beaches of *la Côte d'Azur*.

The movie was called *French Kiss*, and it starred the ever-adorable Meg Ryan playing Kate, a buttoned-up history teacher who'd never been to Paris, and the hilarious Kevin Kline as Luc, a swindling but sexy French conman. Kate left behind her boring, predictable life in Canada to fly to Paris, where she planned to steal back her fiancé from the irresistibly voluptuous French woman with whom he'd fallen in love. On the plane ride over, Kate sits next to the ultra-French, ultra-sexual Luc, who hides a stolen necklace in Kate's bag, and henceforth follows her around the country pretending to help her win back her fiancé's love, but really trying to get his necklace back.

Of course, being the telltale romantic comedy that it is, the unlikely schoolteacher-conman pair *do* fall in love over the course of their own little tour de France, and in the final scene of the movie, we see them kissing in a vineyard to Louis Armstrong's version of "La Vie en Rose."

It was the quintessential France romance, and for me, it was love at first sight.

One of my favorite scenes in the movie is when Kate and Luc are taking the train through the French countryside, and Kate is marveling at just how gorgeous those rolling green hills of France are. That image of the French countryside as seen from the train window has been dancing through my mind ever since I watched the movie, and every time I've traveled to France since, I find myself sighing in awe at that very same sight when I take the train.

My time on the train in France is sacred to me. I don't spend it reading or planning or worrying. I listen to music, lean my head against the window, watch the beauty of France pass by and usually, at some point, I drift off to sleep. I treasure these moments alone on the train. It's my time in a country I love deeply. And now that I am single, now that I am free, I can breathe a little easier and simply...*enjoy.*

LATER THAT night, I am sitting on the terrace of a charming little wine bar on the Presqu'île, enjoying a buttery glass of

Mâcon Chardonnay with my friend who makes me laugh harder than anyone in the world—a tall, blue-eyed Brit from Liverpool named Mark.

I first met Mark back in 2003 when I was studying abroad in Lyon and frequenting a little English pub called The Smoking Dog several nights a week with my girlfriends. A lot of drinking and debauchery went down in that place, and Mark was a regular debauchery creator there as well. Soon our crowds collided and we became close friends.

We did more with Mark than just drink, of course. We watched movies at his place and compared his British vocabulary words to our American ones—for example, I loved when Mark would offer me his *jumper* in reference to his sweater, or ask to bum a *fag* off one of his friends, but of course he was talking about a cigarette. We even went with him to pick out his kitten from the pound. Being from Liverpool and an obvious fan of the Beatles, Mark named his little kitty Ringo.

Ten years later, Mark still lives in Lyon, he still frequents The Smoking Dog and even bartends there on occasion, he still has Ringo, and he has a son now too—an adorable little mini-Mark named Alfie. Mark and Alfie's mom split a few years back, and tonight, as we discuss the topic of his sweet Italian girlfriend, Camilla, whom he's been dating for a few years now, Mark lifts his big blue eyes to mine and says in his lovely accent, "Camilla and I are engaged. We're getting married."

My wine catches in my throat. *Mark, married?* He never married Alfie's mom, so this would be his first trip down the aisle, and even though I've seen him and Camilla together and know what a perfect match they are, the idea of my friend Mark saying vows doesn't quite register.

Or maybe it's the fact that I've just left my marriage, and my view on the institution of marriage as a whole is a bit jaded, to say the least.

"Wow, congratulations! I'm so happy for you two," I say, meaning it from the bottom of my heart, even if my head is still processing this big news. "So when's the big day?"

What I really want to ask is, *why lock it down by signing a marriage certificate? Why not just be together and live together and love each other until it doesn't work anymore? Why the need for marriage?*

He takes a sip of his wine. "Not sure. We're not rushing or anything. I mean, it's marriage. *Marriage.*"

"Yes, *marriage*," I say, a supreme heaviness leaking through my voice as I say that word. "Crazy that we're switching places," I say, taking another sip of wine and thinking about how strange timing can be sometimes. Of all the years I've known Mark, up until now, I was either dating or married to my husband. And now, when I am free, when I am setting off into the land of singledom, Mark is preparing to tie the knot.

If I'm being honest, it's bittersweet for me. I've always held a special place in my heart for Mark. To have a friend who makes me laugh to the point of tears every time I'm with him; to have someone I can see once a year or less, but we still pick up every time as if not a single day has passed; to have that kind of ease and compatibility with a man is such a gift. The days I've spent with Mark over the past ten years have been some of the happiest, most carefree, loveliest days of my entire life, and I only hope that his getting married won't change that.

I simply adore him, and I always will. As we sip our wine and talk about his upcoming marriage and the end of mine, I hope with all my heart that no matter where life takes us, we will always be close friends.

Toward the end of our evening together, Mark asks, "Are you seeing anyone?"

I hesitate for a second, running my fingers up the stem of my wineglass. Finally, I say, "No...no one special." It's a lie, of course. But how do I share with my dear friend who is preparing to embark on his own marital adventure that, just before leaving my own, I took on a married lover? This decision of mine to have an affair with a most unavailable man is not in any way a smart one, and I fear Mark will say as much.

So, I keep my secret a secret, and I realize that in doing so, our friendship has already changed.

THE NEXT day, Dimitri and I are lying in the grass near the rose gardens at Le Parc de la Tête d'Or, a massive, lovely park just down the street from my host family's apartment, where I used to spend many a day jogging, strolling, and doing just this—lying in the grass and loving life.

Today we are pondering our eternal debate between wanting relationship stability versus a life freedom and adventure.

"I want both," Dimitri says. "I want to build a life with someone one day, get married and have children. I really do see myself doing those things. But you know how it is, Juliette, being a writer. At the same time, I want freedom, I want to experience many women, many adventures. I don't want to be limited."

Dimitri and I are kindred souls on this front—well, except for the fact that I would like to experience *many men*, not women. Otherwise, I couldn't agree more.

"I know," I say. "I'm exactly the same. It's a constant struggle between wanting stability and craving independence. I would love to find a relationship where, somehow, I have both."

We lie in the grass in silence for a little while, until I decide to tell him about my latest irrational romance.

"I'm seeing a married man," I say.

He props up on one elbow, lifts a brow. "Oh?"

I launch into the entire story of me and Nick. How we met. The initial affair. Our four intoxicating days together in Los Angeles. How I have never, in my life, felt this way about anyone. But the story always ends the same way—he's married.

He's married.

He's fucking married.

"Do you think he'll ever leave his wife for you?" Dimitri asks.

"No," I say. "That's not on the table, and I don't think it ever will be."

"I couldn't live like him," Dimitri says. "In a marriage like that, where all of the passion is gone. That is like death."

"I know," I say. And I do know. I left my own marriage precisely because I felt that the death of my soul was imminent if I didn't get out.

As Dimitri and I leave our quiet spot on the grass and stroll down the tree-lined path that lines the park, our feet crunching over fallen leaves as we go, I realize that I am just as much of a mess as he is. But he isn't judging me for that, and I'm not judging him either.

We messes understand each other. And for that, I am grateful.

"Want to go eat lunch, and more importantly *dessert*, at Pain et Cie?" I ask him.

"That's your favorite café, near Cordeliers, right?"

"That's the one. They have the best tartines—I always get the pesto mozzarella one, and it is so damn good."

Finally, Dimitri smiles and his big brown eyes light up. *"Mais, bien sûr, ma chère Juliette. Allons-y!"*

THE NEXT night, Isabella and I are devouring pizza at Pizzeria Carlino, a charming little Italian restaurant a few blocks away from Hôtel de Ville, and she is catching me up on her latest man gossip.

Jean-Michel, the architect, is old news. Even at the young age of twenty-four, Isabella knew herself well enough to know that she'd be bored to tears if she continued on in that relationship. So, shortly after I first met them together at her apartment, Isabella asked Jean-Michel to move out. She continued seeing Jean-François, the forty-nine-year-old sex god, but he didn't want to make a commitment. So, now, at twenty-five, she is dating *another* Jean! This one is a thirty-two-year-old restaurant owner named Jean-Sébastien.

I can hardly keep all of the Jeans straight; how in the hell is *she* doing it?

"He's great, you know," Isabella says, referring to her latest Jean. "He absolutely adores me, we have a wonderful time together, and my family loves him."

Still, I detect a hesitance in her voice. "Do you see it really going somewhere?" I ask.

"He would marry me in a heartbeat. Have kids, the whole thing," she says, waving her wineglass around before taking a sip.

"But is that what you want?" I ask.

"I do," she says, "but there's one tiny problem."

"Uh oh...what is it?" I say through a mouthful of melted cheese. God, even the pizza is amazing in France.

"The sex," she says. "It just isn't...exciting."

"Oh no. That is a big problem," I say. "So, are you still seeing Jean-François?"

She giggles suddenly, her entire demeanor loosening up, becoming more flowing and free. "You know us. We just can't stay away from each other. I've never felt this way about any man."

"Then break up with Jean-Sébastien and be with Jean-François!" I tell her. "You can't deal with boring sex for the rest of your life. And this thing with Jean-François has been going on for well over a year now, right? Just go with it."

"But I'm not sure that Jean-François will really commit to me if I end things with Jean-Sébastien. I think he only wants what he can't have."

"It's always that way with men, isn't it?" I say, but then I wonder if it isn't that way with me too. Why is it that I have chosen a man I really can't have, not on a full-time basis anyway, rather than focusing on finding an available man for my first relationship out of the divorce gate? Is it because I, too, only want what I can't have?

"It is. They're all like that," Isabella says before taking a long sip of her red wine.

"Well, regardless of whether or not Jean-François will commit to you one day, you have to evaluate your relationship with Jean-Sébastien for what it is. Sounds like he's a wonderful guy, and you two are compatible in many ways, but you certainly can't marry the man if you're already bored in the bedroom. You'll never stop seeing Jean-François on the side if that's the case. And that's not sustainable."

"I know you're right," she says. "But Jean-Sébastien is so lovely. And he treats me so well."

"Well," I say, rethinking my statement, "*perhaps* keeping Jean-François in the secret garden *is* sustainable. Maybe it's simply not possible to find everything we need in one man. Maybe we need *at least* two men to be fulfilled on the relationship front, and sexually and romantically too. In Jean-Sébastien, you have all the good relationship stuff—the daily companionship, compatibility, stability. And with Jean-François, you have the passion, the excitement, the romance. Maybe it *can* work," I admit.

"But it's not fair to Jean-Sébastien," she says.

"True, it's not," I say. "Do you think Jean-Sébastien would see another woman on the side?"

"No, he's not like that. He only wants me."

"Then you'll have to make a decision at some point," I tell her. "But it doesn't have to be tonight. You'll know what to do when the time is right."

"Things always have a way of working themselves out, don't they," Isabella says, her blue eyes twinkling with optimism.

"They do," I say. Although when I think about my affair with Nick, and how *I* am the woman hiding in *his* secret garden, I wonder how this complicated situation will ever work itself out. How long will Nick want to keep me in his secret garden? And how long will I be okay with hiding out in there before the weeds take over and crush the roses?

If Nick were ever to leave his wife for me, would our excitement and passion for each other eventually die down, the way it always does in a relationship once the business of real life enters into the equation? Does our romance exist only in a bubble, the way Jean-François and Isabella's does? If we were to pop that bubble, what would become of the sex, the passion, the unadulterated desire to be in each other's arms, connected at the hips, kissing and making love all day, all night?

Would we one day tire of each other and want out? Or would we create our own new secret gardens, with new lovers and new complications to go with them?

Is that simply human nature?

Is there any other ending to this story?

THAT NIGHT, I am crossing le Pont Morand by myself, strolling past couples holding hands and teenagers out causing trouble and students on their way to the same bars I used to frequent ten years ago.

I stop walking for a moment, wrap my hands around the railing of the bridge, and inhale the cool night air, admiring the beauty splayed out before me. The way the moon sparkles on the dark blue waters of the Rhône. The unique bridges that stretch across the river, bridges I have walked across hundreds of times. And most of all, the familiarity and peace I feel in a place that has always loved me just as much as I have loved her.

I close my eyes for a moment and allow myself to feel—*really feel*—the love and the warmth that pours through my veins every time I am here.

And it is standing here with my eyes closed, on my last night in Lyon, that I realize I *did* have my own secret garden all the years

I was married. But growing in my garden wasn't another man, or another lover—*it was France.*

I never wanted to hide my love for France in a secret vault, lock the door and throw away the key. I wanted to share this love with my husband, but that's not the way things worked out.

I smile to myself, overjoyed that I no longer have to keep France locked away in a secret garden. I can love her freely, with abandon, without apologies.

I can travel here anytime I wish.

I can even move here one day.

Opening my eyes, I set off across the bridge back to my host family's apartment, beaming the whole way as I envision living in my very own apartment in Lyon, surrounded by some of my dearest friends, and finally, *finally,* taking France out of my secret garden and declaring to the world that *I am in love.*

Chapitre 21

I AM adding a new item to the recent divorcée's itinerary: Get a divorce and go to Saint-Tropez. Then, once you're in Saint-Tropez, eat cake! But not just any cake, specifically you must—*must*—eat *la Tropézienne*.

I am sitting in a crowded little café in Saint-Tropez with my friends Marie So, Chris, and their two kids, doing just that. Devouring my own rather large *Tropézienne* and wondering if this delightful brioche cake filled with fluffy, velvety cream and sprinkled with big grains of sugar isn't the entire reason I became single. Maybe I had to leave my husband just so I could come to Saint-Tropez and eat this cake. As I close my eyes and take another sinful bite, I think this just might be true.

"All divorced women need to come to Saint-Tropez and eat this cake," I say to my friends. "Really. I'm so happy right now I could die."

Marie So would never have to divorce her husband so that she could travel and eat cake because Chris is all too happy to join her. In fact, *Chris* is typically the travel instigator in their relationship.

Marie So—short for Marie Sophie—and her husband Christophe are jazz musicians with a flair for adventure, and the fact that they have two small children never stops them from traveling the world and taking their little ones along for the ride. The couple first met in a jazz club in Paris, and after spending several years traveling and making music together, they had two children—a beautiful, spunky little daughter named Soléa, and the cutest, cuddliest little boy in the entire world, Tao. A few years after the babies came, Chris and Marie got hitched in Vegas on a whim. These two don't do anything by the book, and they live an extraordinary life because of it.

I first met them on one of their many adventures, while they were doing a one-year home exchange, swapping houses with a family in Cardiff-by-the-Sea, California, while that family lived in their adorable house in La Ciotat.

Mutual friends introduced us, and as soon as they found out I was a writer, they asked me to write a few sets of song lyrics in English for Marie So's third album. With my lead character, Charlotte, from *Sleeping with Paris* in mind—well, let's be honest, Charlotte is really *me*—I got to work on my first song, "City of Lights."

It's about—*surprise!*—a girl who has left all of the men in her life for Paris, her true love. But to think this girl could run off to Paris and not have a little romance? Not a chance. At the end of the song, a man comes along—"the one she swore never to love... and by the Seine, their lips met."

Ah, so our girl gets a little action in Paris, after all.

Over the coming weeks, I wrote two more songs for the album—"One Night in Paris" and "A French Girl in California." We spent many an afternoon at Chris and Marie's cute little Cardiff home tweaking the lyrics while Chris composed the music and Marie So sang. Writing can be such a solitary profession, so to be able to weave a story with my words and watch it come to life in their music was such a beautiful, fulfilling process. The three of us were forever bonded from that point on, and when the time came for Marie So and Chris to return back to their home in France, I promised them I'd be back to see them later that fall.

And now, here I am.

Having an intense food-gasm in Saint-Tropez and admiring the way Marie So and Chris have synchronized their dreams together so beautifully, so seamlessly. One of them thinks up an adventure, they work together to make it happen, and then they do it! They don't spend hours arguing about *how* to do it or *if* they will do it. They simply decide and *do*. On top of that, they share their art and create music together, all while being responsible and earning a living to support themselves and their two children.

Wow.

"*Un peu plus?*" Chris says, offering more cake.

I hold my plate out and smile at the two of them, thinking, *yes, I'll have what you're having.*

We spend the rest of the day taking a leisurely stroll around this magnificent town on the French Riviera, and once again, I am falling in love. This is a totally different side of France than what I'm used to experiencing in my two beloved cities of Paris and Lyon, but it's equally as charming, alive, and gorgeous. A talented line-up of artists circle the port, each of them showcasing their own unique flare in the way their paintings reveal the beauty of *la Côte d'Azur*. Nearby, sailboats and yachts wait patiently for their owners to take them out for a spin. There are ice cream shops and cafés and breezy, upscale clothing shops everywhere we look. Marie stops to take a photo of me in front of one such shop, next to the sign on the door that reads: "Your husband called. He said to buy anything you want!"

I may not have a husband anymore, or the money to buy anything I want, or the money to buy anything at all except the cake I just ate, but as my feet carry me along the rocky shores, as I hum along with the musicians strumming their guitars, and as I hold onto little Soléa's hand, my heart feels full again. I feel alive, thankful, and loved. And that's all that matters.

ON MY last day with my friends in the South, I am tapping my foot and singing along as Marie So, Chris, and their jazz band give an informal performance of their third album, *City of Lights.* All three of the songs I wrote for them are featured on the album, along with several exquisite songs in French written by a poet named Sasha, who is sitting by my side, a picture of elegance with her wine in hand, her head swaying to the music.

With the plucking of the bass, the jazzy piano rhythm, a lively drum beat, the melodic guitar, and Marie So's smooth voice rounding it all out, the words I wrote alone at my desk in that apartment overlooking the canyon are coming alive before my eyes, in this living room in the South of France.

It's amazing how life weaves together such beauty if you just follow where it leads.

I'm smiling in gratitude, my eyes teary, as I listen to Marie So sing a story I wrote in a song.

This story, of course, is my own.

The City of Lights

She follows her own path
She never was like the others
Those lights, they drew her in
On the Seine, she fell in love

Heartbreak used to be her pastime
But now, she has a new love affair
Those lights, they won't break her heart
Not like the men...
Never like the men

She dances under the lights of Paris
The moon, sparkling on the Seine
This is her one true love
Those lights, those brilliant lights
This is where she fell in love

She guards her heart
A treasure all to herself
No man can touch it
Only the lights she lets in

She left it all behind
Her loves, her broken heart, her hope
She sent them away
Down the river

She dances under the lights of Paris
The moon, sparkling on the Seine
This is her one true love
Those lights, those brilliant lights
This is where she fell in love

He came along one day
The one she swore never to love
She already loved the lights
By the Seine, their lips met

She couldn't resist him
A thief, he stole her heart
It was night, on the Seine
Where she fell in love

She dances under the lights of Paris
The moon, sparkling on the Seine

This is her one true love
Those lights, those brilliant lights
This is where she fell in love

Of course, I haven't yet fallen in love with a man while kissing him along the Seine at night. But in only a few short days, I have a feeling that the final verses in this song may finally come true.

Chapitre 22

I HAVE three more days to spend alone in Paris before the arrival of my lover, and with a last-minute cancellation on the Airbnb flat I'd booked, I'm on my way to the apartment of one of my dearest Parisian friends, a man I refer to as: *The Publisher.*

This French publisher does have a name, though, and it is Stéphane.

Rain is drizzling over Paris as the cab pulls up in front of Stéphane's apartment, which is situated in a prime spot right on the bustling, tree-lined Boulevard Saint-Germain. With one foot out of the cab, a memory of the first time I met The Publisher flashes through my mind.

It was one year before I met Nick, and I was at my favorite yearly writers' conference. Amid the sea of 2,000 fairy-tale-loving, wild, raucous romance writers, I met a French publisher named Stéphane. Little did I know that night, but meeting him would change my world forever.

At this time, my husband and I had been trying to get pregnant for a year, I hadn't had my period in several months, and

I was battling severe PCOS. My skin was breaking out, my hair was thinning, and I was the lowest I'd ever felt in my marriage, although I didn't want to admit it to anyone.

But at this writers' conference, when I finally had a few days to breathe and be myself, I admitted this truth to a French man I'd only just met. Over wine and books, I told Stéphane the story of my struggle to get pregnant and how this had led to the downward spiral of my marriage. I told him all about how much I loved France and how I'd based every single book there so that at least I could travel back through the eyes of my characters on a daily basis.

Stéphane listened, and then he told me all about his own views on marriage. He found it to be an ancient institution that doesn't at all honor human nature.

"It's not natural or realistic or fulfilling to spend your life with one person, and one person only," he argued. "Think of all of the interesting people you can meet and the incredible experiences you can have when you're not tied down to one person for the rest of your life."

"So what's your answer?" I asked him. "How do you live your life?"

"I don't have exclusive relationships anymore," he said, not batting an eye. "And I *don't* fall in love."

This from a Frenchman at a romance writers conference.

"You don't fall in love?" I asked, baffled. "But how do you stop *that* from happening? And don't you *want* to fall in love?" Even though my marriage was falling apart, I still wrote love stories. And I wasn't yet so jaded that I believed those stories were crap. No, not yet.

My disbelief in love and happily ever after would come later.

But that night, as I discussed marriage and love and relationships with the only Frenchman for miles, I couldn't imagine a world in which I didn't ever again want to fall in love.

What had happened to Stéphane to turn off his heart? I wondered.

I didn't have to wonder long. Stéphane was like an open book—he told me all about the long, exclusive relationships he'd had in his twenties and thirties, all of which had ended in heartbreak. A few years before we met, he'd decided he was finished with all of that. Since then, he'd carried on in a few long-term open relationships, where the women were fully aware of the arrangement, and they were free, in turn, to have other relations with other men. And in between his passionate, romantic nights with *those* women, he would travel to conferences and book fairs and meet other women, and have what he called in French, *aventures,* whenever he so pleased.

And since he was so honest about the whole damn thing, where was the harm?

Huh.

This new way of experiencing relationships really opened my mind. That night as we drank more and more wine by the hotel pool, I felt envious of Stéphane's way of life. Of his freedom. Of the constant excitement and passion and romance he could experience with this lifestyle he'd chosen.

"This way things don't get old and stale," he said, "the way they do in marriage."

Old and stale. Yup, that about summed it up.

"But don't these women get jealous that you're sleeping with other women? And don't you get jealous that they're sleeping with other men?" I was still trying to wrap my head around this so-very-French arrangement he'd worked out to essentially have an unlimited number of mistresses who all knew about each other and were seemingly okay with it.

"Of course there is jealousy at times," he admitted. "But who am I to tell any of these women who they can sleep with or how they should spend their lives? I don't own them, and they don't own me. I think this is one of the biggest crimes in marriage— this assumption that you *belong* to your husband, and he *belongs* to you. That the two of you own each other—own each other's hearts, souls, minds, and bodies. It's ludicrous."

I was nodding, almost furiously, in agreement. Marriage w*as* like that. And I was so, so tired of it.

Later that night, as I lay in bed unable to sleep, my conversation with Stéphane whipped my married mind into a total frenzy. The notion that I belonged to my husband physically, emotionally, sexually, and in every other way *did* seem ludicrous when I really thought about it.

Was I not my own individual adult woman who could make her own choices?

How thrilling would it be to have an *aventure*, to feel butterflies again, to kiss a new boy, to forget about all the troubles that awaited me at home and let myself go?

As Stéphane had said to me earlier, what reason do I have to deny pleasure where pleasure can be had?

Well, the vows I took, the marriage I was still in, and respect for my husband and our relationship, to name a few. But what did I think of this marriage thing I'd signed up for so long ago? These days, I was having a hard time believing in marriage, especially in my own, and I was certainly having a difficult time enjoying it.

Is that how we're supposed to live? Just sucking up the displeasure and getting through another day because we made this commitment long ago when we were too young to know what we would want in five years, ten years, twenty years? Do we not have the right to question the decisions we've made in our past, and re-evaluate them when they don't seem to make sense for our futures?

When I returned home from my conference, nothing had changed for my husband, but everything had changed for me. Meeting Stéphane had opened my eyes and made me remember who I was and what I truly wanted out of life. I didn't want to be held down, controlled, made to feel bad for my creative dreams and passions.

Now that this fire had been lit inside me—a fire I thought had died a sad, pitiful death long ago—I could no longer stand to stay complacent in my restrictive marriage. I began speaking my mind, announcing my truth, and refusing to mold to my husband's every desire and demand.

I was allowed to be me! I didn't belong to him! And I would fight until he finally accepted me for the strong, independent woman I was.

Which, of course, was the beginning of the end of my marriage.

So now, here I am. Back at Stéphane's, feeling so thankful to be able to spend time with a man I hold so dear to my heart. For it was he who first lit my fire and helped me come alive again. For this, I am eternally grateful.

When I arrive at Stéphane's door, dripping from the rain, giant suitcase in hand, he smiles.

"Welcome back to Paris, *ma chérie*."

I SPEND the next few days frolicking around the City of Light, devouring its decadent cuisine and drinking in its vibrant, artistic culture with a myriad of Parisian friends, all of whom are so refreshingly candid about their lives that each conversation is as rich and fascinating as visiting a new art exhibit at the Musée d'Orsay or watching a ballet at the Opéra Garnier or perusing the shelves of old books at Shakespeare & Company. With the romance of Paris as our backdrop and a glass of wine always in hand, we discuss art and literature, careers and friendships, spouses and lovers, marriages and divorces, but time and time again, our conversations go back to one topic, and one topic only: *love*.

On an especially chilly fall day, I'm tucked inside Café de Flore, enjoying the clanking of dessert spoons and wineglasses and the bustling excitement that can only be found swirling around a Parisian café. I take a sip of my steaming *chocolat chaud* as Anne-Laure, a talented French painter and one of my closest Parisian friends, fills me in on the latest in her love life.

Anne-Laure has been in love with a married Austrian violinist for years—the man actually composes music for her, how could she *not* fall in love with him?—yet she is tied to her own financially stable, rather unfulfilling marriage to a Frenchman.

"If I leave my marriage, my art doesn't provide me with enough of a stable income to survive on my own, and on top of that, my lover is married with a child, and he is never going to leave his wife." She says this with a haunting sadness in her big brown eyes, but I also detect in her a certain level of exhilaration over having this secret lover—the thrill of those stolen kisses, the passion she feels each time he touches her, tells her she's beautiful, holds her in his arms.

This is a feeling with which I am becoming quite familiar, now that I have taken on my own married lover.

Despite the thrill of this forbidden romance, it seems Anne-Laure is bound to her marriage and destined to pine away for the true love of her life for the rest of her days. In the rare moments she gets to spend with her lover, they are practically undressing each other on the banks of the Seine at night, and while they know they will never be together, that doesn't kill the love.

Always, it's about the love.

On another breezy autumn evening, I am drinking champagne and circling my friend Sylvia's apartment at the book reading she is hosting for me, and it is here that I meet Roniece, a glamorous, blonde New Zealand beauty whose husband of thirty years has recently left her for another woman. Immediately upon signing the divorce papers, Roniece packed her bags and headed straight for Paris because, just like me, she is in love with this city.

There it is again, *the love.*

And on my last night at Stéphane's, while we are out to dinner at a charming Italian restaurant near Odéon, Stéphane admits that I am the first woman about whom he has had what he calls *la fantasie de l'épouse*, or *the fantasy of the spouse*.

At this, I can't help but smile.

"Stéphane, this is why I love you," I say. "While everyone else in the world is stuck in a marriage, having fantasies about taking a lover, here you are, with more lovers than you know what to do with, fantasizing about what it would be like to take a wife."

What I don't admit is that I find it incredibly sweet and endearing that he is fantasizing *specifically* about what it would be like if that wife were *me*.

With his Casanova lifestyle, it's not what Stéphane truly wants, of course, to take me as his wife. And considering I've only just initiated my divorce, *and* I have my married-but-in-an-open-relationship lover descending upon Paris in just a little over twenty-four hours, it's clearly not what I want either. But still, because we are drinking wine in Paris, and because we have the most candid, thought-provoking conversations about everything under the sun, it's fun to discuss.

As our spoons crack the golden brown layer of our crème brûlée, Stéphane brings up the topic of my divorce. "I didn't think you were ever going to leave him," he says. "I thought you were going to stay unhappy in that situation...forever. I must admit, I'm shocked you really did it."

"I'm just as shocked as you are," I say. "I still can't believe I actually did it. You were the initial catalyst, you know, to helping me realize that I was living a life that didn't fit me anymore. I will always be so grateful to you for that," I tell him. "*Thank you.*"

Stéphane's smile is as warm as the crème brûlée melting on my tongue, and I just adore him.

Ahhh, the love.

The next day, after I say goodbye to The Publisher, I lug my giant suitcase out of his apartment, cab it over to the Marais, and check into the chic little flat my lover and I will be romping around in for the next few days.

In the depths of my suitcase, I find my hidden bag of lingerie and hang each delicate piece in the closet, running my hands along the satin and lace, imagining instead my lover's hands and what they will do to me the first time they gain access to my hungry body.

I spend the evening outlining my screenplay on index cards, blanketing the bed where we will be making copious amounts of love with notes on how my leading lady will meet her own Paris lover.

Late that night, as I am trying in vain to sleep, I check the clock and realize that Nick is at the Chicago airport right at this moment, waiting to depart for Paris.

And so, I send him an e-mail with a photo attached. It's one of the photos that he specifically told me *not* to send, but assuming he has nothing left to focus on except our Paris adventure, I decide a sneak peek of what is to come won't hurt anything.

The photo I choose is tasteful and soft and intimate. It's a picture of my profile as I am holding my hair up, a few loose strands falling, brushing my cheek. My arms are bare, and only the straps of my bra are visible on my tanned shoulders.

The picture says so much about me these days, but as I send it across an ocean to Nick, I know it really only says one thing: *love.*

Chapitre 23

THE SUN has barely said *bonjour*, but I am wide awake, my heart pounding, as I stand on my tiptoes in a crowd of strangers, craning my neck to watch for Nick amid the sea of passengers filing out of the baggage claim area in the Charles de Gaulle Airport.

Come on, come on, come on...

And just when I feel like I may die of sheer anticipation, *there he is.*

As soon as our eyes meet, his grin lights up the entire airport. His smile is brighter than the sun, the stars, and the moon combined. And it's all for me.

He rushes to me, drops his bag and wraps me in his arms. His lips are soft and warm and hungry as they press into mine. We don't care that we are surrounded by all of these strangers with their different languages and their mountains of luggage.

We are together.

We are together.

I feel such relief in his presence, in his arms; I wonder how I have survived so many weeks without him.

On the train ride back into Paris, we are still kissing, still wrapped around each other, one long male-female body made of hormones, lust, desire, and pure, unadulterated joy. When we finally take a brief moment to breathe, Nick smiles sweetly at me.

"I brought you something," he says, reaching into his bag.

"You brought me more than *you*?" I ask. "You know that you being here is already the best gift of my entire life."

His pale cheeks blush in appreciation, and he hands me a book titled *The Dud Avocado* by Elaine Dundy.

"I was in an old bookstore when I saw this and thought of you," he says. "It's about an American girl who moves to Paris in the 1950s, and all of her affairs and adventures abroad. Obviously, I had to get it for you."

I clutch the book to my chest, smiling like a fool. How is it that I have only known this man for a few months, during which we've spent less than a full week together, and he already *knows* me, he already gets me?

What a gift that I don't have to fight to be myself any longer. What a gift that I can relax in Nick's arms and know that he adores me for exactly who I am.

"Thank you," I say. "This is perfect. I can't wait to read it."

What I want to say is *you're perfect, and I want to be with you. Forever and ever and ever more.*

There is simply no other way for me to feel when this man has flown halfway across the world to be with me in Paris. When he shows up and showers me with kisses and brings me the most perfect gift. When I know he is about to make my every sexual desire and fantasy come true inside our own little flat in the City of Love.

Honestly, how else could a girl feel but wanting to keep this sweet and sexy man all to herself for the rest of her days?

When we arrive at our flat, I barely have a moment to show Nick around before he strips me down and buries me beneath the red sheets, a torrent of heat and passion and breath steaming up the window beside our bed.

Beyond that window, Paris is waiting patiently for its newest set of lovers to set fire to its streets. But first, we have to set fire to each other.

THE TREES, sidewalks, and apartment buildings are bright and sparkling with the midday autumn sun as we emerge from our newest love nest, satisfied, giggling, and intoxicated with each other. We meander through the Marais, past the towering Hôtel de Ville, and across the Seine, holding hands all the while. Even though I feel an inevitable stab of jealousy at the sight of the silver wedding band glued to his left hand—a firm reminder that I am not, and never will be, the only woman in Nick's life—I tell myself that nothing will ruin these moments we have together in a city that seems to be made for us.

Our first stop is Notre Dame. We don't actually go inside, but instead we cozy up on a set of bleachers facing the cathedral, and we talk, so breezily, so easily about where we grew up, what we were like in high school, and how we were both troublemakers in our own ways.

"I once outran the cops in a cornfield, after they busted a party I was at," I tell him. "I was wearing the tiniest little tank top, the shortest shorts *and* high heels, and I still outran them. We hid in the fields for over two hours. I've never had so many mosquito bites in my life; I was covered."

Nick laughs, his eyes lighting up at my stories. I think I could tell him the dumbest, most boring of stories and he'd still be lighting up like this. He does the same for me. We are the light in each other's lives—a light we didn't know we needed so badly until we first met.

"Wild Ohio girl, running through cornfields," he says, squeezing my thigh and scooting closer to me. "Probably driving all the boys crazy..."

He runs his lips up my neck, not caring that we are facing a cathedral. I don't care either. I am more concerned with our ridiculously amazing compatibility. Stunned by it, actually. It seems that not only was Paris made for us, but that we were made for each other.

Later, we have moved our cozy chat to Malongo, a trendy coffee shop nestled on the Left Bank on rue Saint-André des Arts. After Nick gets our strong French espressos, we settle into a cushy love seat in the back corner, and it is here that Nick finally asks me how everything went down at home when I told my husband I wanted a divorce. I give him the basic story, not sugarcoating it, but certainly not letting on just how devastating it really was to make the official break.

"Have you been in touch with him at all since you arrived in France?" Nick asks.

"Only for a few administrative details," I respond. "It's all business between us now, which feels really weird, but at least he's being kind. When I get home, we'll be living together for three more weeks before he moves out of our apartment, so I'm hoping we can keep things calm and amicable, the way we have so far."

Nick shakes his head. "I can't believe you did it."

"I know it was the right decision," I affirm. "And I'm doing really well now. I mean, I'm running around Paris with a lover, so I'm doing *really* well."

He laughs, wrapping his arm around my shoulders. "You do seem happier. A liberated woman. A *sexy* liberated woman."

"Why thank you," I say with a giggle, loving the way he looks at me, like he could devour me again at any second, and then devour me a third time, immediately after.

"So how are things going at home for you?" I ask. I know I shouldn't even bring up his home life, but I can't stop myself. I want to know if this—*if we*—have impacted his marriage.

He shifts in his seat, a sigh escaping his lips. "To be honest, I've never been so distracted before. Both with work and my marriage. It's just...*this*...*you*...*us*...it's..."

"I know," I say. "It's crazy."

"It is," he agrees. "I've been having all these negative thoughts about my marriage. You know, noticing all of those little things that have always been there, that I've just overlooked for years. You can't have everything with one person, and I know that, but the things that are missing in our marriage seem to be so glaringly obvious now that I've met you."

After a long pause, I say finally, "I don't want to mess anything up for you."

"I know you don't," he says. "And I'm a willing participant here, obviously."

"Seriously though," I say, "I want you to know that I have no intention of meddling in your marriage. I get what it's like to be with someone for so long that you can't imagine your life without them. And I also get what it's like to want to experience other people and other relationships, even while you're in your marriage. But if this relationship is screwing with your marriage too much at any point, you know I'll understand."

He pulls me close, and with the scent of coffee swirling around us and his lips brushing over my cheeks, I want to retract my last sentence. I won't understand. I am falling too hard for Nick to be able to imagine a time when I wouldn't want his arms wrapped around me, his heart pressed against mine, his lips hovering near.

"Don't worry," he says. "I don't have any regrets about coming to Paris. Already, it's been the best morning I've had since I woke up with you in LA."

This gets a grin out of me. "Are you sure you're not jet-lagged? You don't want to head back and take a nap?"

"No way in hell am I going to sleep until you're wrapped in my arms, fast asleep yourself. And even then, I may stay awake and creepily watch you sleep." He stops talking for a moment, those handsome eyes of his drilling into my soul. "I don't want to miss a second with you, Danielle. Not a single second."

As we walk out of the coffee shop attached at the hip and the heart, I think that if I could count the number of seconds I have in the rest of my life and then spend every one of those seconds in Nick's arms, it still wouldn't be enough.

I'd still want more of him.

"ISN'T THIS just the most charming little *quartier* you've ever seen?" I say to Nick as we wind down rue de Buci, past bustling brasseries and sweet-smelling boulangeries and vibrant flowers and tempting gelato.

But when I look up at Nick, I don't find him gazing around in awe at the beauty of this lively 6th arrondissement neighborhood. Instead, he is gazing down *at me* in awe.

"You know I've been to Paris several times," he says, "and I've always loved it. But watching the way you light up here, seeing the streets through your eyes, puts a whole new spin on this city."

He kisses me then, in the middle of this Parisian street, and as the scent of flowers and chocolate and coffee envelop us, I know that I, too, will never see Paris in the same light after I've walked these streets with Nick by my side.

All of this kissing and giggling has gotten us hungry, so I lead Nick down a picturesque cobblestone alleyway just off Boulevard Saint-Germain, and we settle on a classic French bistro called La Jacobine.

Inside, we are so delirious for each other that we can barely hold a conversation without breaking into a fit of laughter or smiles or intense glances as we drink our wine and try crazy dishes on the menu like *le foie gras de canard au pain d'épice—*

duck foie gras with gingerbread—and not so crazy things like *la soupe gratinée maison aux oignons*—homemade onion soup. After lunch, Nick leads me straight into *la chocolaterie* across the cobblestones and we spend far too long eating mouthwatering samples and combing over row after perfect row of delectable chocolates before we make our final choices.

With full stomachs and a little sack of raspberry, caramel, and ganache-filled chocolates to tide us over until our next decadent meal, my lover and I take to the streets of Paris, grinning like idiots.

"Thank you," I say. "For lunch, for the chocolates. You know I don't expect you to take care of everything." I am referring to the fact that Nick has paid for everything, and I can tell he plans on continuing to do so.

"You don't have to thank me," he says. "This is the advantage of being my mistress." That devious, boyish smile lights up his face as he says this, making it obvious that he enjoys the thrill of having a Paris mistress, and the power of being the man who treats his mistress to whatever she wishes—fancy meals, wine, chocolate, and mind-blowing sex.

"I'll take it," I tell him. And while I am enjoying this mistress thing too—it *certainly* has its perks—I can't deny the deeper feelings bubbling up inside me, wishing I could be so much more to Nick than just his mistress.

OUR POST-LUNCH stroll takes us to the Pont des Arts, a charming pedestrian bridge whose railings have been smothered from end to end in recent years by love locks—little padlocks that tourists have engraved with their own messages of love in a city that is already bursting at the seams with romance.

I'm not going to ask Nick to do a love lock with me—that seems entirely too cheesy for our sophisticated, secret affair. But there is a question I've been wanting to ask him all day, one that I haven't worked up the courage to ask until now.

"Want to take a picture?" I say. "Together?"

Nick hesitates, and for the first time since he arrived, I detect that same look of fear in his eyes that I first noticed back in LA, when he decided he couldn't handle seeing the psychic with me.

"I'll never share it with anyone of course—it's just for me," I clarify.

Still, he's hesitating.

"I'll hide it in a secret file—I promise."

He takes a deep breath, relaxes a little, and smiles. "Okay, sure."

An American couple is passing by just as I pull out my camera, so I ask them to take the photo for us. Nick puts his arm around me, and we smile for the camera, these two lost lovers who have found each other on a bridge laced with love.

"What a lovely couple," the woman says as she hands me my camera.

"Thank you," I say, suddenly feeling awkward about the whole thing. Did she see Nick's wedding ring? Does she think I'm his wife?

When Nick and I check out the picture, my eyes aren't drawn to the beaming smile on my face or to the hesitant grin on Nick's. My eyes don't go to his uneasy stance or to the way I've never looked more comfortable.

Instead my eyes go straight to that silver wedding band.

The photo is tainted.

But so are we, I realize.

Even the city that is made for lovers can't erase the glaring symbol of Nick's love for his wife, smack in the middle of our picture together.

LATER THAT afternoon, we are back at the flat, unable to put off our desire for a second longer. I have slipped into the transparent gray and peach lingerie that I bought at Darjeeling in Lyon, and with my legs wrapped around Nick's waist, he removes my shirt, grinning in delight at the sight before him.

"Of course you would wear something beautiful." He kisses my collarbone, neck, and shoulders, and then he runs his fingers along the straps of my bra and down to my breasts.

"Delicate, tiny, and soft, just like you," he says.

He picks me up, lays me on my back, and runs those fingers down, down, and still further down, until I am moaning with pleasure, never wanting this moment to end.

OUR FIRST shower together in Paris is both sexy and hilarious. The shower handle is the kind that we must hold in our hands, and as Nick turns it on, a spastic blast of hot water shoots out in all directions. We've both just had the most amazing orgasms, so we are still delirious and giggly, and as Nick hoses me down in the tiny shower, this only makes me laugh harder.

Plus I just adore the way he looks in the shower. Those long, dark lashes filled with big drops of water, his dark hair all slicked back, and water dripping down his handsome cheekbones as he grins at me. That never-ending, sexy hot grin.

"What am I going to do with you?" I say as I kiss him over and over and over again on his wet lips.

"Never stop kissing me," he says.

"I won't," I promise. "Never."

And I don't stop, for the rest of our entire first day in Paris. We kiss and hold hands and kiss some more, all the way to a café near Châtelet, where we try all different kinds of crazy French cheese and drink wine and champagne and talk about when we are going to see each other again after Paris.

"Two months was too long to go without you," he says.

"It was *so* long," I agree.

"Are you taking any trips in the coming months?" he asks. "Trips that I could join you on perhaps?"

"I'm heading to Seattle next month to see a few friends and visit my publisher," I say.

"I've only been to Seattle once," he says. "A long time ago. But I loved it. And one of my new clients is up in that area, so I can always arrange some business there, no problem."

"Perfect. So you want to come?" I ask.

"Do you even need to ask?" he says.

We both sip our wine at the same time, then break into our ridiculous lover grins. He leans forward, kisses me over the table, and feeds me a melty piece of Camembert cheese.

"God that's good," I say before returning the favor.

After he eats his cheese and licks his lips, he lifts his bright green gaze to mine. "And after Seattle...what's next?"

And so we discuss all the cities we both may be traveling to over the next year—LA, San Francisco, Las Vegas, Santa Barbara, Rome, and New Orleans—and we plot out how we can make each one of them work. As a successful businessman, Nick already travels a lot for work, and per the hall pass arrangement he has with his wife, he may have already been having one-night stands during any of his travels, so I figure those nights might as well be spent with me. And now that I am officially single, I can take a lover on my trips without any guilt or lying.

It's the perfect set up.

But as we spend the evening talking about our incredible connection, and Nick admits that he has never taken an affair this far, or felt even remotely this strong for another one of his conquests, I wonder what exactly, this is setting us up for.

Knowing that he has no intention of ever leaving his wife, and that we are falling harder and harder for each other with each passing look, each kiss, each time we make love and please each other more than we've ever been pleased, I think that we are, quite possibly, setting ourselves up for disaster.

But it's a disaster I can't walk away from.

A disaster I *won't* walk away from.

Instead, after more drinks and more laughs and more exciting talks, Nick takes me back to our flat, and I change into the raciest little red slip and the skimpiest little red thong, and I dare that disaster with a dance that Nick will never, ever forget.

Lorde's new album, *Pure Heroine,* is playing as I sit him down in a chair in the middle of the room, straddle him, and let his hands have their way with me. The album title could not be more perfect, and as our sexy soundtrack rolls from "Tennis Court" to "400 Lux" to "Royals," I give Nick the biggest, deadliest dose of my "heroin" that he's had to date.

"I must be imagining you," he says.

"I'm as real as it gets," I whisper in his ear.

Later that night, we are lounging naked on the violet couch in our flat, and Nick feeds me a square of raspberry-filled dark chocolate from our visit to *la chocolaterie* earlier that day. The food-gasm I experience as the chocolate melts on my tongue is only intensified by the fact that I have just had one of the most intense *actual* orgasms of my life.

Yes, this falling for a married man thing is certainly a disaster waiting to strike. But at the moment, I am too high on Nick, on his sex, and on his chocolate to care.

Chapitre 24

OUR FIRST day in Paris is *still* going.

After all the cheese and the chocolate, the wine and the champagne, the walking and the talking, the dancing and the sex, Nick hasn't slept in over twenty-four hours, and he is *still* going. I adore this quality in him to say *yes!* to every adventure. To love life and our time together so much that sleep isn't even an option.

Which is perfect because tonight in Paris is *Nuit Blanche.*

On *Nuit Blanche*, which happens once a year, every October, Parisians take to the streets all night long for a rich celebration of the arts. There are free dance performances, art exhibits, and musicians blanketing the streets, and the city is *alive.*

Nick and I have weaved our way through the music and the booze and the art, all the way back to rue de Buci, where we are having dinner at a chic restaurant called Germain.

Dim lighting, sleek modern décor, and a background beat of sexy music set the stage for our first incredible dinner in the City of Light. Even better than the cool spot we've chosen to dine in or the scrumptious food we're eating is the effortless conversation we have when we're together. On tonight's menu: what I'm looking for in a partner now that I am officially *single and fabulous!*

"I want a partner in crime," I say. "I want someone who will take adventures with me, who will travel with me, not only to France but all over the world! Someone who will really *live life* with me, who won't hesitate to jump out of his comfort zone and try something new. I've never liked staying in one place for very long, and I'm tired of pretending that I'm okay with monotony, with doing the same thing day in and day out. I'm not. I'm a writer—it's in my blood, in my bones to make adventures and to write about them."

"Well, you haven't waited long to get started on that," Nick says with a lift of his brows, clearly referring to our scandalous Parisian adventure.

"And sex," I say. "I need to have a lot of it, consistently and frequently. This is non-negotiable. I will never again allow a relationship to get so stale that sex is an afterthought, something that we schedule in once a month if we're lucky. And if we are headed in that direction, I want to be able to sit down as two flawed human beings who care about each other, and talk calmly about how we have arrived at this point, acknowledging that it is normal to feel like we may want to be with other people, and then make a decision on how we're going to handle it. I don't want to lie anymore. I don't want to cheat. I don't want to deceive anyone. I don't regret us, of course, but I also don't feel good about the fact that I lied to my husband. He didn't deserve that. I don't ever want to be in a relationship where I let it get to that point again. I want to be myself. Unapologetically me, and whoever I'm dating can either take it or leave it. I'm never again pretending to be someone I'm not."

After my speech, I take a long drink of my Sauvignon Blanc, and I wait for Nick's response.

"I love that you've figured all of this out for yourself," Nick says. "I think it's amazing that you had the courage to make a break and move on with your life with such grace. And I love knowing you through this self-discovery period. It's such an important, memorable time in your life, and I'm honored to be a part of it."

"That's sweet of you to say."

"I mean it, Danielle. I've never met anyone like you."

"And I've never met anyone like you," I say.

Nick scoots his chair closer to me, and his soft lips meet mine over the candlelight.

"We are both so sickeningly romantic," I say to him between kisses.

"What can I say? I'm a dude, but I love romance. And I love that you love it too." He kisses me more and more and still more, until I am melting in my chair, ready to have him inside of me again.

"This connection we have..." Nick says, "...it's insane."

"I know." What I really want to say is that all of those qualities I just described about my ideal partner are sitting right next to me in him.

He is my ideal partner. The romance, the love for travel, the zest for life, the sex—*dear God, the sex*—Nick has it all. *We* have it all.

Except, of course, for that one pesky little fact that he is totally and completely unavailable.

And that I am totally and completely falling for him.

For tonight, though, and for the next few days at least, he is mine.

All mine.

THE FACT that our hearts belong together has never been more obvious than in the basement of this club in the Latin Quarter where Nick is swinging me around the dance floor to a live jazz band. The place is called Le Caveau de la Huchette, and even though I lived in Paris for a year, I've never been until tonight. It was Nick's idea to take me here, and I am in heaven.

We are giddy and tipsy and his hands are roaming inappropriately over my body as we sweat and dance and kiss. But appropriate doesn't matter in the middle of the night on *Nuit Blanche* when everyone else around us is swinging and laughing and dancing and kissing too.

"I love this!" I shriek as Nick spins me 'round and 'round and 'round and the sax blares and the drum keeps the rhythm and old men do the Charleston and young women swish their skirts. "It feels like we've been zapped back in time to the 1920s."

"I thought you'd love this place," he says, with his characteristic shit-eating grin.

I also love watching Nick dance in his sexy white T-shirt. He has rhythm, but with his somewhat corny moves, this is another one of those times when our age gap is clear. And I even love that about him.

I love it all.

As Nick dips me back, I feel myself falling, falling, falling... until he catches me in his muscular arms and plants a sweet, happy kiss right on my lips.

Even with his arms wrapped around me, I am still falling.

Hours later, we emerge from the club, our hot breath steaming up the chilly night air, and I say to Nick, "Thank you. Thank you for everything."

To which he gazes down at me and replies, "Thank you for being born."

I think I almost fall straight into the Seine at this line.

Dear God, am I falling for this man.

IT'S THE middle of the night as we tumble back into our flat, and Nick doesn't waste a second before he begins undressing me.

"We have to pace it, lover." I try to bat his hand away from my bra straps, but he's got that thing ripped off before I can say another word.

"I haven't had you in two months," he says, pressing me against the wall, running his insatiable tongue over my breasts.

"You've had me three times today. Do you want me to be limping around Paris tomorrow?" I am only half kidding when I say this. Our lovemaking, while quite possibly being the most intoxicating, satisfying sex of my life, is also excessive and leaves me limping around in pain from the sheer madness and frequency with which we do it.

"You really want to wait until the morning?" His voice is lined with the disappointment of a little boy whose mom is taking away his lollipop after only a few licks.

"Yes, lover. Really, we have to." I say this as I am topless and taking off both his shirt and his pants, so my words aren't at all compatible with my actions, but sex or no sex, I just want to run my hands over his smooth skin, his strong shoulders, his amazing back.

"You're not helping..." he says.

"I know, I know." I walk away from him, throwing a teasing look over my shoulder.

"Damn, woman." He shakes his head as his eyes comb the length of my body, stopping to rest on my breasts. "I'm hungry."

A few seconds later, Nick is standing in the kitchen wearing only his black boxer briefs and his black glasses, devouring figs instead of me.

"I have to get out my hungry, sexual energy by eating these figs," he says. "Figs or Danielle? Close call, but I'm going with the figs."

I want to wrap his shirtless, muscular, glasses-wearing, fig-eating body in my arms and kiss him and never let him go. He is so absolutely adorable and silly and handsome.

After the fig party, we brush our teeth together, then jump into bed in our underwear, turn out the light, and wrap our bodies around each other.

Skin to skin, we are hopeless. My underwear and his are off in less than half a second.

"I can't help myself," he whispers after he is already inside me.

"I'd be offended if you could," I whisper back.

We make love in the dark, like it's the first time all over again. And later, when we are finished, we collapse on each other, satisfied, sweaty, and intoxicated in the pure, perfect bliss of this beautiful Parisian love affair.

Just before sleep finally takes us into another dreamland, Nick whispers, "I've been waiting for this moment, just to fall asleep next to you, for *so long*." He pulls me in tighter, our bare skin meeting under the covers, my head resting on his chest. With full hearts and exhausted bodies, we sleep wrapped up in each other for hours and hours, until the morning sun blankets the city once again the next day.

Chapitre 25

DAY TWO of Paris Lover Bliss begins with a crêpe. Well, it really began with another romp under the sheets, but considering we are secret lovers who have met in Paris, the morning romp is a given. It is precisely *because* of this intense physical activity that we *need* to eat this delicious *crêpe salée* filled with *jambon, fromage,* and *champignons.*

"Sooo good," I coo as Nick and I pass the cheesy ham and mushroom crêpe back and forth on our way to the Châtelet metro.

With a mouthful of deliciousness, Nick takes me by surprise with a kiss. A crêpe kiss. It's my first, and I love it.

"*You're* so good," he says, once he's swallowed his big bite. "God, this morning was..."

"*I know,*" I say. "I still have butterflies just thinking about it."

"I get them too," he says. "The butterflies. I never thought I would have them again."

With our stomachs full of crêpes and butterflies, we squeeze onto the packed metro together.

I'm so short that I can barely reach the railing up above to steady myself, so Nick takes my hand. "Here, hold onto me; I won't let you fall."

We are pressed together, so comfortably, so sweetly. I rest my head on his chest and listen to his heartbeat as the train takes off down the tracks and whisks us all the way up to Montmartre.

We don't notice the uncharacteristic heat of this autumn day until we have climbed up what seems like an endless amount of hills and stairs to reach the grandiose Sacré-Coeur Basilica. Nick has stopped me at various cobblestone courtyards along the way to photograph me. In each picture, I have stripped off more and more layers until I am down to a tank top, jeans, and flushed cheeks. By the devilish grin he is giving me, it's clear he doesn't mind seeing more skin.

If I could strip off my tall black boots and walk barefoot, I would. But cobblestones and bare feet don't go very well together.

When we reach the stairs to the basilica, we stop for a moment, our hands always intertwined, and we gaze up at this massive, white fairy-tale-looking structure. With the bright blue sky and only a few wispy white clouds as the backdrop, it's simply stunning. On the landing of the stairs, a street musician is singing Michael Jackson's "Billy Jean."

"Billy Jean and the Basilica. Perhaps the title for your next book?" Nick says with a cheeky smile.

"They're obsessed with eighties American pop in France," I say. "When my girlfriends and I used to go out in Lyon during our semester abroad, all of the bars constantly played Madonna, Michael Jackson, and George Michael. You'd think we might hear a current French song every now and then, but no. The French are always at it with the eighties pop."

Inside the basilica, we are sweating more than Madonna, Michael Jackson, and George Michael performing on a combined tour in the heat of Las Vegas.

"It's like a sauna in here," I whisper to Nick as we remain smashed between the crowds of tourists, at their mercy as we walk slowly—*so slowly*—past rows of flickering candles and magnificent stained glass windows. "A beautiful, reverent sauna, but still."

"If I could pull down your jeans and take you behind that big pillar, I would," Nick whispers.

I smack him, biting my cheek so I won't break into a fit of giggles. "We are in a holy place!"

"Your ass is holy," he whispers back.

"You are so bad," I say.

"And you love it," he says.

"I do," I admit. I love it so much. And I love more than just his dirty sense of humor and his endless sexual desire that he cannot stifle for even ten minutes inside this steaming hot basilica. I love every single thing about him.

Well, except for the fact that I can't have him more than a few days a month or less. That, I do not love.

Everything else, *j'adore.*

Outside, the refreshing air is a welcome contrast to the cloud of steam we have just waded through inside the basilica, and Nick and I don't waste a moment to bolt down the stairs and escape the crowds.

Once we find a nearly deserted stairway, we stop to kiss over the railing, and I think to myself that this moment would make the perfect book cover. I am constantly writing and creating in my head, and this adventure with Nick has only served to heighten my creativity. I can't help but think that someday, this story—*our story*—would make a spectacular book. I'm not sure how Nick will feel about being the star in my next novel, so I keep my mouth shut on that and instead make a different suggestion.

"Time for a chocolate croissant perhaps?"

Nick whisks me into the first boulangerie we see and lets me order. He doesn't speak French, but he loves it when I do.

"*Un pain au chocolat et un croissant aux amandes, s'il vous plaît,*" I say, wanting to order the entire damn boulangerie. The scent of melted butter and freshly baked baguettes and chocolate is almost as intoxicating as Nick.

Outside on the street, my lover is leaning against a lamppost, eyes closed and moaning as he savors each bite of his almond croissant.

"The marzipan," he moans. "*The marzipan!*"

"It's happening," I say. "You're having a food-gasm."

He offers me a bite, and so we stand there on a bustling sidewalk in Montmartre, having side-by-side food-gasms, and not being quiet about it. French people must be used to loud Americans doing this sort of thing here, though. We simply don't have pastries this orgasmic in the States, and we couldn't stop ourselves from making a scene if we wanted to.

"The marzipan!" Nick says again as he devours the last piece of flaky pastry.

With bellies full of buttery croissant and *marzipan!*, we are both giddy, happy, and alive as we join hands and set off through the winding hills of Montmartre.

Nick takes me off the beaten path in search of hidden courtyards and abandoned alleyways where we look into each other's eyes and kiss and whisper sweet words of adoration.

We are in one such courtyard, admiring the flower boxes, the balconies, and the endless charm that can be found in the simplest of places when Nick says to me, "If I ever moved to Paris, I would buy a place in Montmartre, off a quiet little *rue,* with a courtyard just like this. I love these courtyards."

I would live here with you in a heartbeat. In a half heartbeat. In a millisecond of a heartbeat.

I don't say this, of course. Instead, I opt for, "It's magical here." Magical here *with you*, is what I really want to say. But as Nick leads me up rue Lepic and past the big windmill perched atop a restaurant called Le Moulin de la Galette, I know he knows.

He knows how magical we are together. He knows that living in Montmartre together would be nothing short of a dream come true for us both.

But since that isn't an option, I let the moment pass without telling him how I really feel, what I really want. Today isn't the day to shout our love from the rooftops, or even from the middle of a hidden courtyard on a hillside in Montmartre.

Only the city of Paris will be witness to these magical moments we are sharing in our own little fairytale land of windmills and flower boxes and butterflies.

Yes, Nick is married.

No, he will never be mine.

But this day in Montmartre is ours, and forever will be.

It's a heart-wrenching gift, but a gift nonetheless.

LATER THAT afternoon, after we have sat outside at Café Montmartre drinking espresso and discussing my love of writing; after we have passed by the oh-so-pink Montmartre landmarks of La Maison Rose and Le Lapin Agile; after we have admired the most magnificent paintings of all of the street artists; after Nick has let me take a photograph of him that I will forever cherish, where he is wearing his glasses and tilting his head the way he does every time he smiles at me; after *all of this*, we come across a tall red brick house speckled with black balconies and red flowers spilling over the railings, and Nick says what I've been thinking all day.

"That's where *we* would live. In that house." He squeezes my hand, his eyes getting misty.

"It's perfect," I say, my heart speeding up and constricting at the same time.

"When you strike it rich with your screenplay and your next book, maybe you'll buy it," he says. "And I'll visit you here."

"You have an open door, always," I say to my lover. And I mean it.

He pulls me into his warm chest and we hug in front of the house that would be ours, the house we wish were ours, the house that will never be ours.

LATER THAT night, after the sun has disappeared behind the clouds and the air has finally cooled, Nick and I have emerged from the Châtelet metro totally drunk on each other. And so we decide to heighten the feeling even further by stopping in a bar to have a glass of red wine.

It is in this bar, with alcohol on our palates and love on our minds, where Nick asks me to make him a promise.

"No matter what happens with us in the future, whether you're finished with me after Paris or we can't stay away from each other for the rest of our lives, promise me...*promise me*...that at some point in the next five years, we'll meet again in Paris."

My eyes can't help but take a quick peek at his silver wedding band, the ever-constant reminder that all we will ever have together are secret rendezvous and dreams of houses that will never be ours. That I am tumbling headfirst into a most dangerous territory, one that I have no business being in.

A territory that, in reality, belongs to another woman.

But as I tear my gaze away from the ring, I find solace in my lover's eyes. I find adoration and desire, love and hope.

I know I'm crazy to make such a promise. I'm crazy to continue this affair with even one more forbidden trip together, but I don't care.

All I see is my lover, whom I adore. All I know is how I feel when we are together, in this bar in Paris, as teardrops meet my lashes and my lover grips my hand.

"Hmm. Me, you, Paris, in the next five years..." I say, giving the very false impression that I'm considering my options.

"Promise me," he says, slipping his arm around my waist while his lips meet my neck.

"Yes. I promise." It's only a whisper, but there is more heart and soul in this one sentence than any I have spoken all weekend.

Nick brings his hands to my face, cups my cheeks, and our lips collide. Much like the way our lives first collided, so seamlessly yet so dangerously in a bar surrounded by romance writers.

Except when we leave this bar, the romance of *Paris* is there, waiting for us.

The wind has picked up, the night has settled in, and two of the city's most hopeless lovers have made a promise—a promise they wish, with every fiber in their being, that they can keep.

Chapitre 26

WE SAVED two very important adventures for our last full day in Paris together: a visit to the Opéra Garnier and a visit to the lingerie shop.

Since we know what we'll be doing immediately following the lingerie fashion show, we head to the Opéra first.

"This is my absolute favorite place in all of Paris!" I tell Nick for the tenth time as we hold hands down l'Avenue de l'Opéra and I bounce along like a little girl who gets to go to the ballet and eat chocolate and kiss the boy she loves all in the same day...well, basically because I *am* that girl. "I've been here a million times, but there is something about this place that always draws me back in."

Once we are inside, roaming through the Grand Foyer, admiring the intricate paintings on the ceilings, the golden chandeliers and golden pillars, and the absolute majesty of this historical masterpiece, Nick offers up a suggestion as to why I've always been drawn back.

"Perhaps in our past lives, we met here once, at a masked ball."

"Ohh, I love it," I say. "While we were dancing, our eyes met, and you knew you had to have me."

"I whisked you away from the ball and took you onto one of the balconies inside the theater." Nick is leaning closer to me now, whispering our latest fantasy in my ear. The tourists weaving past have no idea where our dirty minds are at.

"And I slipped your dress up and took you right there. I couldn't wait another second."

"Don't forget, I'd be wearing a corset and all those hot layers underneath my dress," I remind him.

"Oh, I'd still find my way in there," he says with his devious grin.

"I have no doubt you would, lover."

With our cheeks flushed and our libidos in full drive, I wonder if we *have* met before, in another life, in another time.

And what if that life was in Paris, long ago?

Nick and I make our way onto the balcony where he wraps his arms around me and we take in the bustling Place de l'Opéra below. The green awning of the famous Café de la Paix off to our right brings me back to the first time I tasted Paris, when I was only fifteen. I remember sitting out on the terrace of Café de la Paix with my girlfriends on a hot summer day, enjoying my first ever *croque-monsieur* and thinking that was the most delicious ham and cheese sandwich I'd ever had, but even more so, thinking this was the best city in the entire world. By this time in my life, I'd seen New York, DC, Madrid and Barcelona, and none of them held a candle to Paris, in my humble fifteen-year-old opinion.

I've been drawn to Paris since I was young, and I fell in love with the city upon first sight. Then again, I loved Paris before I even set foot on its cobblestone streets. All it took was a romantic comedy starring Meg Ryan and I was hooked. But what if there was more to it than that? What if I already knew Paris? What else would explain the fact that an Ohio girl who grew up in small towns and cornfields would come to Paris and instantly feel at home?

And what about with Nick?

I've been drawn to him like a magnet since the moment our eyes first met, but I wonder if something inside me didn't already know him, before we first shook hands, flirted, and later that night, made love.

Because as he holds me on this balcony and we look out over the city I know so well, the city I love so dearly, the city I trust to keep all of our secrets, I think that knowing him in only one life would never be enough. This love that is unfolding between us is far too big, far too spectacular, far too alive to be taken away by mortal death. This is the kind of love that lasts. The kind of love that carries over from decade to decade, from century to century.

This is a love that was written in the stars.

Since I was too young to understand why, I've always known that Paris was in my destiny. And now, I'm beginning to think that Nick was too.

OUR DESTINY has taken us to a treasure trove of lingerie shops that we discover not far from l'Opéra.

First stop: Darjeeling, of course.

Inside, Nick is seething with desire as we comb the aisles, our hands roaming over lace, our fingers tracing the smooth satin. He chooses more than a few delicious pieces for me to try on, and I choose a few as well, making for quite the lengthy show of bare skin, cleavage, and curves.

Nick is *in heaven.*

I honestly don't think I've ever seen him so excited. He would absolutely take me right here, right now in this dressing room if there weren't a myriad of saleswomen and customers popping in and out of the neighboring fitting rooms every two seconds.

When I lift the curtain, revealing the elegantly seductive white corset Nick chose for me, his eyes widen in delight.

"Oh, we are definitely getting *that*." He pops into the dressing room without warning, closes the curtain behind us. "You dirty little angel, you," he whispers in my ear as his hands roam my curves and find their way between my legs.

"You dirty devil." I take his hands and put them where I can see them. "Now get out of here or we'll never make it back to the flat so we can enjoy these!"

"But we can enjoy them right now."

"Lover. *Go*."

Nick makes our first large lingerie purchase in cash, so as not to leave a paper trail of his infidelities. As he hands over a wad of bills, I think about his wife, and how she has no idea that at this very moment, her husband isn't in a business meeting, but instead is purchasing massive quantities of lingerie for a lover with whom he is totally and completely infatuated.

Or, perhaps she does know. And perhaps, with his constant business trips, she is off enjoying her own secret garden of romance, lingerie, and desire.

It's not for me to worry about, I remind myself. Nick is in an open marriage, and while we are certainly taking things farther than the one-night-stand hall-pass they've agreed upon, I'm not turning back now. And neither is he.

And so we head into our next sensual shop, Orcanta, where I try on even more evocative, racy apparel for my lover. And my lover, who is now *dying* to have me, spends ever more forbidden cash on his secret Paris mistress.

THE SUN is high in the sky, once again radiating heat through what I thought would be a chilly October day. Nick has stripped off his sweater and as he leads me past le Pyramide du Louvre, one hand wrapped around mine, the other holding one of my shopping bags full of lingerie, I stop for a moment to take him in.

He is wearing a simple gray T-shirt paired with dark jeans, but in this moment, I've never seen him look sexier. His dark hair sits messy on his head, and when he looks back at me, with those mysterious green eyes and that come-hither smile, I can't help but take out my camera.

"Let me take a picture of you," I say.

He isn't as hesitant as that first awkward photo on the Pont des Arts, but I know him well enough now to detect just the slightest hint of uneasiness in his stance as he smiles for the camera.

In the photo, that simple gray T-shirt he is wearing is stretched tightly across his broad chest and muscular shoulders, and I think he is the sexiest guy I've ever seen standing in front of the Louvre, or the sexiest guy I've ever seen standing...*anywhere.*

"I love it," I tell him as we join hands once again and walk beneath one of the grand archways of the museum, on our way to the Seine. I can't ignore the look of apprehension on his face, though. He's worried about the photo.

"You need to know that I would never do anything to hurt you," I tell him. "No matter what happens with us in the future, I would never show anyone the photos we've taken. They are for my eyes only, okay?"

He squeezes my hand. "I know. I trust you. I just don't want anyone to get hurt."

"I don't either," I say, but the sinking feeling in my gut is telling me that *I* am the one who is likely to get my heart torn apart in this scenario. Granted, he may too.

But whenever we end this thing—because it will end some-day, somehow—he will still have his wife. The woman he has loved for years, the woman with whom he has built a life.

But I've given up my husband. I've given up my marriage.

And now I'm falling in love with this married man, who, as we stroll down the Seine, has pulled out his iPhone to answer e-mails from his wife.

As he types, his silver wedding band is glinting in the sunlight, blinding me, making me feel sick.

I know I signed up to be the mistress for the weekend. I knew what I was getting into. And I'm in too far to turn back now.

So I walk quietly alongside Nick as he sends his e-mails and puts out some sort of fire that's happening at home. And I only hope that someday, I'll be able to put out the fire inside me, the fire that is blazing only for him.

THAT NIGHT, we are drinking champagne as we lounge in the sheets together. I am wearing one of my new pieces that Nick just bought me—a transparent, lacy white bra with a silky mauve bow in the center and a matching silky white thong. Nick is rocking his own sexy lover look wearing a pair of black boxer briefs and nothing else. We are both tipsy from the champagne, laughing and kissing and chatting. The level of intimacy we've reached in only a few short days in Los Angeles and Paris together is astonishing, as if we've known each other for years but still possess that passion and excitement that you only have with someone you've barely just met.

As Nick brushes a strand of hair from my cheek and kisses me softly there, I know it's time to give him the gift I've been saving for him for the past few weeks. I also know that if I don't do it now, while I'm slightly drunk, I may never do it.

I hop off the bed and head to my suitcase.

"What are you doing, lover?" he asks, propping up on his elbow.

"I have something for you." I return to the bed with a folded piece of paper and hand it over to him. Nick takes it slowly as if he knows that whatever is written inside will take us down an even deeper rabbit hole than the one we've already dived into.

But he's deliberate as he unfolds the paper; he wants to go wherever this is taking us.

"I wrote you a poem," I say. "It's about the night we first met. I wrote it after our Hollywood trip, and I'm thinking of using it in my LA Confessions novella."

He takes a deep breath, then reads my words silently.

Did my soul already know?
Had she already planned that magical night?
The night your eyes would take me hostage
The night chemistry would flow between us, effortlessly
An electric current of heat.

My soul, she must have known
How important you would become to me.
How happy I would be
Knowing you exist.

She knew...that smart, vibrant, sexy soul
She totally knew.

You are a gift
A beautiful, perfectly timed gift.
One I will never take for granted
One I will love, always, for this.
For where you have taken me.

The world has opened
Now that you have arrived.

When Nick's eyes meet mine again, they are cloudy, filled with tears. He grabs me in haste, kisses me on the lips, folds me into his chest as the breath escapes his lungs in short, raspy bursts.

"You're laying down some heavy stuff, lover," he says finally.

I pull back so I can see him, so I can see the way my words, my feelings, have moved him.

"I wanted you to know how I feel. How thankful I am to have met you. Really, Nick. This—you, *us*—it's such a gift."

He pulls me in tight again, one hand squeezing me around the waist, the other stroking my long hair. And it is here that I hear how quickly his heart is beating. I feel it pulsing against my chest.

Mine is beating just as fast, maybe faster.

And I don't ever want it to slow down.

IT IS our last night together in the City of Light, and as we are on our way to dinner, both of us sobered up now and hanging onto each other as if the world might end any minute, we are crossing over Le Pont au Double just past Notre Dame when we stumble upon the most incredible street musician singing and playing his guitar. We join the large crowd that has gathered, and Nick stands behind me, wrapping me up in his tall, safe body as I lean all my weight into him, close my eyes, and listen.

The young musician has chosen to perform "Let it Be" by the Beatles.

Now it is my turn to stifle the tears, but divorce has turned on some sort of crying faucet that I didn't know I had, and I am unable to stop them. Nick is still behind me, though, so he doesn't see the drops streaming down my cheeks. He doesn't know that I am wondering why the Universe would play such a cruel joke on us. Why would I find the loveliest, most intense, intoxicating compatibility in a married man's arms, just as I am jumping out of my own marriage? Why would I find the person I feel I am meant to be with, the person with whom my soul is most aligned, and yet, stand here on this dark bridge in Paris, listening to the sage words of the Beatles, and know that no matter how much I wail at the sky, I simply have to *let it be.*

There is no other choice.

Because somewhere, across an ocean and half of a continent, there is a woman who has chosen this man as her husband. A woman who believes that *he* is *her* other half. And even though I don't know her, even though I am falling for her husband, who am I to take away such a wonderful man from the woman who loves him?

Then again, who am I not to follow my heart? Not to at least take these beautiful moments as I can get them—sparing though they may be—and cherish them for what they are. Gorgeous, heartbreaking, and full of love.

I may be Nick's Paris mistress, but tonight, as he rocks me back and forth on this bridge, as the words of the Beatles serenade us beneath the moon and the stars, tonight, I am his and he is mine, and nothing else matters.

THE NEXT morning, we are both sad messes. We only have a few hours left together before we have to head to Charles de Gaulle, board separate planes, go back to our separate lives, and wait almost another two months until we can see each other again.

We are strolling around Place des Vosges, kissing and whispering and holding hands in this quiet, sun-kissed courtyard in the heart of the Marais, wishing we never had to leave.

We stop in front of the fountain, listening as the water trickles down, and watching as the sun disappears behind a cloud.

"Maybe we can just disappear in Paris," I say. "Miss our planes. Never go back."

Nick kisses my forehead, pulls me close.

"I wish we could," he says. "I wish for that so badly."

He holds on to my shoulders, looks into my eyes as our noses touch. "I'll see you in Seattle, though, right?"

"Yes," I say. "*Yes*," I say it again, so he knows I mean it.

We continue our sad stroll beneath endless rows of archways and into a hidden garden that neither of us has ever seen in all of our Paris travels. In this garden, amid the perfectly trimmed trees, Nick takes the camera, and he photographs the perfect mess of me.

I'm smiling and I'm laughing, but I can't smile away the melancholy in my eyes. It's palpable in each of the photos he takes.

"I want you to look back on these and know that this is how I'll always see you. For exactly who you are, Danielle. You're perfect to me."

On our way back to the flat, we pass by the window of a men's clothing store and Nick points out a collared shirt that is covered in...butterflies.

"That's how you make me feel," he says. "Covered in butterflies. I think I should get that shirt."

"That shirt is ridiculous. But yes, it's perfect for this trip. Perfect for us," I say. And after a long pause, I tell him, "My butterflies are crying."

"Mine are too," he says. "Such sad, pitiful butterflies."

BACK AT the flat, we only have a few minutes until the Australian family who is taking over our love nest next is set to arrive—small children and all. As I'm finishing my last bit of packing, Nick comes up behind me, grabs me by the hips, and runs his fingers between my legs.

Even though I have had him more times than I could possibly count in these past few days, my desire for this man hasn't waned in the slightest. I lean back into his chest, let him press his fingers into me.

"I need to have you one more time," he whispers in my ear.

"That family is going to be here any minute," I say. "We can't."

"Let me take you into the bathroom. We'll be quick; I promise."

I don't have much time to make a decision, and as I look into his hungry eyes, I know there is only one answer.

Like two horny high schoolers who don't want to get caught in the act by their parents, we dash into the bathroom together, giggling all the while, and close the door behind us. Our laughter stops as Nick slips my leggings down, bends me over the sink, and pushes into me from behind. Our last time together is hard and nearly frantic—one last shot of heroin before we have to go cold turkey for the next several weeks.

With his hands wrapped around my hips, his body pulsing into mine, I turn around and give him my most sultry look, a look that I've only ever given to him. It is this look that does him in. He finishes and nearly collapses on me, wrapping me up in his arms, our bodies once again merging as one.

Not more than ten minutes later, the Australian family bursts through the door, all lovely smiles and perky accents. As I hand over the keys and tell them how much we enjoyed our stay, I notice that Nick is passed out on the bed, a heap of total sexed-up exhaustion.

Apparently I've taken every last bit of energy he saved for me. With the intense aching I'm feeling between my legs, I think that perhaps a break will be good for us. While we are so good for each other and so astonishingly, unbelievably compatible, we are also each other's kryptonite.

We are total addicts, druggies who can't get enough.

Judging by the sickly, gray look on Nick's face when I tell him *we have to go,* it's clear that these two lovers have a serious problem.

AT THE airport, Nick's flight leaves first, so I walk him as close as I can get to his terminal, and we sit down together in silence. You would think someone has just died.

"You said you have one of your books with you, right?" he asks.

"I have a copy of *Sleeping with Paris,*" I say.

"I want to read it on the plane. Can I have it?"

I pull the book out of my bag, but I'm hesitating to hand it over. "Remember, I wrote this when I was only twenty-four, and it's really girly, and—"

"Danielle. It's you, and I want to read it. Don't worry, okay?" He takes the book from my hands and opens it immediately.

My heart is racing at the idea of Nick reading an entire novel I've written. While I've had no problem exposing myself to him in every way imaginable over these past few days, exposing myself *in my writing* is another story. It's such a significant part of me that I can't bear the thought of him finding my writing silly or boring or fluffy.

He is lighting up as he thumbs through the pages. "I can't believe you've written so many books already. You're so young. It's amazing."

"Thank you," I say.

"I can't wait to read it." His lips find mine; our kiss is desperate, sweet, sad. "And I can't wait to see you again," he whispers.

"I can't wait to see you again, too," I say. "I had the most incredible time with you this weekend. The best three days I've ever spent in Paris."

"These were three of the best days of my entire life," Nick says. "Thank you."

"*Thank you.*"

The time comes for Nick to head to his terminal, for these two lovers to say goodbye.

And so, as much as we want to fall into some sort of lovers' abyss and never emerge, we must return to real life.

We kiss, we hug, and we hold each other one last time.

And finally, we let go. I walk away. I look over my shoulder again and again and again, and my lover is still standing there, planted to the same spot, tears in his eyes, waving and smiling his brokenhearted smile at me.

I have to force myself not to run back to him. Not to beg him to stay here in our lover's paradise forever. Instead, I turn away and walk toward my gate, alone, clutching my heart.

I don't feel it beating anymore, though.

I've left it behind, in my lover's hands. I only hope he'll keep it beating until we meet again.

Partie V

UNE CATASTROPHE ÉMOTIONNELLE ~
AN EMOTIONAL CATASTROPHE

"These violent delights
have violent ends
And in their triumph die,
like fire and powder
Which, as they kiss, consume."

~ William Shakespeare,
Romeo and Juliet

Chapitre 27

AFTER A long, lonely voyage, I've made it back to Los Angeles. I'm regrouping at Katie's house before I make the last leg of my trip down to San Diego. Katie wants to know *everything* that happened after she left Paris, and while I am once again tempted to tell her about my whirlwind romance in the City of Light, with her daughter on her hip and her husband in the next room, I keep my mouth shut. But as we chat about how much she loved the city and how we absolutely *must* make another trip back someday—*after* she has had her second baby and after that baby is old enough for her to jet off to Paris child-free, of course—I am distracted.

My mind is only capable of thinking one thing: *Nick, Nick, Nick.*

I still hear his boyish laugh. My stomach is still melting over that deadly grin. My insides are fluttering as I remember the way he took me in the bathroom of our Paris flat less than twenty-four hours ago. I can still feel him on me. Still taste him. Still smell him...even though we are now thousands of miles apart.

Katie is midsentence when my phone rings. A quick glimpse of the caller ID makes me realize that I'm not the only one jonesing for more.

"Katie, would you excuse me? I have to take this." I don't even wait for her to respond. I am so desperate to hear his voice, I can hardly think straight. My heart is pounding as I dash out of her house like a madwoman. When I've made it to the sidewalk in her picturesque little neighborhood, I answer.

"Hey," I say, trying to sound sexy and calm and easygoing, like this whole affair thing is just so *natural* for me.

"Hey, you," he says. I can hear him smiling. "I miss you." And now I can hear the sadness in that smile.

"I miss you too," I say hastily. Fuck acting calm and natural. I miss him so much that my heart may burst right here, shatter into a million pieces on this sidewalk.

"I'm sorry to call so soon, I just couldn't wait—"

"It's okay," I interrupt. "I'm so glad you called. I can't believe Paris already happened."

"It was so magical," he says. "More intense than I ever imagined it would be. Overwhelming."

"I know," I agree. I'm now pacing up and down the sidewalks of Katie's neighborhood, past picket fences and flower boxes and perfectly painted shutters. I'm the woman who gave all of that up. The mistress who is dying to be in her lover's arms again, to feel the weight of his body once more.

I don't belong in this neighborhood. In fact, I don't know where I belong anymore. Home is only a word I used to know.

"Are you doing okay?" Nick asks.

"Yes...just scared to go back to San Diego. I have no idea what it's going to be like. My ex and I have to live under the same roof for the next three weeks until he moves out."

"It's just a few short weeks, lover. It will go fast. And remember, Seattle is only a few weeks after that," he reminds me. "In the meantime, I was thinking that e-mails aren't going to cut it. What would you say about a Skype date every now and then?"

"I would *love* that."

"It may have to be *Silent Skype* on occasion, for obvious reasons, but if you're okay with that...we could even spice it up with a little Darjeeling and dancing..."

The obvious reason is so very obviously Nick's wife. Does he really plan to Skype with me while she is *in the house*?

"You know I'm always happy to dance for you," I say. "But only if you're sure it won't cause any trouble for you, and I'll need to be careful too as I'll still be cohabitating for the next few weeks..."

"I can't wait almost two months again to see your face," he says.

"I know. I can't even think about that right now."

"Later this week, lover, I'll see you on Skype."

"It's a deal," I tell him. What I don't tell him is that this new addition to our arrangement is making me feel queasy.

When I was a little girl, I never once said to my mom, "Mommy, when I grow up, I want to be somebody's mistress. I want to be the woman he has to hide away and keep a secret from everyone in his life. Mommy, I want to fall in love with a married man, a man who can never be mine."

That just isn't what we want as little girls. We want the fairy tale. We want to meet our Prince Charming and claim him for our own, for ever and ever more.

I did meet my Prince Charming, when I was nineteen. But our fairy tale is over.

Instead of happily ever after, I am heading home to help my husband pack and move out of our apartment. I am heading home to file for divorce. To officially end the fairy tale that started so long ago, the one I thought would last forever.

And amid all of that, I'll be dancing in lingerie for my lover over Skype, while his unassuming wife is sleeping in the next room.

No, this isn't at all the fairy tale I had in mind when I was a little girl.

But I'm a woman now. A grown up. And messed up though it may be, this is the life I am choosing.

WITH MY massive suitcase in tow, I tread carefully into my San Diego apartment, not sure what I will arrive home to.

Inside, the late afternoon sun is streaming in through the windows, but it feels as frigid as ice in here. Our wedding photos have been taken down, some of them turned over on the shelves. My husband has moved his belongings into the spare bedroom, and he is nowhere to be found.

My cats are happy to see me, though. Sweet and cuddly and purring, they are the only things keeping my heart warm in a place that now feels so cold, so foreign, so unsafe.

THE NEXT few weeks are filled with what I call "Shoot Me in the Face Divorce Moments."

Watching my husband iron his clothes and gel his hair before he goes out on another date.

Hours spent drowning in divorce paperwork, trying to do everything on my own without the aid of a lawyer so that I can save money, but worrying that I will check the wrong box and sign my entire life away.

Going through every closet and cupboard and crevice in the apartment with my husband by my side, as we decide, item by item, who will take this, and who will take that.

The worst of those items being our photos, our memories of our beautiful life together. Because it was beautiful. For so many years, it was happy and warm and loving and amazing. It was a dream come true. *He* was my dream come true. He rescued me from an inundation of dysfunctional family situations. He kept us financially stable during all the years where I was writing and teaching and not making a lot of money. He took on my student loans as if they were his own. He took me to the movies, where we would cuddle up close and whisper in each other's ears at random moments during the film, "I love you."

Despite all the ways in which the spark of our love has died, I know he loved me dearly, and he still does.

And now, we have to decide who gets this album, who gets that one, knowing that neither of us will have the heart to look at these photos, to be reminded of all the good times, for months or years to come, if ever.

Another Shoot Me in the Face Divorce Moment is the day I go to the courthouse to file the paperwork that I have spent endless hours preparing, but learn that I haven't filled everything out correctly. I cry the whole way home, wondering why it is necessary to sign legal agreements to be in relationships with people we love and call it marriage. Can't we just *be* with them, live with them, and love them until it doesn't work anymore? Ending a long relationship is hard enough. Why must the breaking up also involve filling out a gigantic stack of legal documents that are so confusing and intricate, they've had me in tears each time I've tried to finish them. And those tears were in vain, because now I need to hire a lawyer anyway.

It is in this state of condemning the entire institution of marriage that I do a Google search for divorce mediators in my area. My husband wants me to file as quickly as possible so we can get this over with and move on with our lives, so it's time to call in some help.

The first place that comes up is just down the street. I call, and it turns out they have just had a cancellation and can see me in twenty minutes. With my mountains of divorce paperwork, I fly out of the house and zoom up to the Divorce Help Clinic. Just before I turn into the parking lot, I notice that their office is directly across the street from a fertility clinic. It's the same fertility clinic I spotted when we first moved to San Diego, the one I thought we might have to visit in our quest to have a baby.

How ironic that here I am, a mere year and a half later, visiting the *other* clinic—the one across the street where people go to end marriages, not to bring new life into the world.

Inside, my new divorce lawyer helps me work out all the kinks in my paperwork, and when we are finished, I want to hug her. I want to cry on her shoulder. I want to tell her that all I have needed these past few weeks is to have a friend or a family member—anyone—sit with me and help me the way she has today.

"Thank you," I say. "Really, thank you so much. You have no idea how helpful this was. You should call yourself The Divorce Angel."

This gets a chuckle out of her, but she remains all business. I'm sure she's used to emotional women coming in and sobbing on her desk. That's what I feel like doing.

The next day, I drive back to the family courthouse downtown. I wait in line, I pay $465, and I watch a woman I've never met stamp the papers that I've just filed to end my marriage. She hands me my copy.

"Thank you," I manage to say before I dash up the stairs and out of that sterile building, holding in the tears that are ready to burst. When I make it outside, I cry, in public, all the way to my car. I cry the entire way home, my eyes so blurry I can barely see the highway.

Right when I walk in the door, my mom calls. She knows I'm getting a divorce, but she doesn't quite realize how hard it has been for me. She doesn't know that I've just filed. I don't tell her much of anything these days, but still, when I see her name on the caller ID, I am flooded with the desire to hear her voice over the line telling me she knows how I feel and that I will be okay. I want her to tell me I haven't just made the worst mistake of my life.

When I answer, and she asks what I'm up to, I tell her I've just filed at the courthouse, and I break down once more.

The minute she hears me crying, she tops me with her own deep sob. She quickly becomes more hysterical than I am, and while I know this is simply because she loves me and she can't bear the idea of knowing her daughter is hurting, I can't handle it. I need her to be strong, just this once, to listen to *me* cry, without breaking down herself.

But this is something she simply isn't capable of.

I dry my tears while I listen to hers pouring over the other line.

"Mom, I love you so much, but I have to go. I'm sorry, I can't comfort you right now. I need to get through this on my own."

She sniffles and sniffles and tries to control herself, but she just can't.

"It's okay, Mom. I know you love me. I love you too. But I have to go."

I hang up the phone and feel like throwing it through the window. I want to run out to the canyon and just fucking *scream!*

Instead, I settle for being a total divorced lady cliché, and I spend the day on the couch eating a family-sized serving of Stauffer's macaroni and cheese, an entire pint of Häagen-Dazs chocolate ice cream, and I barely even feel the food going down. I take a Xanax. And then another. And another.

I just want this whole day to go away.

Before my husband returns home from work, I manage to get myself up and into the shower. I drive over to my friend Kelly's house, where she is hanging out with Hayden, a cool California surfer dude who always makes us laugh.

I am sitting on the floor of her bedroom, a slumped-over mess of despair, when they look at me, then at each other, and back at me.

"I know exactly what you need," Kelly says. She opens a drawer, grabs a pipe and some weed, and they smile at each other. Kelly and Hayden know that I've never smoked pot and they think it's hilarious and absurd that I've never tried it. They've always made me promise to smoke with them the first time I do it, and while I've made the promise, I've never had any intention of actually smoking the stuff.

But today, I don't care.

So Kelly and Hayden teach me how to smoke a pipe, and since I've never smoked anything before, it's all a totally ridiculous scene with me coughing and laughing—yes, this got me to laugh—and them laughing *at* me. Finally, I get the hang of it. The smoke fills my lungs, and I puff it out, hoping it will help me feel better.

And it does make me feel better. Only a few puffs in, and all of my tension is melting away. I feel neutralized, as if the storm of emotions weighing down on me today has lifted, and I am calm, still, at peace.

And laughing. Laughing so hard at absolutely nothing.

"Why haven't I done this before?" I ask my friends later on while we are wolfing down beans, rice, and guacamole at Chipotle.

"Shit, Danielle," Hayden says. "Why the fuck *haven't* you been smoking pot?"

Kelly pats me on the leg. "I knew we'd convert you."

Later that night, I return home to find my husband making his dinner.

"Hey," I say, all cheery and giggly.

He shoots me a curious glance, then turns back to the stove. "Hey. Out with friends?"

"Yeah, Kelly and Hayden," I tell him.

"What did you guys do?"

"Just hung out at Kelly's for a little while, then had some dinner."

"Where did you eat?"

But I don't answer him because I'm off in some far-away la-la land, happy as could be.

"Where did you eat?" he repeats.

"Hmmm?" I say. "We didn't eat."

"You just said you ate dinner," he says.

"I did? Humph." I'm really stumped at this one. All I want to do is laugh, but I'm trying to hold it together. Then it comes to me. "Ohhhh, yeah. We ate at Chipotle!"

A long pause as he stares at me. And finally, the question of the year: "Are you on *drugs?*"

This pulls the laughing fit right out of me. When I finally calm down, I say, "Yes! I smoked pot for the first time. You should really try it. I have like zero anxiety right now. I mean, you could say anything to me, *anything,* and it wouldn't bother me."

My husband looks at me like an alien has invaded his home.

And I suppose I am an alien in that I am certainly not the girl he married long ago.

I'm a girl who had an affair she hasn't told him about, a girl who jets off to Paris to see her married lover, a girl who takes loads of Xanax and then smokes pot so she doesn't have to feel how badly it hurts to watch the life she once knew crumble before her very eyes.

That's the girl I am. But tonight, I don't feel any of that. I don't worry about it, either.

Instead, I head to my side of the apartment, write my lover an e-mail telling him about my first pot adventure, and then I drift into a dreamless sleep.

It's the first good sleep I've had since I was wrapped in Nick's arms in Paris.

THE NIGHT before my husband is set to move out, we are sitting opposite each other on the kitchen counters, drinking and eating pizza. We have split up all of our belongings, we have packed all of his things in boxes, and now we have one last night together before he moves into his own apartment, before we are both living alone and taking on the world by ourselves.

Before we launched into packing, we decided that the only way we'd get through this particularly painful Shoot Me in the Face Divorce Moment is with alcohol. I am now a few glasses of wine in, and he is several beers deep.

We spend the rest of the evening talking candidly about his dating adventures for the past two months. He tells me about how crazy some of the women have been, and how he realized this week as he began to pack up his entire life, that he isn't at all ready to be with someone else. He hasn't even begun to process the fact that we are really, truly, getting a divorce, and that will certainly take some time.

And so, as his soon-to-be ex-wife and friend, I give him dating advice. I tell him how I think he should handle these crazy women who want to get married immediately. I advise him to be honest with them, to let them know that he's not ready for much at this point.

He takes another swig of his beer while I take another sip of my wine, and I think about how we have sat on the kitchen counters like this so many times in our marriage, talking and laughing and sharing our lives with each other, and how this is the last time we will ever do it.

And how insane is it that our own fairy tale is ending with me giving my husband dating advice on the night before he moves out?

I keep drinking my wine so I don't have to think about it too hard. And he keeps drinking his beer so he doesn't have to, either.

The next morning, I help my husband move all of his things out of our apartment, and when everything is packed in the U-Haul, he comes back inside one last time to hug me.

We squeeze each other tight, and I will myself not to break down in his arms. I force the question out of my mind, the question that has been swirling around in my head day after day, night after night since I got back from Paris: *Am I making the right choice?*

Instead, I say, "See you soon." Even though I don't know if I will see him soon. I don't know when I will see him again.

And then he turns and walks away. My husband leaves.

And I am left all alone in the silence, wondering what I have just done.

I AWAKEN to the sound of birds chirping outside my window. When I open my eyes, the bright orange sun has just risen over the canyon, and swirls of pink clouds are floating in the sky.

Outside, nothing has changed.

But as I climb out of bed and walk through my half-empty apartment, I know that everything has changed. I feel elated and euphoric at the idea of being a single gal with her own apartment, but I am simultaneously heartbroken knowing that my marriage is over. It's really over.

We've filed for divorce. He has moved out.

And life must begin anew.

In a knee-jerk, panic-mode reaction the very morning after my husband has moved out, I grab my laptop and create an online dating profile on OK Cupid.

An hour later, I double-check my work.

Pictures of me looking *fabulous!* in France: *Check.*

An alluring profile that presents me as a romantic, sensitive, strong-minded but easygoing girl that you won't meet every day: *Check.*

A mention in the profile about my career as a French professor and novelist—intelligence, sexy language skills, and creativity combined: *Check, check, and check.*

I decide to leave out the part about my husband moving out *last night* and the part about me having two massive cats who sleep in my bed every night. I'm not sure which my prospective dates will think is worse—the fact that I am so very recently split from my husband or the fact that I have two gargantuan felines who will blanket their clothes in fur if they come to my house.

Oh, and then there's the whole thing about my married lover. Clearly, *that's* not going in the profile.

On my first week of online dating, I have four dates with four different guys. I alert my married-but-in-an-open-relationship lover to the fact that I'm dating now, just so he is in the know, but I don't go into specifics.

When we were in Paris and the topic of me dating came up, I told Nick that I did hope to begin dating again at some point, especially since there was no hope of ever actually being with him.

"Do you want to know?" I asked him. "When I'm dating other people?"

Nick nodded, seeming entirely too cool about this whole thing. "Yes, I think we should be open with each other as you start dating. I want you to be happy, and I certainly can't expect you to only be with me when I'm married."

His response stung even though I knew I should be pleased that he was being so open-minded.

"*How much* do you want to know?" I asked him. "Do you want to know details...like if I'm intimate with someone else?"

He paused, his face suddenly looking a little pale. "I can't even think about you sleeping with other people."

A sad silence settled over us as Nick held my hand a little tighter.

"I'm sorry," I said finally. "But I want to have a chance to be in a real relationship with someone who can actually be with me. I've felt alone in my marriage for so long now, and what you and I have together is...well, it's extraordinary, it's magical...but you're..."

"I know," Nick said. "And you deserve to have everything you've always dreamed of in a relationship, with an available man. I would never want to hold you back. But for today, the thought of you being with other people is just..."

"I understand," I said. "We can talk about it another time."

And when we did discuss the dating issue again, Nick told me that he *did* want to know when I began dating, and he *did* want to know if I was intimate with someone else, although the idea of it seemed to make him sick.

The idea of him going home to his wife after our beautiful Paris affair made me sick too.

That is just the nature of the affair beast.

I can't put my life on hold for Nick. So, I dive into the jungles of post-divorce online dating, having no clue what to expect.

Bachelor Number One is a handsome Asian photographer who is raring and ready to jump straight into a serious relationship. The date is fantastic, but the midnight text a week later telling me he misses my smile? Not so much.

Bachelor Number Two is a tall, sexy entrepreneur who has just moved to San Diego and lives right down the street from me—how very convenient. A few moderately fun dates and a few steamy make-out sessions into this one and the man still won't talk about anything other than work and the weather. I am getting the impression that he ran from something, or someone, on the East Coast, and he has no intention of ever opening up about his past. The only photo I spot in his house is a picture of a baby on his nightstand. Being the novelist that I am, I immediately begin concocting a story about his secret baby back east. Then, the first and only time he comes to my house, my cat Charlie stares him down like the creeper he can totally be and freaks the poor guy out.

I never see him (or the photo of his secret baby) again.

Bachelor Number Three is a divorced guy with a kid who invites me to dinner at a really posh restaurant on the beach, but when we walk in, he suggests that we sit at the bar and only order drinks. I didn't eat beforehand because I thought we would be eating together. So now, in addition to being exhausted and devastated because my husband just moved out and brokenhearted because I miss my married lover, I'm starving too. Not a great setup for a successful date. And now I have to sit here all night and listen to this guy talk and talk and talk...and *fucking talk*! The man doesn't shut up about himself for almost three hours and barely asks me a single question. I almost have to hold my eyes open to avoid falling asleep because I'm so bored. After that winner of a date, he walks me back to my car. The waves of the Pacific are crashing on the shore nearby and the stars are twinkling overhead, and just as we arrive at a set of train tracks, the gate goes down and a never-ending train barrels past.

So, *now* we have to stand here in what would have been a beautifully romantic moment had the date gone better. Instead I am avoiding eye contact and shuffling my feet, praying to the heavens that he doesn't try to kiss me.

He takes a step closer and says, "Well, I guess if I was going to kiss you, this would be the right moment."

Ugh! Why? Why? Why?

And so he does it. And it is the most lackluster non-kiss of a kiss I've ever had in my life. Even my first kiss as a ten-year-old playing spin the bottle was steamier than that.

Needless to say, we won't be having another date.

Bachelor Number Four is a swing-dancing physicist.

Uh-huh, you heard me: *a swing-dancing physicist.*

After a few dates with this one, I finally get to see him dance. It's like a fucking episode of *Dancing with the Stars.* He's swinging and shimmying and throwing women around and dancing up an absolute storm! He pulls me up to the dance floor to spin me around, and while I haven't a clue what the hell I am doing, being a ballet dancer for most of my life, I can at least wing it and I end up having a ball.

On our one and only overnight, the swing-dancing physicist arrives at my house with a rolling suitcase in tow. I almost ask him if he's planning to stay the entire week, but I bite my tongue. He's a sweetheart—a quirky one, but still. And clearly he just likes being prepared!

On our final date, when I realize just how awkward this dancing scientist is in the daylight, and when we accidentally take a walk to the *exact same cliff* where my husband and I said our vows, I realize I just can't do it. I can't be with a swing-dancing physicist right now, and that's not because he's a swing-dancing physicist—I kind of love that about him—but because I am so not ready to date *anyone* at this ultra-emotional juncture in my life.

The final straw with OK Cupid is when I sign on one day and find that my top match is—yes, you guessed it!—none other than *my husband*.

According to OK Cupid, we are a ninety-two percent match! Shoot Me in the Face.

Honestly.

I delete my account and decide that online dating isn't for me. Or that dating, in general, in the state I am in, is not for me.

In the weeks following my OK Cupid debacles, I spend my time *not* writing the screenplay I have promised to write, *not* writing my next book or writing anything, really, but instead walking aimlessly around my apartment, feeling like my arm has been chopped off. And even though that arm was sick and dying and needed to go, even though I *chose* to remove that arm, I still miss it. I miss it so much that I can barely function.

And so my dependency on Nick grows. Without him even knowing it, I am hanging on to his every word, his every e-mail, his every silent smile over Skype. I need him to sustain me because whatever strength I used to have buried deep inside me when bad things would happen seems to be gone.

I can't find it. I've searched and I've searched and I've searched. But all I have found are empty closets where my husband's clothes used to hang and empty spaces on the walls where our wedding pictures used to be, and empty kitchen counters where we used to sit together, and laugh and talk and be in love.

I am breaking. I am broken. And while I do have friends who love me, these sweet friends of mine have their own lives, their own husbands, their own children to take care of. They can't stop their lives to come take care of me, nor would I ever ask that of them.

And so I suffer alone, again numbing myself with Xanax when I get too hysterical to breathe. On the mornings when I think I simply cannot get out of bed, on the mornings when I am tempted to pop another Xanax and keep sleeping, the only thing that gets me out of bed, quite literally, is my cats. They walk over my chest, sit on my pillow, purr in my ear, nibble my arms, my knees, and every bare piece of skin they can find so that I will wake up and feed them. They are the size of small toddlers—Bella is nearly twenty pounds, and Charlie nearly fifteen. Which means they are always hungry and they are impossible to ignore.

And thankfully so; otherwise I may never get up again.

ON ONE particularly gruesome night, after I have spent the afternoon sitting in a downtown jeweler's office selling my beautiful engagement ring so that my ex and I can use the cash to pay down a mutual credit card, I am curled up on the couch alone, writing the only words I am able to write these days: *the truth.*

Tonight's truth is a tear-stained poem to my husband. A poem I will never give to him, but one I must write all the same.

How?

It is in the worst of times,
When we discover who we truly are
What we are made of.

We are weak, all of us.
We want something firm, something strong to hold onto.
We don't want to be alone.
I don't want to be alone.
I never have.

But you weren't there, when I needed you.
You couldn't meet me where I was at.

We failed, we both failed.
I never wanted it to turn out this way.
I didn't marry you thinking this would happen.

That I would have to leave you to survive.
That I would feel like part of my soul, half of my heart
Had been ripped, torn, shred to pieces
After you left.

After I got what I wanted.
What I thought I wanted.

Now I am here.
Alone.
Lost.
Wishing you were here.

But not you.
The you I wanted you to be
The you I always hoped you would be
The you who you never became
The you who you will never be.

You'll never be him.
And I'll never be her.

But we did love each other.
I did love you.
I still do, and I always will.

Which is why my heart is broken
Totally, utterly, desperately broken.

I am so sorry I couldn't be what you needed
That you couldn't be what I needed.

I'm sorry I fell in love with someone else.
Someone who can't be with me.

Karma, right?
A sick twist of fate.

Will I ever smile again?
I don't know.
I honestly don't know.

I can only hope.
I can only believe in a better time.
A better life.

The life I hoped for when I told you I couldn't be with you anymore.

But now, sitting here in our home, without you,
I wonder what I have done.
What on earth I was thinking when I told you I was leaving you?

How will I survive this?
How will I get through the day?
The week?
The month?

How will I write?
I don't have the energy to dance, the creativity to write.

I am zapped, exhausted, tapped out.

I am limp, desolate, alone.

And I just want to be happy.
I want something strong to hold onto.

Once, you were my life vest
Together, we became a sinking ship.
I jumped off to swim to sunnier skies, safer shores.

But I am stranded in the middle of the ocean
The waves are crashing over me
And I don't know if I will ever breathe again.

Chapitre 28

IN THE days leading up to my Seattle trip—the trip my lover and I are counting down to the week, the day, the hour, the minute, the second—both Nick and I separately make a visit to see a psychic. I call my best girlfriend from home, Angie, to fill her in on my latest lover gossip.

"So, my married lover went to see a psychic," I begin, "and then I did too."

"Oh dear God," she says, not stifling her laughter. "You do realize how ridiculous that sentence sounds." Angie is a very practically minded therapist who doesn't believe in psychics, but instead in dealing with problems in a more realistic, concrete way. She has been extremely helpful to me on the many occasions when I have called her in despair as I've plunged deeper and deeper into my new life status as a depressed divorcée/mistress.

"I know," I say. "My *life* is ridiculous right now. But we already knew that. Want to know what the psychics said?"

"Well, *yeah*."

"Okay, Nick saw his first, and she immediately picked up on the fact that he's seeing someone outside of his marriage. She said his sexual chakra is spinning out of control and that I am all over his aura. Whatever that means. She thought that *I* was over ten years older than *him,* even though it's the other way around, and she warned him to be careful with me—not to lead me on. But she also remarked that she saw in him no intention to end things with me anytime soon."

"Of course he has no intention of ending things with you," Angie says. "As long as he can have the wifey at home keeping the stability in his life and his mistress dancing naked for him over Skype and meeting him all over the world to fuck his brains out, of course the man will keep having both! He's a *man.*"

"I know," I say with a sigh. "*I know.*"

"And what about your psychic?" she asks. "What did she say?"

"Mine said that it's likely that Nick and I were lovers in a past life. She said that I was most definitely French in one of my past lives, and that I was in the court in the time of Marie-Antoinette. Apparently I was a true French woman—very tiny and delicate, and also extremely promiscuous, taking lots of lovers and having an absolute ball."

"Well, not much has changed where promiscuity is concerned," Angie says with a snort.

"So true," I admit. "She also told me that Nick will never make a choice between me or his wife unless I force him to by ending the affair. And she advised me to '*clearly walk in the other direction.*' Basically to get as far away from this man as possible so I can begin to heal and move on with my life."

"I could have told you that for free," she says. "Jumping into a relationship with a married man who is never going to leave his wife isn't exactly the healthiest move while you're going through a divorce. And you know I'm not preaching to you—I've made more than a few unhealthy choices when it comes to men. I mean, haven't we all?—but I'm just reminding you, as your friend, that this is dangerous territory."

"Healthy, schmealthy," I say. "If you had one night with this guy inside you, you'd understand."

"It's that good?"

"It's the best sex of my life."

"Sex that good is like a drug," she says. "Guys like Nick are drugs. It's always the most dangerous ones that we get most hooked on."

"I am *so* beyond hooked," I admit.

"Just be careful, Danielle," she warns.

"I will," I say. Although I know that I have no intention of doing so.

IT'S MY first trip to Seattle, and even though it's absolutely freezing outside, my heart is overflowing with warmth, relief, and joy now that I am back in Nick's embrace.

Our first time back together is slow and soft and sweet. Nick kisses me and touches me in a way that is different from our hungry, wild romps in Paris. He takes extra care with each caress of my skin, each stroke of my hair, each long, meaningful gaze into my eyes.

His big green eyes are filled with total and complete adoration for me, and it is the sweetest thing I've ever seen.

As Nick buries me beneath his tall, strong, beautiful body and pulls the sheets over our heads to block out the rest of the world, our noses touch, our lips meet, and I know, without a doubt, that I am in love with him. Totally, insanely, head-over-heels in love, and I am bursting at the seams to tell him.

As Nick cherishes every inch of me and every synchronized movement of our bodies, there is no hiding it in his eyes or in mine that we have crossed into a new territory. One that isn't covered in his hall-pass marital arrangement, one that doesn't come with a rule book, one that neither of us was prepared to enter, yet here we are—under the sheets, making each other's toes and hearts curl, and falling harder than we ever could have imagined back when my hand first slid into his only a few months ago.

"I missed you so much, Danielle," Nick whispers in my ear as he moves so perfectly over top of me.

I wrap my arms tighter around his shoulders, squeeze my legs around his waist and pull him even deeper into me.

"I missed you too. So much," I say.

"I don't know how we went so long again," he breathes.

"Me neither."

"I don't ever want to wait that long again to see you," he says. "I need you."

"I need you too," I admit. Because I do. I need him in so many ways, and I am so sublimely happy to know that he feels the same.

After nearly an hour of this intense reunion of hearts, minds, and bodies, Nick finally collapses on top of me, and I lie there, beneath the weight of him, feeling his heart beat into my chest.

And I think, *I could die right now.*

I could die a happy woman.

LATER THAT night, we are all bundled up in our hats and scarves, coats and gloves, cuddling in the backseat of a cab as it whisks us through the bitter cold Seattle night and drops us off at a little Italian joint.

Over wine, mozzarella, pasta, and warm bread, with the candlelight flickering and Nick's hand wrapped around mine, I am not able to keep my feelings for him bottled up any longer.

"There's something I need to tell you," I say.

"What is it?" Nick's voice is open and sincere.

"I want you to know that if anything ever changes in your situation at home, in your marriage...you need to know that I would love to be with you. *Really be with you.* As more than just a lover."

He is quiet, seemingly taken aback by my words.

"I don't expect anything to change on your end, of course," I say quickly, "but I just want you to know that if it ever does, I would love to have a real relationship with you. This isn't just sex for me, obviously. I love spending time with you, and our connection isn't the kind of thing you find every day. So, if anything ever changes—again, not that I think it will, but if it does—I'm here, and I'd love to be with you."

I have laid my heart bare on the table, and it is beating, frantically, waiting to hear what my lover will say.

But he is still quiet, and something in him has shifted after hearing my words. It is nearly undetectable, but I can see it in his eyes. A hesitance. A fear.

"Wow..." he says finally. "Wow, I...I wasn't expecting that."

"I don't mean to—"

"Thank you," he says. "That means so much to know that you feel that way. But my marriage isn't...it's not going anywhere. You know I'm not planning to leave—"

"I know." I swallow the knot in my throat and tell myself *not to cry.* "I wasn't asking that of you, or expecting it. I would never do that. I just felt that I needed to be honest with you and let you know how I'm really feeling."

"Thank you," he says again.

And then he goes on to say once more how sweet my words were, but how he has no plans to change his current marital situation, and that had we met under different circumstances, yes, it would be wonderful if we could really be together...and on and on...but I barely hear him. I have pulled my hand away from his, and I am silently begging myself not to break down over my eggplant mozzarella penne in this adorable little restaurant in the middle of a wintry Seattle.

I let him talk, and when he is finished, I excuse myself.

"Are you okay?" he asks.

"Yes, fine. I just need to use the restroom."

I can't dash away from that table fast enough. Inside the bathroom, I splash water onto my blazing cheeks, take a few deep breaths, and look at my tear-stained eyes in the mirror.

I didn't reveal my feelings to him with the expectation that anything would change, but by the way I feel like I could collapse in a heap of tears on this dirty bathroom floor, my heart was clearly *hoping* that Nick would say: *I feel the same. You're my soul mate, and I can't live without you. It may take some time and it won't be easy, but let's figure this out. I want to be with you.*

He didn't say any of that, though. Instead, he reminded me that he's not leaving his wife.

He's never leaving his wife.

I shake my head at myself. *Don't be such an idiot, Danielle. You told him your piece, now get your shit together, go back out there with a smile on your face, and be the strong woman I know that you are.*

But as I walk back out to the table, my hands shaking, and my fragile heart breaking even further, I want to run away. I want to run straight into the arms of a man who will love me the way I love him.

But I don't have that man.

I have a married lover and a husband I have chosen to leave.

So, really, I'm alone.

BACK AT the hotel, as if I haven't already laid my withering heart bare enough for this man, I slip on my ballet shoes, and I dance for him.

It is a dance I have choreographed just for Nick. In some of my saddest, most desperate nights alone in my apartment this past month, I have found solace in the simple act of putting on my ballet shoes, turning on some music, and dancing in the empty bedroom where I used to sleep with my husband.

One of those nights, a dance emerged, a dance that I knew I would do for Nick one day.

And so, here I am. Dancing to "Stay" for my lover. It's a tune that was originally sung by Rihanna, but I have chosen the version by Shaun Reynolds, featuring Laura Pringle. The words and the slow, sad melody are full of depth and longing and love, and my dance for Nick captures all of those things...and more.

It is full of *me*. This dance embodies my very being, my essence, and although I realize that Nick will never fully be mine, I still want to give this gift to him.

Nick has seen me dance before, of course, but those dances have been tipsy and lustful and sexy and dirty.

This is something else, altogether—a lover, a writer, a dancer, performing for the man she has fallen in love with, knowing she will never truly have him as her own.

After my dance, I turn to Nick and see a tear streaming down his cheek. He stands from the bed, walks over to me, wraps me up in his arms and breaks down.

"Danielle, that was so beautiful," he says, his head buried in my hair. And I think that finally, his heart may be breaking the way mine broke over dinner earlier.

Not that I want him to hurt, but it's comforting to know I'm not alone in the way I feel about us and our connection.

"I'm sorry that I shut down at dinner," he says. "It's just that what you said, it meant so much to me, and I have to be honest with you—my wife was the first person I fell in love with. She was the only person I thought I would love for my whole life. And then I met you. And the way I feel about you...it scares me."

"I know." I reach up, running my hands through his hair then pulling his lips into mine for a kiss. I want him to know that it's safe with me, that I'm safe. That I won't hurt him.

Nick picks me up, carries me to the bed, and we make love. It's even more intense than when our bodies first connected in this same bed only a few hours ago. It's harder, more passionate, and more lustful but also laced with a new level of intimacy and emotion.

After we are finished, I am still lying on top of him, when he looks into my eyes and asks, "Are we falling in love, Danielle? Is that what this is?"

Even though I wish he didn't have to ask, I wish that he would declare his love for me, loud and clear, I am so relieved that Nick is finally acknowledging what this really is. And so I tell him what I think.

"I'm bursting with it, Nick. I'm bursting with love for you."

He smiles and pulls me down into his chest, wrapping me up in him.

I know he is scared; I am too.

But nothing has ever felt more right than our bodies wrapped up in each other, our hearts beating together, our love warming up this cold Seattle night.

THE NEXT day, Nick and I have pushed off all of our work commitments until the afternoon so that we can spend the day together on Bainbridge Island. Even though the wind is fierce and the air is bitter cold, the ferry ride over is spectacularly beautiful. The winter skies are clear, the sun is shining, and the snow-capped mountains off in the distance are breathtaking.

Nick takes a photograph of me outside on the ferry. Despite all of my thick layers and the hair whipping my face, I am beaming. His acknowledgement last night that he is falling just as deeply for me as I am for him has warmed my heart and calmed me down. I know that despite our intense feelings for one another, we may never be together, but knowing he is falling in love with me too makes all of this turmoil worth it.

"Can I take a picture of you?" I ask him.

This time, he doesn't hesitate the way he did in Paris. The sun lights up his already bright smile, his chest is broad in his gray sweater, and he looks so ridiculously handsome, I could just die.

Bainbridge Island is quiet and charming, the perfect haven for these two lovey lovers. We meander through the quaint downtown, past shops and restaurants that haven't yet opened, until we find the perfect place to warm up: Blackbird Bakery.

Inside, we are welcomed by an array of warm pastries and delicious scents. One cranberry orange roll and one lemon poppy seed muffin later, and we are cozied up at a corner table, drinking steaming hot mugs of chamomile mint tea and talking about my divorce.

This time, I tell Nick the truth about how very hard it has been to watch my husband move out and to start life anew on my own, even though all of this was my choice. He listens patiently and quietly as I give him all the dirty details, and when I am finished, he takes my hand.

"You are so strong. I don't know if I'd ever have the strength to do what you did."

"Thank you," I say. And today, I do feel strong. I feel like a woman who has made a most impossible choice and who is beginning to emerge on the other side, painful and excruciating though it may be. And it is so nice to have someone who will listen to the whole story without judging me. Nick understands marital discontent, even if it is clear that his is not great enough at this point to choose to leave.

After our pastries and tea, we hold hands and stroll through the little town until we reach a path that leads through the woods to the water. Our walk beneath the pines is cool and refreshing and quiet. Sometimes we talk, and at other times, we remain comfortably silent, just listening to the sounds of our feet crunching over the dirt and the trees swishing in the wind.

Soon we find our way to a little grassy beach that juts out into the water. There are a few gorgeous waterfront homes nearby and some boats tied to a dock not far away, but there is no one else in sight. This little slice of heaven is all ours.

We walk out onto the sandy grass, connected at the hip, and take in the pretty view. And since I can't stop myself from being romantic, I turn to Nick and smile.

"I have something for you," I say. "For your birthday that's coming up."

"You didn't have to—" Nick starts, but when I hand him another folded piece of paper, he grins so sweetly. "You wrote me something?"

"I'm a writer. I couldn't help myself."

I take his hand and lead him over to a nearby bench, where we sit together, and he silently reads the birthday poem I have written for him.

On your Birthday...

I want you to know
That of all the souls,
Who have crossed paths with mine,
I am happiest to have found yours.

I want you to know
That wherever you go,
Wherever I go,
I will always think of you.

I want you to know
That you have brought to my life
A bliss, a fever, a dance, a desire
I've never known before.

I want you to know
That for me, you are
More than a body,
More than a lover,
More than your handsome smile
Or your sexy boy band hair.

For me,
You are a connection, an arrow
Straight to my heart,
Into my soul.

I want you to know
That my soul was waiting for you
And when she found you
She breathed a sigh of relief...

You do exist, after all.

On your birthday, Nick
I want you to know
That I am forever grateful
Forever filled
With desire, passion, and joy
Just to know you.

And whatever happens,
Whether our paths stay on this same intense journey together...
Or veer far away from one another

I will always feel
Your heat, your warmth,
Your sweet, adoring smile
Right next to me.

I want you to know, too
That I would follow you to the ends of the earth...
Or to a motel in the middle of Kansas.
I don't care, really.

It's you I want
Plain and simple
It's you.

Happy Birthday, Lover.

Once again, my heart is laid bare for my adoring lover. And he is, once again, touched to the point of tears.

In our secret little beach on this secret little island, my lover gives me the sweetest of kisses and holds me in his arms.

"I love it," he says. "*Thank you.*"

AFTER A late lunch back in the tiny downtown of Bainbridge, we are on our way to the ferry when we realize that we're running late.

"We need to run if we're going to catch the ferry on time to make it back to the city for our meetings," I tell him.

"All right, dancer, let's see what you've got." Nick takes my hand and we bolt through the town, two crazy lovers on a mission.

We reach the ferry terminal out of breath and sweating. Then we dash down the long corridor to the boarding area only to find that the ferry has just left.

"Shit," Nick says. "When's the next ferry?"

We find the timetable pinned to the wall. "The next one leaves in an hour," I say. "Are you going to miss your meeting?"

"Yeah," he says. But he doesn't look too disappointed. And truth be told, I'm not either.

"I'm sorry," I tell him. "But kind of not."

"Want to get a hot chocolate?" he asks, his grin back in full force.

"You should know by now that I *never* turn down chocolate."

We wind back into the town together, and over hot chocolates and whipped cream, I suggest to Nick, "What if we never made it off Bainbridge Island? What if we never left?"

"I could disappear here with you, happily," Nick says.

"Me too. It would be magical."

"Maybe we'll miss the next ferry too..." Nick says with a wink.

"Maybe..." I say, wishing we could miss every ferry that takes us back to real life. I want to stay here with him, eating pastries and drinking hot chocolate, kissing and trading love poems, forever.

EARLY THE next morning, before the sun has even risen, Nick wakes me up to kiss me goodbye. He has tears in his eyes as he holds me and my messy bedhead in his hands. I'm too tired, too sad to cry. So I just hug him and kiss him and tell him I can't wait to see him again.

"Only three short weeks this time, lover," he reminds me.

"It will go fast," I say, although I don't want to think about what even one day will feel like without him.

After Nick leaves, I lie there in the silence, hoping that he will miss his plane and come back for me.

But as much as he's falling for me, as much as *love* may truly be entering into the equation, Nick is never going to miss the plane that takes him home to his wife.

Chapitre 29

IN A swanky hotel room in San Francisco, only a few weeks after our trip to Seattle, Nick finally says the three words I've been waiting to hear.

He says them after he left me alone in our hotel room for hours while he was out drinking and eating with friends who don't know about me, friends who *can't* know about me. After he told me he'd be back to take me out for dinner and dancing, but instead stayed out with his friends because they know his wife— they *love* his wife—and he couldn't tell them he had to leave to tend to his mistress back in the hotel room.

He told me after I considered packing my things and leaving, finally beginning to realize just how fucked up this whole affair is. I'm in love with a man who has to hide me away, who can't tell a single person in his life about me, and who never plans to.

I never wanted to be a mistress, but here I am, nonetheless, waiting in a hotel room, pining over a man who will always prioritize *everything else* over me.

I don't go anywhere, though, even though I wish I had the strength, the self-worth, to walk away.

I love him too much to leave, as messed up as it all is.

And so, late that night, when he arrives at the hotel room full of apologies, for the first time ever, I am cold as ice to my lover.

"It's not too late to go out dancing," he urges, nuzzling his nose into my neck.

I turn away from him. "I'm tired," I say. "I waited all night for you, and I'm too exhausted to go out dancing. I'm going to bed."

And so I do. I fall asleep barely touching him, barely talking to him.

In the middle of the night, he is tossing and turning, not sleeping a wink, when he wakes me up with his lips on my neck, my collarbone, my breasts. Even though I'm still angry, I fall back into him so quickly, so easily.

While he is on top of me, making love to me, holding me with the desperation of a man who will do almost anything to keep me in his arms, our eyes meet in the darkness and he finally says the words, "I love you."

"I love you too," I tell him, gripping his shoulders for dear life, kissing him and holding him as if the past several hours never happened.

As if I didn't overhear Nick making the obligatory phone call home to his wife earlier this same day...as if I didn't hear him tell his wife that he loves her, too.

OVER THE Christmas holiday, Nick can't see me; he can't whisk me away on another trip. Instead it is his wife he is whisking away.

They are leaving tomorrow for some exotic location where he will barely be able to be in touch with me for two whole weeks. We have been e-mailing every single day for months now, sometimes several times a day. We talk on the phone, we talk and don't talk over Skype, and we communicate over all sorts of secret apps so that his wife will never find out. Even though our calls are frequently cut short due to the fact that I can't *exist* in his life—at least not where any of his friends, family, or coworkers are concerned—we are constantly in contact all the same. The way he must squeeze me in between meetings or while he is riding on noisy public transportation or just before he walks in the door to kiss his wife or late at night after she has gone to bed makes me feel cheap and desperate, like a woman with little to no self-worth, a woman who will accept being last priority in a man's life, even when he tells her it's just the opposite.

All the same, it's contact with my lover, and I crave that more than I crave anything these days.

But for the next two weeks, it will be radio silence.

With Christmas just around the corner and no family or friends coming to see me, no husband to celebrate with, and no lover to correspond with, I am spiraling into my deepest depression yet.

I know I must do something—*anything*—to save myself because no one is going to do it for me. So I e-mail Nick, the night before he is set to leave with his wife, and I tell him that I need to take a break from this, from him, from us, in order to try to take care of myself.

He responds immediately asking me to sign onto one of our secret apps and have a live chat with him. He can't FaceTime because his wife is nearby, but he needs to talk to me, he *must* talk to me, even if it is only typing in real time from halfway across the country.

I am a twisted pretzel of emotions, and I am so easily persuaded. Nick talks me through my doubts, reminds me that we are in this "life raft" together. We have made it this far, this deep, and he asks me to hang on, at least until our next rendezvous a few weeks out, so we can talk things through in person.

Although I feel sick about it, although something inside me is screaming *No!*, I agree that I will wait to take a "break" from him and from this sordid affair that is tearing me apart.

The In-Between

I am in the in-between

In love
Total, relentless, all-consuming love

But protecting myself
From the way
You shatter my heart

Every sunrise
Every sunset
Every moment in between

Is it an illusion?
To think we could have a happy ending?

To think that one day
You will choose me.

Am I crazy?
Straddling this line?

Some days I am sure
Absolutely certain
You will come to me
Only me.

Other days
I am
Tormented, tortured, heartbroken

Because you are far
So far away

That is my reality
You are not here.

I am alone
And in love

A most intoxicating love

Which keeps me in between
Love and sanity
Joy and heartbreak
Reality and illusion

Which will it be, lover?

OVER THE next few days, as Christmas nears, I am alone in my apartment with my cats, crying from dawn till dusk. I am barely eating. I am taking Xanax again.

On December 23rd, I recall that nine years ago today, my boyfriend proposed to me in the rain by the Christmas tree at Rockefeller Center. That boyfriend became my husband—the husband I have left, the husband I miss so dearly today and every day, despite the fact that I have fallen in love with someone else.

My love for my husband exists in a bubble all its own—one that, apparently, is immune to the harsh realities of divorce or an intense infatuation with a married lover.

The idea that my life has plunged so far from our happy engagement night is too much for me to bear. I miss my husband. I am sick with myself for thinking life would be better without him.

It certainly felt better while I was prancing around Paris, eating chocolate croissants, drinking wine, and having too many orgasms in a day to count.

But the cold, hard reality is that my day-to-day life isn't better without him. It's a disaster.

A disaster of my own doing.

I fucked up. I never should have left him.

I ruined my own life.

This realization punches me in the gut. I am hunched over on my kitchen floor in hysterics, gasping to breathe, when I pray for a way out. I crawl over to the kitchen table where my laptop is sitting, open it up, and begin a Google search on ways to end my life.

First up: *overdose.*

I certainly have enough pills in the house to pull it off. And no one is planning to come over tonight or tomorrow or even on Christmas, so it's not like I'd be found quick enough to be rushed to the hospital and saved.

But suppose I didn't take enough pills, and I did end up being rushed to the hospital? The whole idea of getting my stomach pumped and then having to be hospitalized for severe depression? Not an option.

The same could happen with slitting my wrists, and I'm entirely too weak-stomached to even contemplate that possibility.

If I'm going to do this, it needs to be something sure. Something solid. Something that won't fail.

The train.

All it would take is a perfectly timed jump. There would be no near-misses with that approach, that's for sure.

I think of the Coaster train that runs up and down the Pacific Coast. The Coaster that first inspired me to write my fourth book, *Midnight Train to Paris.*

Where has that girl gone? The one who used to be inspired, who used to love to write. Who could write ten to fifteen pages a day on deadline and whip out books like it was her job.

Well, it *was* my job.

And it still would be if I could do it.

But how am I supposed to write when I'd rather be dead?

Sylvia's words from the balcony in Paris come rushing back to me.

You're going to be okay.

You're going to be okay.

Now I understand why she was looking at me with such intensity. She knew. She knew it could get this bad. And yet she insisted that I would be okay.

I *was* okay in Paris. But ever since I got home, life has gone to shit. If only I could get back to Paris, maybe I'll feel better. No, that's not a maybe. I *will* feel better. Paris heals me. I love it there.

If I end my life, I'll never see Paris again.

And just as I begin imagining what it would be like to never again set foot in France, my cats appear, all purrs and fur and cuddly faces and giant, adorable paws. They are rubbing on my legs, meowing, and begging for food.

If I leave, who will take care of them the way I do? My husband loved them, especially Bella, who he rescued from the pound and gave to me as a Christmas present six years ago. She was, without a doubt, the best present he's ever given me.

But even he wouldn't love them the way I do.

The idea of leaving my cats behind is somehow worse to me tonight than the thought of all of the people I would hurt by ending my life.

So, in the end, it is for my cats and for Paris that I take another Xanax—only one—and decide that instead of ending my life, I will just go to sleep.

Death will always be looming there, as an option, I remind myself. Even though my entire body is aching and my heart is dying, I can manage another day.

With tear-stained, sunken-in cheeks and shaky hands, I lie in my bed with my laptop before the Xanax kicks in, and I write the poem I would leave in my absence, just in case.

If I Go

If I go, I want you to know
How much light you brought to my life
How I loved you
More than I loved myself

Which is why I'm here
On my knees
In despair
The darkest darkness
A night with no stars

Except I know the stars are there
Waiting for me
They are my home
And I am ready to go

Will you stand by me
When I have lost everything
When I have nothing left to give
When I am no more
Than the tears streaming down my face

Because I have stood there, by you
By all of you
In the worst of times
Yet I am here
Alone

A father who never wanted me
A mother who doesn't believe I love her
A husband who couldn't grow with me
A lover who hides me in the shadows

So where does that leave me?

My friends are my true family, my love, my rock.
Thank you, friends, for being there.

If I go, you should know
That I'm not leaving because of you.
I'm leaving because there was nowhere left for me to go.

And I love you
Each and every one of you

The father who never wanted me
The mother who doesn't believe I love her
The husband who couldn't grow with me
The lover who hides me in the shadows
And my friends, my dear sweet friends

I love you. Every single one of you.
And when I am gone, I will continue loving you.

I WAKE up at 4:30 the next morning, still wanting to die.

I write my lover an e-mail telling him that I'm not doing well, that I'm in a fragile state, and asking him to really think about what his intentions are in continuing this affair. I tell him that I don't want to be stuck in a life raft in class 5 rapids, nor do I want to be in a relationship which we often compare to a drug addiction. It's not only that I don't *want* those things, it's that I don't have the strength in me to survive the rapids, the drugs, the withdrawal, and I tell him as much.

But my lover is frolicking around somewhere on a tropical island with his wife, in a place where he barely gets service, and it could be hours, or even days before I hear back.

And so, as I begin to imagine more ways to end my life, as I really, truly contemplate how wonderful it would be to just disappear, finally, I reach for my phone and dial the one person who I won't feel embarrassed being this much of a mess in front of. The only person who will know what to do.

My husband.

"Hey..." I say through my sobs. "I'm so sorry to call you like this, on Christmas Eve, but..."

"You're not doing so well," he says, not hiding the worry in his voice.

"No," I manage to get out. "I'm so sorry. Can you come over?"

"I'll be right there," he says.

And so the husband I have left drops whatever he was doing, races over to my apartment—*our apartment*—and takes care of me.

He hugs me, calms me down, feeds me, and talks to me. I feel sick with myself that I'm not telling him the entire truth about why I am breaking down—the truth about my lover—but considering suicide is on my mind, I don't think it's the time to introduce that scenario into the equation. I just need to be strong again so that I can take care of myself.

But for today, the man who has loved me for over twelve years—that is the man who takes care of me when I am too weak to do so myself.

He only leaves that night when he is certain that I will be okay. And before he goes, he makes me promise that I will go to the doctor and get on an antidepressant.

"It's time," he says. "You can't live like this, and there's no shame in taking medication."

I have resisted the idea of taking a daily antidepressant for so long, but I know he's right. I'm beyond the point of needing help, and I have to do something about it.

ON CHRISTMAS morning, my husband returns and I make him eggs, bacon, cinnamon rolls, and toast. We don't exchange gifts, but we do make jokes about how we should get an ornament that says *First Divorced Christmas!* or send out a Christmas card photo of the two of us each holding one of our cats with a jagged line drawn down the center of the card, indicating our new split-up family status. Our dark divorce humor finally gets a laugh out of me, and by the time my husband leaves, I am feeling stronger.

I know I'm not alone, and I have my husband to thank for that.

That night, I join my sweet Argentinian friends and their son for Christmas dinner. After a night of food and laughter—oh, it feels so good to laugh again!—I get up to leave, but I notice that my backside feels wet. A quick trip to the bathroom reveals a massive amount of blood has soaked through my underwear and all over the back of my dress.

My doctor has advised me to take my birth control pill straight through the month so that I don't have to endure the horrendous periods I normally have. Which means I shouldn't be bleeding...*profusely*.

My girlfriend, Jimena, who is eight and a half months pregnant and ready to pop, gives me a change of clothes and hugs me as my hands shake and my heart pounds.

"What do you think it is?" she whispers so as not to alert her husband or her son to the girl drama going down in their home on Christmas Day.

"I don't know. I don't get my period anymore, and even if I were to, this is a *ton* of blood."

She takes a deep breath. She knows about my affair. "Do you think you could have been...?"

She doesn't finish her sentence, but I know what she's asking. *Could I have been pregnant? Am I having a miscarriage?*

I shake my head. "No, I'm on the pill."

"But sometimes things happen anyway." Jimena rubs her belly as proof of what can happen.

"Well, if I was pregnant, I'm certainly not now."

I don't want to know if I was pregnant, so instead of going to see my gynecologist, I make an appointment with the psychiatrist.

I'm still bleeding, a lot, the next day when I visit my new doctor and she puts me on an antidepressant, anti-anxiety medication called Lexapro. Within hours of taking my first dose, my head launches into an even thicker fog than I've already been living in. I feel as if someone has been pounding my temples with a hammer for days.

And I feel even sicker, even more depressed than I felt before. And I am still bleeding.

I only give it three days before I decide there is no way I'm going to take something that makes me feel worse, and I kick Lexapro to the curb. Knowing that something still must be done, I find a dance studio nearby and sign up for one month of unlimited classes.

The pirouettes and the jetés and the sheer movement and beauty of dance certainly lift my spirits. But I'm still a wreck, and by the time Nick returns back from his lovely vacation, and we are set to meet again in another hotel room, for another secret rendezvous, I am not sure I can go.

I call my best friend, Angie, to talk it through.

"Maybe I'll go just this once, and it will give us a chance to talk things through and decide what to do next," I tell her.

"Yeah, just like heroin," she says, not hiding her sarcasm. "I'll just do it *one more time*, and maybe this time, it won't hurt me."

"I know," I say. "I know you're right."

"Danielle, this man, this relationship, is the emotional catastrophe of your life. One more weekend in a hotel room isn't going to change that or make it better."

Of course I know that Angie is right, but as is the nature with drugs, the promise of the high is so alluring that, later that night, I find myself alone in my car, flying up the 101 to meet Nick in Santa Barbara. And later that same month, I am back in the car, speeding through the desert to meet him in Las Vegas.

In addition to the fancy dinners and the all-night sex marathons, the love declarations and the dancing, we have now added meltdowns and crying and exhausting all-night-long discussions about the status of our relationship. Nick is now talking about the possibility of leaving his wife, and he knows that without this possibility on the table—weak and unlikely though it may be—I am close to ending our affair.

Because while the highs are delicious, the lows are nauseating.

They are unbearable.

So unbearable that the following month, even though he is now in talks with his wife about the status of *their* relationship, I cancel my flight to see him in San Francisco. And I'm back where I was at Christmas, thinking of suicide, missing my husband, and hating myself for knowingly bringing all of this on.

Once again, when I reach the lowest of the lows and can't scrape myself up off the floor to eat or get dressed or write, my husband comes to the rescue. And once again, he tells me I *must* go on an antidepressant.

So, back to the psychiatrist I go, this time with a sincere desire to try anything until I find the magical drug that gets me back on track.

I want to ask my doctor if she has a drug that will make me forget Nick ever existed so that I can erase this emotional catastrophe from my consciousness and start fresh. Because as long as I know he exists, as long as I know he is out there and he loves me and still wants me, despite all of the drama I am now bringing into his life and all of the pain he is bringing into mine, I fear I will never be able to get off of this path of destruction that is leading me to him and straight to the middle of nowhere, all at the same time.

THE MAGICAL drug turns out to be Wellbutrin. Before I took my first dose, I had been crying incessantly for days. I was barely able to eat and I weighed less than I did when I was in junior high.

Within twenty-four hours of taking my first little blue pill, the faucet of tears that has been pouring rivers for months, stops.

Just like that.

The tears finally relent.

And I can breathe.

Chapitre 30

NOW I'M not only *single and fabulous!*, I'm *single and fabulous and proudly taking my shiny new antidepressant!* What could be better?

With my new attitude on life—namely that I *want* to be living it—I am back on a plane, jetting across the country, but this time I'm *not* going to see my lover. I'm heading to DC to speak on a panel at Georgetown University, my alma mater, and, more importantly, to spend time with my friend Karen who is nearing the end of her battle with brain cancer.

My close friend and Georgetown classmate, James, organized an event to bring back a panel of 2004 grads to speak to the upcoming 2014 grads about what life is like ten years after graduation. Since I didn't choose any of the typical Georgetown career paths—medicine, law, or business—and instead went the less practical, creative route, James offered to fly me out for the event in the hope that I would spice up the panel a bit.

On my first night back in DC, I'm out with James, his partner Shawn, and three of my very best girlfriends. We are drinking cocktails and eating the most delicious local organic fare at Farmers & Fishers on the Georgetown waterfront. I'm in my old stomping ground with my best friends, I'm tipsy, and I feel like myself again. It's amazing.

Over dinner, when the topic of our Georgetown panel comes up, I tell James and the rest of the crew exactly what I plan to tell these naïve, innocent, soon-to-be grads: "In ten years, kids, you could be divorced and childless, in love with your married lover, scrounging to pay the bills, and barely surviving on a cocktail of Xanax, Wellbutrin, wine, and chocolate. That's where being creative will land you!"

The girls laugh while James shakes his head at me. "Ummm... let's keep it real, but not *that* real."

James knows all about my sordid affair because he is one of my only friends who has actually met this mystery man I speak of, in the flesh and blood.

James works on Wall Street as a corporate attorney, and he's as blunt and hard-hitting as they come. He's also hilarious and full of gossip and sage advice for anyone who is willing—or not willing— to listen. He was on vacation on the West Coast when he met me and Nick for dinner in the lovely town of Santa Barbara.

James doesn't have time for bullshit, and he loves me like a sister, so while he sat in his seat all relaxed, eating his expensive Italian food and drinking his expensive wine, he grilled the shit out of Nick.

And I have to admit, I kind of loved it.

"So, what exactly is your one-year plan?" James asked Nick. "Specifically in regards to your relationship with Danielle."

Nick is a successful businessman and is used to dealing with pushy types like James, but as he shifted in his seat and took another sip of his wine, I could tell this particular question paired with the way James was staring him down was making him uncomfortable.

"My one year plan?" Nick repeated. "Well, in one year, I hope to be with Danielle."

"Could you be more specific?" James asked. "Does that mean exclusively with Danielle? As in you've left your wife, filed for divorce, and moved in with Danielle all by next year at this time?"

"I don't know all of the logistics yet," Nick concedes, "but yes. I would love to have Danielle move to Chicago with me by this time next year."

"Ummm...Danielle *isn't* moving to Chicago," James says. "She's finished moving all over the country for a man. Why don't *you* move to California?"

And so it went, for the next hour, while James drank more wine and Nick grew ever more uncomfortable.

Even though Nick voiced his intention to be with me in a real relationship, *sans* wife, I know deep down that he doesn't mean it. Not that he doesn't *wish* for that intention of his to be true, but he still loves his wife. He still enjoys their life together. And until the day when I force him to choose between us by ending our affair, I don't believe he will make a choice.

And the thing is, while I so wish we could be together too, I get it. I don't want to add another tragic divorce to a world that is already stocked full of them. Mine was enough. I don't know Nick's wife, but she sounds like a perfectly lovely woman, and I don't want to steal her husband.

As I have told Nick several times during our last two trips, when the topic of leaving his wife has come up, "I don't want you to leave your wife *for* me. You should only leave if you were going to leave her already, without the promise of me waiting on the other side. You need to evaluate your marriage independently of me, and only then, if you decided to leave, would you have a chance at not regretting your decision."

But, as Nick would remind me each time we'd discuss this, "It's impossible not to factor you into the equation, Danielle."

And he's right, of course, but tonight, in the company of some of my dearest friends, in the city where I went to college, a city Nick and I have yet to taint with our love, our sex, and our tears, I am worlds away from him and our sad story.

And for the first time in months, I feel happy again.

I feel like myself.

IT IS a good thing I have stored up a bit of strength because as soon as I walk into my friend Karen's home, I realize I am going to need it.

It has barely been two years since Karen's initial diagnosis, but the cancer has taken everything. She is now lying in a hospital bed in her downstairs den—the same den where we used to hold some of our writing meetings, where we would discuss our characters and storylines, our husbands and her children, and drink tea and laugh about it all.

It is in this room where I find my friend Karen asleep in her bed, swollen from steroids, and barely recognizable as the bright, bubbly, fabulous woman I first met over five years ago.

My friend Sharon has warned me that Karen may not wake up for my visit. She has been sleeping for a few weeks now, barely waking for visitors or even to eat. She is on morphine to keep her comfortable and out of pain, and the end is near.

But when I sit by her side and take her hand, Karen rouses. Her eyes flutter open, and I smile at her. The lump in my throat makes it difficult for me to get a sentence out without breaking down, but I force myself to be cheerful for Karen. She knows she's dying. She doesn't need me making this any harder for her than it already is.

"I've missed you so much," I tell her. "I'm so glad I got to make this trip."

In her slow speech that is barely audible, she finds her words. "Me too."

Now she is asking me to do something, but I can't understand her. She looks as though she's uncomfortable and possibly in pain, and I'm not sure what to do. Her husband is nearby, though, and in a flash, he is by her side.

She needs him to roll her onto her side, because she can't do it alone. He reaches beneath her and carefully moves her limp body until she's in the right position. Then he brushes the hair out of her eyes and looks down at his wife with a gaze that is so full of love, it's heartbreaking.

This man loves his wife so dearly that he has watched her body disintegrate over the past two years, yet he still looks at her with total and complete adoration. He has done everything in his power to take care of her and keep her comfortable throughout this nightmare of an illness.

Pure and simple, total and unending, *this is love.*

I can't help but wonder what will become of me if I am ever sick one day. Who will be by my bedside? It would have been my husband. He would have taken care of me the same way Karen's husband has taken care of her. There is no doubt about that.

But I gave him up. I walked away.

Now isn't the time to wallow in my divorce pity, though. I must be strong for Karen.

I stay by her side for the afternoon, talking at times, and at other times sitting beside her in silence, holding her hand as she drifts in and out of sleep.

When it is almost time for me to leave, I wake her with a soft touch on her arm.

"Karen, I have to go soon," I tell her.

"Thank...you," she says.

Her words are barely making it out, but I hear her and I know she is in there. My beautiful, sweet, talented friend is still in there. It is only her body that has decided to leave.

"It was so good to see you," I say softly.

And then I know that whatever words we share next will be our last. And I hate it. I hate her cancer. But there is nothing I can do to change it. I am lucky to have this opportunity to be with her before she goes, and so I must say the things I need to say.

"Karen, thank you so much for being such a wonderful friend to me. And for everything you've done to help me become a better writer. I would never be where I am without you, and I'm so thankful."

I lean down to hug her, and it is here, with her frail body in my arms that I break down. I don't want to lose my friend. I don't want her husband to lose his amazing wife. I don't want her three sweet boys to lose their loving mom.

I hold her for a few minutes, unable to stop the tears, and when I finally lift my face to hers, I blame it on the divorce.

"I'm so sorry, Karen, it's the divorce. It's turned me into this blubbering idiot who cries *all the time*." I wipe at my tears, laughing at myself.

Karen squeezes my hand. "I'm so sorry about your divorce," she says slowly. "I wish there was more I could do."

That's Karen. Her body is dying, and still, she wishes there was more *she* could do for *me*.

She is the embodiment of selfless love.

Karen is now trying to tell me something else, but I can't make out the word.

"Can you repeat it again?" I ask, feeling horrible to make her use her energy to talk, but whatever she is saying, she seems adamant about getting it out.

After a few tries, I still can't understand the word she is trying to say, so I ask her to spell it.

Karen takes several deep breaths, then puffs out a letter with each exhale. Slowly, she spells her word for me:

"B-A-S-T-A-R-D."

"Bastard?" I say, not sure if I've heard the spelling correctly.

"Yes," she says.

"My husband?"

"Yes," she says.

"Well, he's actually been really kind and wonderful through the whole thing," I say through my mixture of tears and laughter.

That's Karen too—to bring humor into such a sad moment when she can barely get a word out. God, I love her so much.

Before I leave, I am telling Karen how happy I am that she has so many wonderful people by her side all the time—her closest friends, her neighbors, her mother and mother-in-law who've flown in from England, and most of all, her adoring husband and three sons.

And the last words she says to me are, "I'm *so* lucky."

I hug her one last time, feeling like *I* am the lucky one. I am lucky to have Karen in my life, to witness her grace, her beauty, and her bravery. There is so much to learn from her, and I only hope I will be half the woman she is when I reach her age.

"I love you, Karen," I tell her. "I'll see you soon, okay?"

She nods ever so softly and drifts back to sleep.

When I stand to leave, I find her husband in the foyer and as we hug, I break down again.

"I'm so sorry," I tell him. "I just don't want to lose her."

He hugs me tight. "It's okay," he says.

Although we both know it's not. It's not okay. A world without Karen in it will never be okay.

But I must go. And so I walk away from Karen, from her husband, and from her home that I have visited so many times, knowing that the next time I am here, my dear friend will be gone.

A COUPLE of weeks later, I receive the call that Karen has passed. She died peacefully, in her sleep, once everyone had left the room.

"I think she was waiting for you to come back and say goodbye," my friend Sharon tells me over the phone. "You were the last person, and I think once you came, she knew it was okay to go."

The idea that Karen may have waited to see me touches me so deeply that I am having trouble breathing.

My dear friend. She is gone.

That night, I sit alone at my bedroom window, looking out at the inky black night and the stars twinkling over my canyon, knowing that Karen is up there somewhere. I know she is looking down on me, on all of us now.

And I am so relieved for her that she doesn't have to endure such pain any longer.

Still, though, my heart is broken. There is no other way to feel when such a bright, shining star has left your world to move on to the next.

I can't sleep tonight. And so, I write Karen a letter. I know that wherever she is, she'll get it, and she'll be happy that I'm still writing.

Dear Karen,

I knew the day would come when I would be writing you this letter, and I am just so thankful I got to see you in person, hold your hand, hug you, and tell you one more time how much you mean to me. Writing novels was my dream, and you helped make my dream come true. I cannot even begin to express the gratitude I have for your friendship, your humor, your fabulous purses, scarves, and earrings, your smiley faces on my manuscripts where you would write: "No conflict in this scene, sorry! :-)", your posh British accent, your writing advice, your life advice, but most of all, your love. I felt such love coming from you when I heard the news that you had passed. I will miss you forever, and I am eternally grateful that you came into my life right when you did.

You were the first person to truly "get" my writing, and as a writer, there is no greater gift than someone who understands your work, loves it, and helps you to make it better. Karen, you were this friend, this writing angel, not only to me, but to so many others. Writing for us really was a team effort, and without you on my team, I don't know where I would be. Our meetings were the highlight of my week, and I have missed them and you immensely since I moved out to California. You changed my life, Karen, and I will be forever grateful. I will never forget you, or what you have taught me. And I promise you that the witty, beautiful stories you were working on when this all happened will still find a home. I will make sure of it.

After I heard the news of your passing, I gazed up at the moon and the stars, wondering what the world will be like without you in it, my dear, sweet friend. It is unimaginable. But then I remembered that you are still here, in my heart, where you will always be.

Love,
Danielle

THE DAY of Karen's funeral, it is brutally cold in Virginia. I drive to the church alone, dressed in a black dress that is practically hanging off of me from all the weight I've lost, but I don't have any dresses that fit right anymore, so it will have to do.

When I pull into the church parking lot, I am the first to arrive, so I blast the heat in my car and pull out the eulogy I have prepared for the service. Karen's husband asked both me and Sharon to speak on Karen's behalf, and while I am honored, I am also scared that I won't be able to get through it.

As I am practicing the words I've written for my friend, I notice that I haven't shaved my legs in far too long. I'm not wearing tights, which is ludicrous considering how cold it is outside, and I have the hairiest knees ever. Of course no one is going to be analyzing the hair growth on my knees, but still, Karen was always a picture of style. I can't walk into her funeral with hairy knees.

In my makeup bag, I dig out my tiny eyebrow scissors, and I begin trimming away at the small forest on my knees.

It is only about halfway through this hair-trimming madness that I realize how utterly ridiculous this is. And I start laughing. I laugh so hard that I cry. Karen is probably watching me right now and laughing at me too. And that makes me smile.

Once my knees are hair-free—or as hair-free as I can get them with these pathetic little scissors—I dash through the winter freeze and into the church. I am holding it together until I sit down with my friends in one of the front pews and see the massive, smiling picture of Karen placed on the altar.

Sitting to either side of me are my friends Sharon and Mary, the two women who completed our amazing writing critique group.

There were four of us for so long—four writers sharing chapters and writing tips and publishing advice. Four women helping each other through life's ups and downs. Four friends who have loved and depended on each other in so many ways.

Now, there are only three.

Sharon and Mary each have their husbands by their side, but with their free hands, they are holding mine. And when I break down, Mary, one of the kindest, strongest women I know, pulls me into her chest and holds me the way a mother would her child.

This is the hug I have needed for so long now. A mother's hug. I am so grateful to have Mary here, holding me when I am too weak to do anything but bury my face in her shoulder and cry.

She doesn't let me go until I have calmed down.

When it is my turn to walk up to the podium and speak about my friend, I am feeling stronger and determined. This is about Karen; it's not about me.

And so I speak about Karen's life, about her gifts and talents, about her brilliant sense of humor and her brilliant scarves. And at the end, I read her my letter, the letter I wrote to her on the night she died.

After I speak, Sharon gives a beautiful talk on Karen's bravery, and then Karen's oldest son and her husband speak as well. Their words are so personal and so heartbreaking, and they all weave together to honor Karen as the magnificent mother, wife, writer, and friend that she was.

Later, the female pastor is addressing Karen's boys, who are all sitting in the front row in their suits, wiping their tears. She tells them, "Your mom has given you the best gift of all, a gift you will carry with you forever—her love. This love she gave you, it will never die." She pauses, and then says it again. "*Love never dies.*"

This realization on the nature of love makes me think that amid all of the loss I have experienced this year: the loss of my marriage, my husband, and the dreams I once had for our future; the constant feeling that I am losing Nick, even though he says his heart is always with me; and now the loss of my dear friend— amid all of that, the love hasn't died.

I still love my husband and he still loves me. We will always love each other. I will always hold our love in my heart, which is, of course, what has made saying goodbye so difficult.

And Nick. I already know that I will love him for the rest of my days, no matter where our paths take us.

And, of course, Karen. This gift of love she has given to her boys, she has also given it to me, Sharon, and Mary; to everyone sitting in this church; and to every single life she has ever touched.

What an incredible gift this love is.

I gaze up at Karen's bright, shining smile and remember her last words to me: "*I am so lucky.*"

Karen understood that thing about love, how it never dies. She knew she was lucky to have been surrounded by so much love, to have had the opportunity to give so much love.

And now it is my turn to tell her how lucky I am, how blessed I am, how thankful I am to have her love. I will cherish it, always and forever.

Chapitre 31

I AM standing next to the Barnes & Noble on M Street in Georgetown, and normally this quaint street in my favorite DC neighborhood is bustling with tourists and shoppers and students. But today, the street is clear. I glance up and down the long city blocks, and there isn't a person in sight.

I begin walking down M street, when I notice an older man walking beside me. I don't know him, but it isn't his presence that is concerning me. It is the massive tornado I have just spotted whipping down Pennsylvania Avenue, in the direction of the White House. The monstrous gray funnel is like something out of a movie. It can't be real.

But it is. I have to get out of here.

I run back to the Barnes & Noble where an older woman is waiting for me. She ushers me inside and takes me down into the basement. There is a car parked there, also waiting for me. She opens the door.

"Get inside," she says.

"No, I want to stay here. We can't drive outside right now. We'll get killed!" I shriek.

"You have to get in."

She is adamant, and I see that this is my only choice.

I climb into the backseat, and there are three older men in the car with me—one at the driver's seat, one in the passenger's seat, and one in the backseat with me. I don't know them, but I feel that they are safe.

We pull out of this Barnes & Noble basement and head into a desolate DC. We race through the city, and when we reach the Key Bridge, I get a full view of the twister that is ripping apart the nation's capital. All of the boats on the river have gone up in flames, the buildings are demolished, and the city of DC, the city I have loved since I first arrived on its doorstep as a wide-eyed, naïve college freshman, that city is no more.

It is ruined.

We zoom away, and as I watch the destruction unfold, strangely I don't feel afraid. The only thought that is passing through my mind is: *Nothing will ever be the same.*

Suddenly our car has plunged into the water, but it's safe in here. The car morphs into some sort of submarine, and we can breathe just fine inside our little pod. As the submarine takes us further and further away from the tornado, I only think of Karen. I feel connected to her here, under the water. And even though everything else has fallen apart, I know she is here with me. And I am with her.

I AM curled up on Angie's couch in my pajamas, sipping hot tea, when I tell her about my tornado dream.

"I have a few ideas as to what the dream might mean, but I'm curious. What do you think?" I ask her. "It felt really significant."

"That's an easy one," she says. "Nick is so obviously the tornado. He is total and complete destruction for you. Your husband is Barnes & Noble because you always used to go there together, and because he was the safe option. You go to him for safety while Nick just keeps destroying everything. In the end, you had to leave them both in order to be okay. And with you just losing Karen, she is on your mind. Your connection to her is strong."

"Wow," I say. "Nick is the tornado. That's a pretty strong message from my subconscious."

"A tornado that you're walking into later today."

My forehead plunges into my hands. "What am I doing?"

Neither Angie nor I have a good answer to that question, and still, later that morning, I take the metro to the DC airport to pick up the man my subconscious believes will destroy me if I don't hightail it out of here fast.

When Nick and I arrive at The Melrose Georgetown Hotel, I realize just how accurate my dream was. The hotel is located down Pennsylvania Avenue, en route to the White House, *exactly* where the tornado was tearing through the city in my dream.

Nick is holding my hand and beaming at me as we glide over the marble floors of the lobby, and while I'm thrilled to see him too, my stomach is tied up in knots, and I'm queasy.

Was my dream a premonition?

Am I walking straight into a tornado when I need to be running in the other direction?

IT'S TOO cold to go anywhere, so on our first day in DC together, we leave the hotel only to eat. All other hours of the day are spent curled up in bed together, making love. Nick's body, his lips, his sweet words and adoring looks are such a comfort after the devastation of losing Karen. His embrace is so strong, so reassuring, that I only wish he could have been at the funeral with me. Although, given the dodgy reality of our situation, that never would have been possible.

At least he is here with me now, keeping me warm, making me forget, at least for today, that outside of this hotel room, I have lost so much. Outside of this hotel room, I don't even have him.

There may be a tornado on its way, but here, in our secret bubble, we are safe. We are warm. We are ever so hopelessly in love.

NICK AND I are sitting cross-legged on red cushions eating dumplings and drinking hot tea at Ching Ching Cha, a teahouse in Georgetown. It is inside Ching Ching Cha that I notice something rather unfortunate—the butterflies that were flittering around my insides all day yesterday have been replaced with pangs of anxiety and sadness...and a rather large dumpling.

The problem isn't that I'm *not* head-over-heels for Nick—clearly I am—it's that I feel *so* strongly for him that on Day Two of our wintry DC affair, I am crashing under the weight of the realization that I want to be with this man more than anything in the world—I want to spend my life with him—and yet our situation is impossible. *His* situation is impossible.

"Even if I do decide to leave my marriage," Nick points out, "it will have to be a long, thought-out process. I can't just walk away from the last fifteen years without warning."

I would think that barely having sex for years and agreeing to sleep with other people is at least a small hint, but who am I to say?

"Of course." I push my dumplings away, clutching my stomach. "And I would never want you to do that. It took me over a year and a half of deliberating and counseling and reading and working on my marriage to finally make the decision to go. You owe that to yourself and to your wife; otherwise, you'll always wonder—what if you had given it more?"

"Exactly," he says.

I am slumping now on my red cushion, the most miserable person to have ever sat on the floor of Ching Ching Cha.

"The situation is still making you feel awful, though, huh?" Nick says.

"Yes. What are we going to do?"

"I don't know," he says. "I need time. I have to do things on my own timeline."

"And I need to move forward with my life. Being stuck in a holding pattern, waiting for you on the off-chance that one day you decide to leave—it's not healthy for me."

"I don't want you to wait," he says. "I want you to live your life." Nick's hand slides onto my lap. "But I don't want to lose you."

"I don't want to lose you either."

I don't believe Nick will ever leave his wife, and when I say that I don't want him to leave only for me, I mean it. Leaving my husband was the most agonizing decision of my life, and even though I didn't leave my husband *for* Nick, even though I thought it all out and gave it everything I had, I still wake up many days regretting my decision.

Despite Nick's affairs, despite the fact that he has fallen in love with me, he still loves his wife and their life together dearly. He doesn't want to go. And he also doesn't want to end this affair.

He wants her *and* he wants me.

But he can't have both of us forever. It's not fair to anyone.

It will be up to me to leave; I know this.

Our blissful days in Paris are only a distant memory now. With each subsequent rendezvous, we are consumed and tortured by the extremes: joy and sadness, ecstasy and misery, love and heartbreak.

There was only one Paris, and now that we've used up our only ticket, it seems we are doomed for eternity to both love and hate our situation.

Well, not for eternity. Only for as long as I decide to keep this damn thing going.

I HAVE been a mess all day. Depressed and desolate, just like the city was after the tornado ripped through it in my dream. Nick hasn't seen me in this state before, and I think it's scaring him. Later that night, after our walk around a frozen DC has sufficiently chilled my hands and my heart, we are back in the hotel room, warming up.

Nick turns on his music, adding to our already sexy soundtrack with "Nirvana" by Sam Smith. "I want to see you dance," he whispers in my ear.

For the first time in our relationship, I feel rage boiling over inside of me. I want to tell him that I'm not a fucking dancing puppet! I don't dance on command, like some sort of doll without a brain or feelings!

I'm a real person, with real feelings, and I feel like absolute shit.

"I don't feel like dancing," I tell him as I walk away and sit on the couch, hugging my knees to my chest. "*You* dance," I say, not hiding the bite in my tone. "I always dance for you. Why don't you do it?"

He hesitates, but he can see by the look on my face that I'm not budging.

"Do it," I order. "Dance for me."

"Okay...what song should I dance to?"

"Hmmm...let me think...how about 'Stayin' Alive'."

"Oh, you want a little John Travolta action, do you?" His grin belies the hesitance in his voice, but I don't care if he doesn't want to do it. That man is going to dance for me.

"Yup," I say. "Put it on and shake that booty."

Nick does as I say, and before I know it, my tall, manly, sexy lover is standing in front of me wearing long johns and a T-shirt, doing a cheesy, older-man boogie to "Stayin' Alive."

And finally, after a day of tears, long talks, and general misery in his company, I am giggling.

"You're ridiculous!" I tell him.

"Hey, you wanted to see my moves!"

"I love them," I say. "I love your moves." Tears of laughter are pouring down my cheeks now, and I am so grateful that for tonight anyway, Nick understands that it can't always be me on the stage, doing the seductive mistress dance. Sometimes he needs to meet me in the middle and do his own boogie, hilarious though it may be.

I LOVE birthdays. When I was a little girl, my mom always made such a fuss over my birthday, and I adored her for it. There was the My Little Pony cake she always ordered special for the big day, and the birthday parties she always threw with all of my girl-friends and tons of presents. She may not have had much money, but whatever she had that month went to making sure I had the best birthday ever.

My husband did a beautiful job taking over where my mom left off and making birthdays special and sweet. He always gave me a thoughtful gift, but more than his presents, I treasured his cards. In his man handwriting, he'd always fill up the entire card with his words of love to me, telling me how much he appreciated and adored me, and how lucky he was to have me as his wife. I always made a big deal out of his birthday, too, even when he didn't want me to. For his thirtieth, I threw him a big surprise party complete with a slide show of all of our most beautiful moments together. I always wanted him to know how much I loved him, and birthdays were the perfect opportunity to demonstrate that love.

It is the morning of my thirty-second birthday, and instead of waking up with my husband, like I have for the majority of my past twelve birthdays, I wake alone in a hotel bed, wondering where my lover has gone. Before I emerge from the sheets, an image pops into my mind. It's not my lover, but my husband. He is young, in his mid-twenties, and he's holding a cake he made just for me. It's a double layer yellow cake covered in vanilla frosting—

my favorite—decorated all the way around with sliced strawberries. Candles in the shape of the number "23" light up the cake, but my husband's grin is brighter. He is so proud of himself for baking this culinary masterpiece all on his own.

I took a picture of him holding that cake, only a few months after we first moved in together and got engaged. We were happy then. Blissfully happy. And so in love.

The sound of my lover walking around our suite snaps me from my birthday memory, and I force myself to refocus. My husband won't be making me any more cakes, and I won't be throwing him any more surprise parties. In less than a month, we'll be meeting in court to finalize our divorce, and then he will no longer officially be my husband.

The weight of that monumental loss is sitting heavily on my shoulders as I shuffle out of the bedroom, a groggy, tired birthday mess. My lover greets me with a kiss.

"Happy birthday, beautiful," he says, ruffling his hands through my hair.

"Thank you, lover," I say, knowing I need to be grateful. Even though it's not conventional, even though it's not my husband, Nick loves me. And I am lucky to have this love waiting for me the minute I rise on my thirty-second birthday, only a few days after I've said goodbye to Karen.

Nick leads me to the little kitchen table in our suite, where breakfast and a wrapped gift are waiting.

I sit down at the table, take a sip of my hot chamomile tea, and open Nick's present to me.

It's a small wooden cylinder...and I'm confused. "What...is it?" I ask, not meaning to sound ungrateful, but I really have no clue what this is.

He holds the end up to my eyes and aims the other end toward the light. "Look inside."

An array of colors and designs and patterns greets my eyes, and as I turn the cylinder, the patterns change, the colors move, and I smile, still a little confused.

"A kaleidoscope," I say. "I don't think I've looked into one of these since I was a little girl."

"It reminded me of you," he says. "All the different colors, the way they move and shift constantly, and each pattern is more beautiful than the next."

Touched, I look at him incredulously.

"What man says things like that? *Who* are you?"

He kisses me and we enjoy our breakfast of eggs, bacon, toast, and tea together. It's delicious, just like my lover.

After breakfast, we are standing at the window together, and Nick's arms are wrapped tightly around my waist as we watch the snow fall outside. There are at least six inches on the ground, and the city has shut down, as it always does when it snows. I grew up in the frozen tundra of Ohio, and while I'm not a fan of the cold, I find it hilarious that the nation's capital can't handle a little snow.

Although today, I'm thankful for the snow and for the city shut-down. It means my lover and I can hole up in our little bubble a little bit longer and keep each other warm instead of having to face the bitter reality of the outside world.

While we do leave the sex nest for food later in the day, we spend most of the day making love on the couch, on the table, in the shower, and buried in the sheets. We make love so many times that late that night, while we are at it again, a sudden, intense pain grips me from deep inside.

"I'm sorry," I tell Nick while he is still inside me. "We have to stop. It hurts."

He stops immediately. "What is it?"

"I don't know." I'm now curled in a naked ball on the bed, clutching my stomach. It feels as if my womb is staging a revolt. "Maybe we've just pushed it too far."

We *have* pushed it too far; we always do. After each of our rendezvous, I have returned home not only suffering from intense emotional pain, but also from intense physical pain. It usually takes my body at least a week to recover, and I have made so many trips to my gynecologist this year that she probably thinks I am having sex with the entire world.

My reproductive organs are not a fan of this affair, not at all.

"What can I do?" Nick asks, leaning over me, a picture of worry.

"I need a heating pad," I say, wincing. "It feels like when I would get my worst periods, but ten times more painful than that."

Nick calls the front desk, but no luck on the heating pad.

"It's okay," I tell him. "I'll be okay."

"You don't look okay." Nick is throwing on his pants, shirt, and boots. I glance at the clock—it's 1:30 in the morning.

"Where are you going?" I ask him.

"There's a CVS down the street. I'm sure it's twenty-four-hour. I'm getting you a heating pad."

"You don't have to trek out in the snow in the middle of the night to get me a heating pad."

"Danielle, I'm going."

"At least look on your phone first to be sure it's open twenty-four hours."

Nick checks and shakes his head. "Shit, it's not open."

The pain hasn't subsided in the least—it has only intensified, and it's so bad that I'm beginning to feel nauseous. "A bath," I say. "A hot bath."

Nick is in the bathroom drawing a bath before I can wince another time. He helps me to the bathroom and lowers me into the bath. I lay my head back against the tiles and close my eyes. The heat soothes me immediately, and while the pain is still there, it finally begins to calm.

"Thank you," I say softly. "Thank you for taking care of me."

He is kneeling by the tub, holding my hand. "You don't have to thank me," he says. "I'm so sorry if I did this to you."

We did this to each other.

I don't say that, though. Instead I squeeze his hand, thinking about my tornado dream. Both my subconscious and my body are smacking me upside the head with signs about how dangerous this affair is, how deeply it is hurting me.

It is hurting him too. And although his wife doesn't know that Nick has carried out one of his hall-pass affairs way past their original arrangement, it is hurting her as well.

I know I must pay attention to the signs and heed the warnings.

But my irrational love for this man is keeping me here, tied to him, pain and all. I'm not sure when I'll have the strength to cut the ties that bind us, to run in the opposite direction of this disaster.

Chapitre 32

MY LEASE is up in my apartment that overlooks the canyon and I've decided it's time to go. It's time to leave behind everything that happened in this place—the hope I felt when we first arrived that *this* would be the home my husband and I would bring a baby into, and then the loss of that dream...along with the loss of our marriage.

But since it's time for this almost-divorced chick to spice things up a bit and have some fun, I've decided that the next logical step is to take my two massive cats and move into a big house on a hill with three guys.

Yes, by some miracle, not one dude, not two dudes, but *three* dudes have agreed to let this almost-divorced girl and her big felines move into their gorgeous house.

And so, I am spending the day packing. Well, if packing is sitting on my closet floor rifling through old memories, photos, and birthday cards from my husband, and crying hysterically, *again*—dear God, will this damn divorce faucet ever turn off?—then yes, I'm packing.

I power through, nonetheless, knowing that I *must* because no one is going to swoop in and do it for me. I have two movers arriving in the morning, and I have to be packed and ready to go when they get here.

Once I have finally managed to turn off the divorce faucet, I am frantically packing boxes when my cell phone dings with a new e-mail.

It's Nick.

We e-mail each other every day, sometimes several times a day, and usually his letters are the highlight of my day. He is an extraordinary writer. Each e-mail is like its own mini love letter, laced with his quirky sense of humor; his dirty, hot sex remarks; and his total and complete adoration for me.

His writing is one of the main reasons I am hanging on. I love hearing from him. I love reading the way he strings words together to tell me how much he loves me.

But today, his e-mail has me slumped on my bathroom floor, back in Tear City.

Nick has informed me that he will be taking his wife on the same trip to Rome that he had originally invited me on. We'd even picked out the cutest Airbnb flat online together, but I had to cancel because the trip coincided with my divorce court date.

So now, he's taking his wife.

I feel like he's punched me in the gut.

I should have expected that he would do this. It's his *wife* for God's sake. I'm only the secret lover, hiding in the wings. Of course he'd take her to Rome. As he should.

But that doesn't make it hurt any less.

I don't have time for this pain, though. While Nick is planning his Italian getaway with his wife, I have to pack up the home I used to have with my husband, all by myself.

I force myself off the bathroom floor, gripping the countertop all the way, and look in the mirror. I'm pale and thin and there are gargantuan circles around my eyes. My normally bright blue eyes are dull and sad and finished. They are just finished with this whole damn thing.

This affair. This apartment. *This life.*

It's time for a new life. A life in a house with three handsome, silly, wonderful guys. I hang on to the hope that the new world I am walking into tomorrow will bring me new friends, new lovers, and new joy, so that I can leave all of this *crap* behind me.

I don't respond to Nick's e-mail. I don't respond to his calls later that day.

Instead, I pack all through the night, and in the morning, I leave it all behind to move into the house with three boys.

IN MY new house, with my new roommates, I finally respond to Nick's e-mail. I tell him that I don't want to be in touch for a little while. I tell him that I need to move on with my life. I tell him that he can't continue to enjoy both me *and* his wife. It's not fair to anyone, and the pain I feel is unbearable. I won't live like this any longer. I can't.

WE GO two days without contact, and then Nick caves. He's lonely in Rome—he is on the business portion of his trip and his wife hasn't arrived yet for their Italian getaway. And so, he's longing for me. Just two days without an e-mail from his mistress, and he's in serious withdrawal.

I read his letter, wishing I were stronger, wishing I didn't feel the same sickening, gut-wrenching, heart-slicing withdrawal. But I do. I am a mess without him.

So, like the weak-hearted woman I have become, I respond and tell him that I miss him more than words could ever express. Which is the truth. A truth that I hate, a truth I wish I could change, but it is there, nonetheless, and I have, once again, admitted this truth to him and invited him back into my life.

A SHOT of much-needed comic relief comes in the form of my hilarious new roommates. The two I am spending the most time with in the house are named Micah and Carl, but they are otherwise known as The Broconuts.

Allow me to explain.

Micah and Carl became close friends when they realized they had an affinity for all things coconut: coconut oil, coconut milk, coconut vinegar, coconut nectar, coconut aminos, coconut flakes, coconut water, and, of course, coconuts themselves. Many days, I will come downstairs to find both Micah and Carl sitting on the couch, cross-legged and shirtless, digging their spoons into their giant coconuts, and then slurping the juice straight from the inside of the coconut.

"*Fuck*, that's good!" Carl will shout.

"*Fuck*, it really is," Micah will echo.

Beyond their extreme love for coconut products, Micah and Carl are like professional Paleo chefs. Each night, they spend hours in the kitchen chopping vegetables, cooking meat, and moaning over the delicious meals they are creating. They are the healthiest boys I know—both of them boasting rock-solid bodies where fat couldn't grow if it wanted to.

Every night, as I am eating my divorced-lady cliché food of macaroni and cheese or Pop Tarts or ice cream, I've been firm with them in that they are *not* to pass judgment. I must get through my court date, and then I will make an effort to eat healthier. I am in survival mode, and while neither of them has been divorced, they are respectful of the process.

Lucky for me, the entertainment they are providing is endless. In the evenings, instead of crying alone in my bed, I am now cooking dinner with the boys, laughing over our ridiculous conversations, and pinching myself, wondering how this sitcom-worthy scenario has become *my life*.

Each day with The Broconuts is like an episode of *The New Girl,* except instead of a bad breakup, the leading lady—me—went through a divorce before moving in with her three dudes. And instead of a PG-13-rated comedy, my real-life sitcom is firmly rated R.

One such R-rated conversation takes place while the four of us are cleaning the garage to clear the way for my things.

We are in work mode, not really joking or laughing about anything, until...

"Hey, Carl, do you need this old microwave for anything?" Micah asks.

"Uh, yeah, I need it," Carl says.

"Why?" Micah says. "We have a perfectly good one in the kitchen."

And then, without warning, and with a perfectly straight face, Carl gives what he clearly thinks is the most logical answer to the question of the old microwave:

"I need that microwave to heat up the rice bags that I use to warm up my penis before I do my penis enlargement exercises."

Now there's a showstopper.

"Wh...what?" I stammer, trying to hide my grin in case Carl is serious. "Did you just say...warming up rice bags...for your...?"

"Yeah, for my penis enlargement exercises," he says, totally unfazed.

"Carl, are you serious?" Micah asks, ready to burst at any moment.

"Yeah, it's a whole method," Carl says. "I have a ninety-page book on it."

"Does it work?" I am still, by some miracle, managing to stifle my laughter.

"Yeah, I've measured. It works. It doesn't get longer, but it's the girth that grows."

"Oh dear God." And that's it, I'm now doubled over in a fit of laughter, and Micah has joined me. Carl is still standing there as if this is all completely normal. He grabs the old microwave, the one he uses to heat up his...*rice bags?*...and then he places it on a shelf above the washer and dryer.

So, we're keeping the microwave.

The story of the microwave/rice bags/penis enlargement is perhaps the best event to have taken place in the house so far. The next best one is that The Broconuts are training for a body building competition. This means that each morning, they arrive in the kitchen, strip down to only their tight boxer briefs and weigh in. This also means that soon, they will be running around the house with tanned, hairless bodies, and practicing their poses wearing only a banana hammock.

One day, when Carl emerges from a ninety-minute meditation and Micah is listening to a Tony Robbins recording, I look at my new friends, my new roommates, my new family, and I tell them, "You know, one year ago, if someone had shown me even a thirty-second snapshot of what it would be like living with you guys and then told me *this* would soon be my life, never in a hundred years would I have believed them."

Micah puts his arm around me. "Awww, D, you love us though, don't you?"

"Of course I do," I say with a smile. And I really do. Living with Micah and Carl has saved me in ways they couldn't possibly comprehend. They have made me realize that laughter really *is* the best medicine, but even more so, it is their friendship which is healing this broken heart of mine, day by day.

DIVORCE COURT. It was something my husband and I hoped to avoid because we agreed on everything and had the most amicable divorce known to man. Our lawyer told us that because of the way we'd chosen to file, we wouldn't have to go to court.

And yet, the court notice came, demanding our presence. Demanding that we stand in front of a judge to end this marriage, once and for all.

It is time to go to this dreaded appointment, and as my friend Hannah drops me off in front of the courthouse, I am a ball of nerves. I walk inside but don't see my husband anywhere. As I'm waiting for him, I imagine that he will be pretty tense when he walks in. Angry possibly. Perhaps we will barely talk. Maybe he'll be a major asshole so I'll feel good about leaving him.

But, no. That's not who he is.

When my husband arrives at divorce court, all tall and handsome and impeccably dressed, he walks straight over to me and hugs me.

My husband is hugging me in divorce court.

What kind of a woman would divorce a man who would actually *embrace her* in divorce court? What the fuck am I doing?

After the hug, we realize we are in the wrong courthouse, and we only have about ten minutes to zoom through downtown San Diego to the right one.

"Shoot...Hannah dropped me off, so I don't have my car," I tell him. "Do you mind if I...?"

"You need a ride?" he asks.

"Yeah, if you don't mind."

"Of course not."

We climb into his shiny new car together and on our way to divorce court, we catch each other up on our lives. I tell him how it's going in the house with three guys, how the cats are doing with the transition, and he tells me how things are going at work and with his family.

I am so happy to be in his presence, to be chatting with him about normal things, that I almost forget where we are going.

Inside the correct courthouse, we weave our way up to the courtroom we've been assigned, and we take our seats. We are only second on a long list of divorce cases, so we're hoping we can get in and out of here quickly. This isn't going to be fun for anyone and there is no need to drag it out.

But, after the first case is finished, the judge calls someone else's name. And after that, he calls another name. But none of these names are ours. And so it goes. We are forced to listen to case after nasty divorce case, and all the while, I am wondering how *we* ever made it into this room.

This isn't how it was supposed to end.

It wasn't *supposed* to end. That's the whole point of marriage, isn't it?

But here we are, and I can't turn back now.

Two hours later, we are the last ones left in this room that has housed the end of so many marriages.

By the time the judge calls our names, I can't remember a single item on the long list of reasons why I left my marriage, and I am questioning everything. I'm questioning my decision to divorce such a kind, loving man, a man with whom I still love spending time. A man who hugs me when he walks into divorce court, a man who is so superbly handsome and sweet. *A good man.* He's not the kind of man who ever would have done to me what Nick is doing to his wife. He wouldn't have done to me what I did to him at the end of our marriage.

He always loved me. And I know he still does.

But now we are sitting on opposing sides of the courtroom, answering questions about our split from a judge who probably thought this was going to be some huge fight, which was why he saved us for last.

We definitely don't live up to that expectation, though, as with each question he asks us, we answer with, "Yes," "Yes," and another "Yes."

Until the final question.

The judge looks straight at me, clears his throat, and addresses my full name. "Do you believe that perhaps with further counseling or work on the relationship, you could save this marriage?"

I want to stand and shout, "Yes! Of course we could do more! Of course we could try harder!"

I want to knock down the podium that stands between me and my husband, I want to take him in my arms and tell him I'm so sorry for all of the pain I've caused him. I'm sorry for being someone who needed to be with other people to feel happy. I want to tell him that it didn't work! I'm not happier! I'm a fucking wreck without him, and this has all been one huge, massive mistake. I want to grab his hand and run as far away from this courtroom as our feet will carry us and never look back.

I want to tell him that I still love him and that I'll do *anything* to make this work.

But this isn't the movies. I've put my husband through enough. I can't change my mind now, at the absolute last second, when the judge has the stamp in hand and he's ready to slam that thing over our names, forever splitting the bond we once had.

But it's not the judge who has broken us.

I broke us. *We* broke us.

And so, as much as I want to take back all of my mistakes and forget this ever happened, I don't. I can't. I made my bed; now I must lie in it.

Finally, after much internal deliberation, I reply, "No, your honor. I don't."

It is the hardest sentence I have ever spoken.

The sound of the judge's stamp echoes through the courtroom.

A finality. A definitive ending.

A death.

"On Monday, the divorce will be final, and you can move on with your lives. You're free to go." The judge has released us into the world, but I don't want to go there. I don't know where I want to be, but it's not in this courtroom or in a world where I chose to leave a man whom I still love.

When we stand, I glance over at my husband, and his eyes are bloodshot and full of tears. Before we even reach the door of the courtroom, I am in hysterics.

In the hallway, lawyers and their clients are swirling around us, but I can barely see them through my tears. The man who will only technically be my husband until Monday leads me down the hallway, and when we find a little alcove where no one will bother us, he holds me in his arms while I cry.

"You're going to be okay," he says.

My entire body is shaking, trembling, crumbling. I am only still standing because he is holding me up. What will I do when he's gone? When he's really gone?

"You're going to be okay, Danielle," he says again.

He says it a few more times, and while nothing in me believes him, I force myself to take a breath.

Finally, after our last hug as husband and wife, my husband turns and leaves.

I walk into the bathroom, collapsing in the stall, and cry until my eyes are raw and dry.

The California sun is relentless when I walk outside. Hannah zooms by in her little blue car and scoops me up.

"It was brutal," I tell her, although she can certainly see that from the way my mascara is streaking down my face.

She hands me a croissant. Such a wonderful friend.

"But it's over," she says.

My hands are shaking as I lift the croissant to my lips.

"Yes, it is," I say, before taking a bite.

It's really, truly *over.*

Chapitre 33

AN INFERNO of unyielding sunshine and hundred-degree weather has descended upon San Diego, and I couldn't be happier to be getting on a plane. New Orleans welcomes me with surprisingly mild temperatures and a hotel full of wild, crazy romance writers.

It is my first time attending the Romantic Times Convention, and it's also my first visit to New Orleans. Nick didn't forget our deal to see a psychic together in New Orleans, but in the weeks leading up to my trip, I vacillated from hot to cold with him—one day telling him that yes, I would *love* for him to meet me in New Orleans, and the next telling him I absolutely could not handle seeing him. I was still burned over the fact that he'd been frolicking around Rome with his wife while I was sitting in divorce court, losing my husband and losing my mind.

I was beginning to seriously resent Nick for stringing me along while he continued to stall on making any kind of definite decision regarding his future with me or his wife.

I knew all along, of course, that it would have to be me to do the leaving in this affair, but since I wasn't quite strong enough to walk out the door just yet, in the end, I agreed to let him meet me in New Orleans. But I told him that he'd have to stay at a different hotel while I stayed at the conference hotel with one of my author friends.

Night settles on New Orleans, and my heart flutters when I check my phone and realize that Nick's plane has landed, and he is en route to his hotel. Not only does my heart flutter, my stomach curls and rumbles, and I feel as though I may be sick.

This affair has been making me sick for a while now. Why can't I stop?

He swoops by in a cab and picks me up outside the hotel. When I climb in, I am still feeling ill. It's the first time in our entire affair that I am not at all happy to see him. I am still so upset with him for taking his wife on our trip to Rome. I am mad at him for not choosing me. It's a rough start to the evening, to say the least.

Nick's lips try to find mine, his hands making their usual tour over my curves in the back of the cab, but I push him away.

"I'm sorry, I'm just not feeling good," I tell him.

Disappointment and confusion line those big green eyes of his, and I know he is probably nearing his limit with my whole love you/hate you routine. I'm exhausted with it too. I just can't force myself to be any other way right now. This is how I feel. I love him and I detest him. But I only detest him because I love him so damn much.

Oh yeah, and I still love my ex-husband too. He is officially my *ex*-husband now, but our stint in divorce court only made me love him more.

What a fucking mess I am. Nick is crazy to be involved with me.

We arrive at the charming room he booked at a lovely hotel in the French Quarter, and inside, we sit on the bed, not ravaging each other the way we usually do within minutes of closing the door, but instead, talking tirelessly about what in the hell we are doing.

It is a conversation we've had before—too many times to count. After we exhaust ourselves and get nowhere, somehow our conversation turns to marriage.

Being a divorce court survivor, I now have a pretty strong opinion on marriage and I don't hesitate to share it with my married lover.

"I don't ever want to get married again," I say. "I don't see the point in signing a legal document to commit to a relationship. If I want to be with you, I will just be with you. And if it's not working someday, we can break up. Why the need to lock it down in the legal system and make it so damn hard to get out of? Breaking up is awful enough; add to that stacks of divorce paperwork which reduce your entire love story to a listing of assets and debts and objects that don't matter, and then top it off with a traumatic trip to court so that you can announce in front of a judge that you and your partner have failed. It's insane."

Nick takes a moment to ponder my bitter diatribe, and then he slides his hand over mine on the bed. "Haven't you ever thought of *us* getting married, though?"

I glance down at his wedding ring, thinking this man *cannot* be serious right now.

"There's an obvious problem with that," I say. "Namely that you are *already* married."

"I know, but if I weren't. If we could be together. Wouldn't you want to marry me?"

"Is this your way of proposing?" I joke, trying not to sound hopeful. He knows how fragile I am. What a wreck I've been. And even though the idea of marriage makes me want to run for the hills, the idea of marriage *with him* is something else altogether.

Something that is making my heart race.

Why would he bring this up?

"Come on," he prods. "Don't tell me you haven't envisioned it."

I *have* envisioned our wedding. Even though I don't want to marry again, even though all faith I used to have in fairy tales has been washed down the kitchen sink in pool of stale, dirty dish water, I *have* imagined myself walking down the aisle to Nick.

While Paris is the obvious choice for our wedding, for some reason, in my wedding fantasy, I see Nick standing beneath a white archway on a tropical island, his head tilted, his smile bright and emotional as I walk, alone, down the aisle. I'm wearing a long, flowing white gown. It's elegant and breezy at the same time, just like our wedding. It's a simple ceremony, with only a few close friends as witnesses, but we don't care who is near. We are so in love and so happy that we can actually be together, that nothing else matters.

That is the wedding I have envisioned for these two star-crossed lovers.

"No," I lie. "I haven't really thought about it. Have you?"

"Well, yeah, I have," Nick says. "If we could be together, there is no question in my mind that I would want to marry you."

We *could* be together. We *can* be together. *It's in your hands!*

I want to shout all of this in his face, but he knows. He knows I'm only hanging on for the day, the hour, the moment, where he says to me, "Let's do this. Let's really do this."

But Nick doesn't say that to me on this day, in this hour, in this moment in our secret hotel room in the heart of New Orleans. Instead, he talks of a fantasy, a fantasy that will never happen.

"I'll admit, I've thought about it a lot. There's something so romantic and beautiful about getting married. I would want to share that with you. I mean, you're a romance writer at a romance writers conference! Don't you want to have that again?"

"Maybe I will someday," I concede. "Who knows? But today... I'm not so sure."

Nick cozies up next to me on the bed, runs his hand through my long hair. "I see us having a small, intimate ceremony on an island somewhere far away. Ocean breezes, sand in our toes, and you. You would be the most beautiful bride."

The island wedding. He sees it too.

We've been envisioning the same fairy tale all along. How crazy. How sweet. How torturous.

I want to resist him. I want to be stronger than this, I really do. But the idea that Nick has fantasized about our wedding has turned me to complete mush in his arms.

And so, I give him more of myself. More than I have left to give.

And even with all the turmoil, the feeling of his love is *sublime.*

I HAD no idea I would love New Orleans as much as I do. Strolling through the French Quarter with Nick, I am transported back to my beloved land of France, only with a Southern twist. The architecture here has more character than any I've ever seen on this side of the Atlantic. There are pink, orange, and yellow homes with blue and green shutters, charming balconies overflowing with flowers, and lampposts speckling the streets. Everywhere we turn, we find bustling cafés, art galleries, live music, and...psychics.

After a decadent snack of deep-fried beignets at Café Du Monde, we take our full bellies across Decatur Street to Jackson Square where the New Orleans psychics are sitting all cozy in their lawn chairs, telling tourists about their destiny.

Nick nods toward a larger woman shuffling her deck of Tarot cards. Her light brown hair is pulled back into a messy ponytail and her skin is dark and course, probably from years of sitting in this sunlit square, telling fortunes.

"She's the one," he says.

"The same woman you spoke with years ago? You're sure?"

"Well, not entirely sure, but from what I remember, she looked like her. Let's have a seat and if we get a good feeling about her, we'll do it." He looks nervous and determined at the

274 | JULIETTE SOBANET

same time. I wonder what he thinks she'll tell us that we don't already know.

We are so obviously in love, and so obviously tortured by that love.

I'm certain this truth is written all over our faces as we take a seat with our woman.

Nick has a little chat with her, and when I smile in his direction, he knows it's a go. He hands her a wad of cash, and she begins her magic.

She shuffles her deck of Tarot cards and lays them out on the table. After a few interesting and not so interesting insights related to the cards, she gets right to the point.

"You two are soul mates," she says all matter-of-fact. "So, what's the problem?"

I raise an eyebrow at Nick, asking silent permission to tell our New Orleans psychic what is plaguing this pair of soul mates. He nods back.

"He's married," I say.

She lifts a hand to her chin, nodding slowly. "There is a difference between a life partner and a soul mate," she says to Nick. "Your wife is your life partner, and this type of relationship works nicely for both you and her. But Danielle is your true soul mate."

She lets this settle in the humid air between us before she continues.

"So, what are you going to do?" she asks Nick.

He runs a hand through this thick, dark hair, not able to hide the troubled look marring his handsome face. "I don't know," he says.

"If you leave your wife, you and Danielle will be wonderful together, and your wife will move on. There is no question about that. But you must take karma into consideration," she says to Nick. "If you leave your wife for Danielle...one day, Danielle will leave you."

No I won't! I want to scream. But then again, I've left one husband. Who's to say I won't leave Nick after the inevitable romance expiration date that all relationships experience?

"I see that you're not ready to leave," she says to Nick. "There are many strong reasons keeping you in this marriage."

Nick gives a silent nod of agreement, his gaze fixed on the cards. Not on me.

She looks to me. "He is the one you love. You've never met anyone who is more suited to you than him. You could learn to live with the situation."

"You mean keep doing *this*?" I ask. "Seeing him in secret while he stays married?"

She shrugs. "Sometimes people carry on these arrangements for years."

"I can't do this for years," I say. "That's not an option."

"It's hurting you," she says.

"Yes," I confirm. "It's hurting both of us. And it's hurting his marriage."

She shakes her head, sadness lining her already weathered eyes. "There is no easy answer to your predicament," she says. "I have been exactly where you are, and I know how heartbreaking it can be to love someone that you cannot be with. I feel for you both, I really do."

Here in this happy, sunny, music-filled square in the heart of the French quarter, our New Orleans psychic looks as though she may cry for us.

Nick looks as though he may cry too.

As for me, I want to stand up on my chair and yell at the Universe. Why did we even have to meet if we can't be together? Is this some sort of cruel joke?

But I don't stand on my chair and yell at the sky. Instead, I sigh in defeat.

God, we're a sad lot, the three of us.

After we thank her, Nick takes my hand and leads me into the park where we sit side-by-side on a bench and stare into space, digesting everything she just said.

"So, soul mates," he says, squeezing my hand.

I squeeze back. "Yes, but we already knew that."

IT'S OUR last night together in New Orleans, and as we walk into an oyster bar off Bourbon Street, we still have no firm solution to our predicament. All Nick knows is that he loves me, he loves his wife, and he can't wait to eat some oysters.

It is while he is sucking down these slimy creatures that he turns to me and says, "So, you really wouldn't marry me?"

"Are you proposing again?" While I know our situation is impossible, I kind of love that he is fixated on this.

He laughs, swallows another oyster, then flicks his gaze on me. "Wouldn't you?"

"I wouldn't marry anyone else. But you? Yes, I would marry you."

"I thought so," he says, all smug and happy.

"You know, when you asked me the other day if I've ever thought about us getting married, I lied. I *have* thought about it."

"You devious romance writer," he says with a smirk. "And?"

"I've envisioned the same island wedding that you described," I tell him. "Somewhere far away and tropical. Small and intimate. Elegant and sweet."

This gets him to stop mid-oyster.

"Damn, lover, we have such an intense, crazy connection," he says.

"We really do," I say, sipping my water and skipping the oysters. Slimy sea creatures aren't my cup of tea, but Nick could eat them all night long. "Now finish your oysters so we can go to dinner. I'm starving."

Nick eyes my black-and-white polka dot dress—it's the same dress I wore on the day I met him in Los Angeles for our first planned rendezvous. And even though he has commented before that this dress is a little too *country* for his big city tastes, by the way he's running his hand up my short hem, I can tell that at least for tonight, he loves it.

"For a country girl from Ohio, you can be pretty bossy," Nick says.

"I get mean when I'm hungry. You should know that about me if we're going to be pretend married."

Nick wraps up his oyster binge pronto and hails us a cab that whisks us across town to a quaint little restaurant he has chosen for our last night together.

The humidity has died down, but as we take a seat on the front porch in this Southern gem, the air is still thick with tension and emotion. We are nearing a turning point in our relationship, a threshold we must cross, and we both know it.

With just a few sips of Chardonnay in me, I find the courage to say the thing I don't want to say, the thing that must be said.

"You're not ready to leave your wife, Nick. You would know it if you were. And that's okay. You know I, of all people, understand how difficult it is to decide to leave someone you have loved for so long. Someone you still love."

He reaches for my hand across the table, and I notice that his fingers are shaking.

"As long as we keep doing this, you will never be able to evaluate your marriage independently of me, of us. And today, you're not going anywhere. We both know that."

He nods, solemnly, not saying a word.

I feel a burst of strength inside me, and I know it's now or never.

"I love you so much," I say, "but this has to end. We have to stop."

He is quiet for a few more moments, and in the silence, I can feel his heart breaking on top of mine.

"I know," he says finally.

Nick's eyes are glossy with tears, and mine are misty too, but I know this is the right choice. For everyone. It has been the right choice for some time now; I just wasn't strong enough to make it.

When the chocolate cake arrives, I can barely eat it, and neither can he.

This will be our last chocolate dessert. Our last dinner. Our last night together, and even though I know this is the only choice for us at this juncture, it is such a wretched thing to have to do that even chocolate is unappetizing.

Nick isn't choosing me today, and it's likely that he never will.

My heart splits open a little further each time I think about this truth, but by some miracle, I am still breathing, torn heart and all.

After our unappetizing chocolate dessert, we take to the streets of New Orleans one last time. Far away from the charm of the French Quarter and the madness of Bourbon Street, we have found ourselves in a maze of big, beautiful Southern houses. They are painted in shades of yellow, pink, and orange, and they have cozy front porches strung with lights and swings and flowers.

"I would love to live in one of these houses with you," Nick says. "We would have so much fun in this city together."

Even though we are over, Nick won't—*can't*—stop fantasizing.

And because he's doing it, I allow myself a minute—only one minute—of dreaming about living in one of these grand Southern mansions with Nick, the man I married on an island far away, the man who is my soul mate, the man whom I love more than I love myself.

When my minute is up, I stroll along with him in silence, wishing I could disappear into one of the jagged cracks in the sidewalk. Wishing things didn't have to be this way.

But no matter how hard I wish, no matter how hard Nick fantasizes, we still find ourselves in a heap of tears the next morning as we say one last goodbye.

"We'll still be in touch sometimes, right?" Nick says. "We can't go cold turkey. I don't think I could survive that."

"I guess..." I say. "But we can't be in touch a lot. That would defeat the purpose of you evaluating your marriage and me moving forward with my life."

"Please don't cut me out completely, Danielle." Nick is desperate now, and I am tired. The past weekend of incessant, explosive sex and all of our exhausting late-night talks about what we are going to do have drained me.

I am feeling dangerously close to that hollow woman who once lay on a hospital cot, writhing in pain, wondering who she had become.

I must turn the other way, or I will be her again.

"I won't cut you out completely, Nick, but I have to take care of myself," I say firmly. "This isn't healthy for me. It's tearing me apart."

"Me too," he says.

I run my hand through his hair, kiss him softly on the lips.

"We'll be okay," I say, although I don't at all believe the words as they are leaving my mouth.

He nods, but he knows we won't be okay either. The pain is written on his face.

"I have to go to my book signing," I say. "I can't be falling apart in there."

"I know," he says, wiping his eyes, then wiping mine.

He pulls me into his chest and holds me, tightly, one last time.

"I love you so much, Danielle," he breathes into my hair.

"I love you too, Nick."

And finally, I let go of this lover I have held onto for almost an entire year. I walk out of his hotel room, I close the door behind me, and I walk through the crowded streets of New Orleans a stronger woman.

On the Streets of New Orleans

The South buzzes around us
Yellow and pink houses
Porches with swings and strings of light
Your eyes, the way they love me

I've never seen anything so beautiful

You tilt your head, sweeter than tea
Smiling at me, talking about our island wedding
You wouldn't marry me, you ask?
As you suck down a slimy oyster

Me, in my polka dot dress, lavender scarf
A country girl for the night,
Simple
And in love

I wouldn't marry anyone else, I say.
But you...yes, I would marry you.

Summer has yet to arrive this night
As we stroll over the broken sidewalks
Wishing these perfect homes were our own

My heart stumbles, dives, lands at our feet
Because we hold hands,
Knowing this is the end

Once again
Clumsy, clutching, wishing
This heart of mine
She hasn't learned

In the cab ride home
I turn my face away
Tears flood my lashes

You are the one I love
The one I dreamt of, searched for, found...
The one I am losing.

You love me
Still you go back to her.

I am a passing love
Wishing I could be more.
Hoping that someday I will be

Because for me,
You are the stars, the moon, my entire universe.

I would give away all the light in the sky
For you, only you

That night in New Orleans
I wonder if the children asleep in their beds
Awoke to the sound of shattering.

Or if the cats roaming the streets,
hungry, prowling, howling...
I wonder if they heard it too.

My heart, smashed to pieces
On the streets of New Orleans.

Chapitre 34

MY SUMMER kicks off with a trip back to DC for the wedding of one of my closest college girlfriends and for my ten-year college reunion. Both of these events have nothing to do with either my ex-husband or my former lover, and I am happily attending each of them *sans* date, with only my friends by my side, so I am hopeful that life is headed in a calmer direction.

Being a novelist who is skilled at ruining my characters' lives by throwing surprises at them around every corner, I should know better.

My oblivious optimism has me bouncing into the downtown Catholic church for my friend's wedding with a smile on my face, and it is only when I see the elegant bride walking down the aisle that my smile turns to tears. My friend is gorgeous, shining, and hopeful. She is about to say *yes!* to spending the rest of her days with the love of her life, and I am sitting in the pew, overwhelmed with conflicting emotions. I don't think I believe in marriage anymore, yet I wish only love, happiness, and success for this sweet couple. I truly want their marriage to work.

Although here I am, the divorced mess in the third pew, doing my best not to sob like this is a funeral. My existence is an ever-constant reminder that even when you pour your heart and soul into your marriage, it *still* may not last until death do you part. As I silently question the institution of marriage and wonder if my friends have any clue what they are getting themselves into, I realize this will be the first of many weddings I will attend alone, without my husband by my side.

I'm in a new land now, embarking on an unknown path all on my own. And while it's certainly scary, there is still something so liberating about the fact that I don't have a ring on my finger anymore, and consequently no man to dictate what I am to do with *my* life. Remembering this prompts me to dry my tears and find my smile again. I've grieved enough this past year. It's time to find the joy in my new life status and embrace the hell out of it.

And the truth is, I'm not all alone. My close friend Lia has agreed to join me at the reception as my "plus one." Lucky for us, loads of handsome Italian men from the groom's side have flown in from Italy, and they are all too happy to drink champagne and dance the night away with us American girls.

When Lia and I invite ourselves to one of their Tuscan villas, I remember that being single can be pretty damn fun. Well, to clarify, this hunky Italian guy didn't actually *say* he had a villa in Tuscany, but he did say that he lives in Italy and would love for us to visit him, so Lia and I are taking the liberty of assuming it's a Tuscan villa because why the hell not?

The wedding turns out to be one of the best dance parties I've attended in years, and the following weekend, I find myself breaking it down again, this time with old college friends at my ten-year reunion. My lawyer friend James spots me at the beginning of the night and pulls me aside.

"So...how are we spinning this whole divorce thing?" he whispers.

Most of our college friends knew my ex since I met him my sophomore year, and they all knew we had gotten married shortly after graduation. But here I am, without my husband, without my wedding ring, and not even a single baby on my hip to show for the whole damn thing. James is asking the same question I've been asking myself all night—how do we explain this to people without putting a dark cloud over the evening?

"If anyone asks, we say that the divorce was amicable, and that we simply grew apart," I instruct James. "And add that my ex and I are still friends...or at least, *friendly*."

"Perfect," he says, but then his gaze catches my nametag. "Um...what's up with that?"

He is referring to the fact that my nametag has a hyphenated last name—my married last name coupled with my maiden name.

I let out a sigh of frustration. "I changed my name on the registration so that it *only* should've been my maiden name, but they messed up and kept my married name on here too *and* took the liberty of hyphenating the names. Pretty awesome."

James grabs a black marker off the sign-in table and crosses out my married name.

"There. Now you won't be having an identity crisis all night."

I love how James takes care of business.

Crossing off my married last name does help me feel more like myself all night as I catch up with old friends, and it turns out that talking about the divorce with the few people who ask why my husband isn't with me isn't too bad either.

What really catches me off guard is the phone call I receive the next day. I'm at Lia's apartment putting on my makeup before our second night of reunion when my phone rings.

It's my ex.

We haven't spoken since divorce court, and as soon as I spot his name on my caller ID, my heart leaps. Despite everything, I miss him terribly.

"Hey," I answer, sounding all too eager to hear his voice.

He sounds eager to hear mine too.

The conversation that ensues is a total shock.

My ex-husband tells me that he misses me, that he's been reflecting on everything we went through, and he's realized some things. He's sorry that he never traveled with me, that we were so busy working and striving and dealing with stressful family issues for our entire marriage that we didn't make time to just have fun with each other.

He tells me that he wants to take me on a date as soon as I'm back in town, and if that goes well, he wants to whisk me away for a weekend, just the two of us.

"I know this probably sounds crazy considering the divorce was only just finalized last month," he says, "but I miss you."

I can't believe that after all this, after I *divorced him*, he still wants to give this a go.

And what about me? What do I want? In this moment, I am so taken off guard that I honestly don't know. I've only just ended the affair with Nick, and even though it's over, we still haven't managed to cut off contact. And I've only just begun to embrace the single life I wanted so badly when my ex and I were struggling through the last year of our marriage. In fact, I was planning to begin the name change process as soon as I returned to San Diego to mark the official beginning of my singledom, a reclaiming of my identity as the woman I always was before *I* became a *we*.

But what if things could change between us? What if we had to get a divorce so that our old ways of being together would die? Is it possible that in the rubble of our old relationship, we could build a new one?

I don't know. This is all happening too fast.

But I do know one thing for sure, so I tell him, "I miss you too."

"When will you be back in town?" he asks.

"I fly back to San Diego tomorrow afternoon."

"Are you free tomorrow night?" he asks.

"Yes..." I say.

"Do you want to go out to dinner with me?"

I hesitate.

"There won't be any pressure for anything to come out of this...
but it would just be nice to talk and see where we're both at."

The love I still feel for him and the hope that things could
change overpowers all logic, and so I say the only word that wants
to pass through my lips, "Yes."

That night, I have a vivid dream where I am driving a car
at night, and I make an illegal turn. I know it's illegal, but I do it
anyway. Immediately, a cop pulls me over. He takes my ID, goes
back to his car, and for some reason I know he has no plans to
give it back.

He has stolen my identity.

I pull away and speed down the highway as the cop races
after me.

Suddenly I notice that I am driving backwards down a busy
highway at night. I zoom past a horrific accident—it is a school
bus full of children, tipped over on its side. It's gruesome, and
there are police cars and ambulances everywhere.

I keep racing backwards through the wreckage, unable to
stop if I wanted to.

When I wake up, I am sweaty and nauseous. This dream feels
just as intense and significant to me as the tornado dream. Lia and
I talk it through later that morning.

"Clearly, the cop taking my ID has to do with the fact that I'm
questioning my identity," I say. "Not only with the obvious last
name situation at reunion, but I'm also questioning who I am fun-
damentally. Am I a single woman who is free and clear of all relationship ties and who can *finally* do as she pleases? Or am I open
to restarting a relationship with my ex and going back to the way
things used to be?"

"Those are good questions...but to tell the truth, I'm much
more concerned about you driving backwards through a school
bus accident," Lia says.

"It feels like a warning," I say. "Like going back to him is going
backwards...with the potential for disaster."

"You need to be careful, Danielle," Lia warns. "If you go on this date with him, I just don't want you to have any expectations that things will really change. You've been through so much this past year. I don't want either of you to get hurt again."

Despite Lia's sound points and my ominous driving backwards dream, I still find myself primping and trying on ten different outfits the next night to get ready for my first date with my ex-husband.

My roommates Carl and Micah look at me as though I have totally lost my mind when I tell them who I'm going out with tonight, and Carl says as much.

"Are you out of your goddamn gourd?" This is one of Carl's signature phrases, with "gourd" being code for "mind."

"D, if you go back to him, things *aren't* going to change," Micah says. "He's still the same person, and so are you."

"We're just going to have a chat," I reassure them. "I don't have any expectations, so everything will be fine. And please hold your horrified reactions for later because he'll be here any minute."

"He's coming here?" Carl asks.

"Yes! Now please act natural."

When the doorbell rings, the Broconuts are on their best behavior. I welcome my ex-husband into my big, beautiful house where I live with three boys, and after introductions, he goes right to Bella, our big, beautiful cat. She hasn't seen him in several months now, but she purrs and rubs his leg like not a single day has passed.

Even though she is a cat, Bella is the closest thing we had to a child, and seeing him with her again both warms and breaks my heart. Bella loved him so much that she actually boycotted food for over two weeks after he moved out, and for this rather obese feline who *loves* to eat, that is serious business.

I am so happy to see my ex again, but I can tell this tour of my new home is making him feel awkward, so I wrap it up and we head out. At a Spanish tapas bar not far from my house, we order wine and food, and we chat. We chat about anything and everything *other* than us, and I am wondering *when* we will discuss exactly what we are doing here and how we are both feeling about revisiting our relationship. His avoidance of the topic has me thinking that perhaps something has shifted, already, since our conversation just yesterday.

So, I bring it up. "How are you feeling about everything we talked about on the phone yesterday?"

He hesitates for a moment, and in that moment, I know. He's already changed his mind.

"It's just so good to see you again," he says, sounding relieved. "It feels like you died."

"I know that feeling," I say. "It's so good to see you too...but is it just that you needed to see me to be sure I'm still here? Or are you still feeling like you might want to explore things with us again?"

He hesitates again, and finally he is honest.

He's had a change of heart. He still loves me, of course. He always will. But he is confused, and he really just needed to see me again to be sure I'm still here.

He doesn't want to sweep me off my feet for the weekend getaway we never had. He doesn't want to try things again.

I told myself that I didn't have any expectations going into this, but I am crushed. Clearly I was more hopeful at this unlikely possibility than I'd realized, and now all I want to do is flee the dinner table and curl up on the floor somewhere and cry. I do my best to get through our meal, but as soon as we climb into the car together and head toward my house, the divorce faucet turns back on.

This particular faucet is more like a fire hose, though.

I am flooded with uncontrollable grief. And my former husband feels awful.

"You can't take me home like this," I tell him through my hiccups. So, we drive to the park near my house, which sits up on a hill and has a stunning view of San Diego, Mission Bay, and the Pacific Ocean. Night has fallen over the city, and while the stars are twinkling overhead, I am clutching onto my husband for dear life, realizing just how badly I was hoping that he had changed, that we had changed, and that we could try this again.

I'm shocked that this is inside of me, after everything, and I think he is too. But he holds me until I calm down, apologizing all the while for the false start. And finally, when the fire hose has run out of water, he drives me home.

The next week is a blur of sleep, crying, Xanax, and more sleep. This event has triggered my depression again, and even my good friend Wellbutrin isn't doing the trick anymore. I'm supposed to be turning in the first full draft of my screenplay to the producer at the end of this month, but I can hardly get food down, let alone have the wits and the energy to finish my screenplay.

Another week goes by, and just when the storm is calming, just when I am finding my groove again with the screenplay, Nick gets in touch to tell me he wants to book a last-minute flight to come see me.

I know what my answer should be: a firm, clear, raging *NO!*

I am in no state to handle seeing the lover that I thought I was never going to see again.

But it is because I am in such a fragile state that I give in and say yes to his impulsive request.

Chapitre 35

THE FIRST item on the lover to-do list as soon as Nick arrives in San Diego is a trip to my psychiatrist to double the dose of my Wellbutrin. In the forty-eight hours leading up to his arrival, I was an absolute wreck. But since he'd already booked the flight, I didn't want to back out. Instead, I let myself fall apart, and now I needed something to glue me back together.

My doctor writes me a script for a stronger dose, and Nick is sufficiently freaked out as I race into the pharmacy and down the extra pill with the fervor of a starving child.

It doesn't take long to kick in. The tears stop, and so do the freak-outs, and I decide that since he is here, I will try to relax and enjoy myself for the next few days. It's either that or hurl myself off a cliff into the Pacific, and I figure that mind-blowing sex and fancy dinners will be more fun than fatal cliff diving.

Nick has picked out an absolutely charming B&B by the beach, and we end up spending a beautiful, mostly drama-free couple of days together.

I've stopped asking him if he's going to leave his wife.

Of course he's never leaving her.

And he is still asking me to continue our affair beyond this weekend. "Next month," he says, "I can make another West Coast trip."

But with each kiss, each romp under the covers, and each heartfelt "*I love you,*" I notice a shift inside me that wasn't fully present when I walked away from him in New Orleans. This time it's not about wanting Nick to choose me over his wife, *or else I must go.*

Instead, it's about *me choosing me.* And *for this reason,* I must go.

My feeling that I am really, truly, finally nearing the end of this affair is only solidified when I take Nick for a visit to my clairvoyant acupuncturist, Ananda. I've been seeing her since the days when I was trying to get pregnant, and she has been one of the most supportive, helpful friends I've had through this entire divorce and the self-imposed shit-storm that has followed. Plus her intuitive insights on people are ridiculously accurate—to the point where I can simply tell her a person's name and she can describe their physical appearance, personality, and many aspects of their life to a T. Which is why I couldn't wait to bring Nick into her lair.

Ananda places Nick in one room and me in another so she can tend to us separately. She starts off with Nick, and after only ten minutes, she comes into my room and announces, "He's never leaving his wife."

I knew this, of course, but to have my clairvoyant acupuncturist affirm the fact helps me feel a little stronger.

"And he's *so* young, Danielle," she says. "I know he's older than you, but emotionally, he's a little boy. He has Peter Pan Syndrome—at heart, he's an eternal boy. He'll never have the guts to leave his wife. She provides structure for him, structure that he needs, and even though you're his true love, he'll never walk away from her."

"Wow...Peter Pan Syndrome. Sounds serious," I say, somehow finding it inside me to giggle.

Ananda continues in her assessment of my married lover and his personal life. "Nick's wife is seeing someone else, too. She has been for a while, and even though it's not as serious as what you two have together, it makes her feel good. But her affair guy is married too, and since he's never leaving *his* wife, she's never going to leave Nick. Which means if you keep seeing him, you're always going to be the mistress. There are great things that come with being a mistress, as you know, but on the other hand..."

"It's dreadful," I say. "Loving someone who will never fully be with me."

She nods and I nod.

I know what I have to do.

When Ananda returns to Nick's room, she finds him looking gray and sickly, on the verge of passing out. She comes to retrieve me, and so needles and all, I pad into Nick's room, sit by his side, hold his hand, and talk him through it...just like a mother would a little boy.

And in this moment, that is how I see him: as a little boy who really does want to have his cake and eat it too. He doesn't want to hurt anyone, but he also doesn't have the balls to do the right thing—whether that thing is to have an honest conversation with his wife once and for all about what they are both doing, or to leave her, or to leave me alone. He doesn't have the balls to take any action except to keep this thing going as long as he can get away with it. And I'm losing respect for him for this reason. Even worse, I've lost respect for myself for being involved in such a plight.

We're right back where we've always been—he's never going to make any changes, and again, I must be the one to end this thing...even though I thought I'd already ended it once.

Of course I was the desperate mess who agreed to let him swoop into town on a whim and re-ignite this whole emotional catastrophe.

The catastrophe of *us* is in full force later that night as we watch a film that eerily mirrors our situation. It's called *28 Hotel Rooms*.

In the film, Marin Ireland plays a married accountant who, on a business trip, has a one-night stand with a handsome novelist, played by Chris Messina. When the pair runs into each other at another hotel, lust overpowers reason, and they begin an affair that lasts over the course of several years and twenty-eight hotel rooms.

Their affair is an emotional roller coaster—an addicting but deadly ride that they *cannot* get off of, mainly because they are so damn good together, and so in love.

Near the end of the film, Nick's eyes are clouded with tears when he turns to me. "Do you think we're going to be like this? Never able to stop? Still seeing each other for years?"

I sigh, exhausted at the thought of continuing this affair into even one more hotel room, let alone twenty-eight.

"I don't know," I say.

At the end of the film, it's not me who's in hysterics...for once. Instead, it's Nick.

He's crying harder than I've ever seen him cry, and through his tears, I feel that he has answered his own question.

No, that won't be us. We can't keep going like this. It's destroying us both.

We still haven't made the official decision to end our affair when I drop Nick off at the airport early the next morning. We kiss goodbye, and I stand on the curb alone, watching as he mouths the words, "I love you," before he disappears into the airport.

When I climb into my car and drive away, for the first time, I don't cry. I don't feel sad.

Instead, I feel relieved.

I know I may never see him again, and still, I feel overwhelming relief.

When I arrive home and fall back asleep for a few hours, I have another one of my crazy vivid dreams that tells me exactly where this thing is headed if we continue.

In the dream, I'm hanging onto the outside of a train as it barrels down the tracks. My cats are below me, hanging onto the outside too. It's just the three of us, holding on for dear life, when suddenly, a truck falls out of the sky, swoops around, and rams straight into the train, causing it to derail.

This is it, I think. *I'm going to die.* And so I begin to pray. I pray that my cats will be okay, that I will be okay, and that we will make it out of this train wreck alive.

To my astonishment, we do. I scrape myself up out of the rubble, I find Bella and Charlie, and I wake up knowing that I'm hanging on by a thread and if I don't do something *now*, the train wreck this affair has become will ruin me.

A few days later, I call Nick and tell him that it's over between us.

Really, truly, forever *over.*

I tell him that even if we were ever together, I would never be able to trust him. I tell him that I want to be with someone who has the courage to make changes in his life when he is unhappy instead of sneaking around and lying to keep the peace.

I am a person who has the courage to live my truth, to change my life even when it's difficult—even when it nearly kills me—and I need someone who has the capacity to do the same. I refuse to be second or third or tenth priority in his life any longer.

I am worth more than that.

I am worth more than a quick hello.
I am worth more than a secret rendezvous.
I am worth more than "if," than "one day," than "hopefully."

I am worth more than the spare time in between your meetings
And your phone calls to your wife.

I am worth more than a vehicle for sex,
Than a pretty girl who dances,
Who you must hide in a hotel room.

I am worth more than your words.

I am worth action.
I am worth true love.
And I will accept nothing less in my life.

I deserve the whole package.

And that is why I'm leaving you.

Chapitre 36

I SO wish I could begin this chapter by saying that I was able to abstain from all contact with Nick after I ended our affair, but that wouldn't be the truth.

When I spoke with him on the phone to bring an end to our madness, I agreed to stay in touch sparingly over e-mail, because we both know that we are hopeless at going no contact, and because, as Nick always insists, what we had was too special and meaningful to go the rest of our lives without talking again.

And there's one other problem with cutting off contact.

Nick has been reading my screenplay as I write and he gives me the most amazing feedback. He gets my writing and my voice, and he loves reading my work. Without Karen here or my critique group still intact to help me with this most important writing endeavor, Nick is the only person who is reading my draft prior to the big day when I will send my baby off to the producers.

I want my first screenplay to be the best it can possibly be, but even more so, I *need* this screenplay to sell. Since I've allowed my turbulent affair with Nick and my grief over the divorce to run my life, and since I've been drowning in the depths of depression for so long now, I've hardly been able to work, which means I have accrued an unreasonable amount of debt.

If I sell the screenplay, all of that will go away.

Not only will the money from that sale pay off *all* of my debt in one fell swoop, it will also set me up to be able to write comfortably and peacefully over the next year or two without having to worry about keeping a day job. What a gift that would be.

Nick knows how important this is to me, so even though it is difficult for him to read my work knowing we have no plans to see each other again, he reads. And as always, he gives me his insightful feedback that is spot-on and so incredibly helpful.

After I make the changes, I send my script—my golden ticket—off to the producers, and I pray with all my might that they will love it.

Only a few weeks later, they write back with notes. They do love where the script is headed, and they have loads of ideas on how to make the story even stronger before we send it off to the director. I dive headfirst into the rewrite, scrapping much of what I wrote the first time around and reworking the entire script to take my visual storytelling to the next level.

On the day that would have been my ninth wedding anniversary, while I am trying to write the next scene in my screenplay, I am distracted. Not with thoughts of the beautiful day when I said my vows...vows that I would later break; I am distracted with thoughts of Nick.

Something inside me is still holding on to him with a death grip, and I simply cannot get that man out of my head, or more importantly, out of my heart.

There is one lingering question I feel I need to ask him before I can truly let go and move forward with my life. So, on this anniversary that is no longer an anniversary, I meet my ex-lover on Skype, and I ask him the question that has been burning in my mind all month:

"Do you feel that you made the right choice in staying with your wife and choosing not to be with me?"

I know that I am the one who has officially ended our affair, but Nick has always had a choice too, and his choice has been clear.

As Nick hesitates, I tell myself that I will be okay no matter what he says. I tell myself that I'm *not* hoping for him to say that it was the wrong choice to stay with his wife, that he still loves me, and that he'll do anything to be with me.

I repeat these affirmations over and over in my head, although I know they are not true.

Finally, Nick looks into my eyes and answers my question.

"Yes," he says. "I made the right choice staying in my marriage."

There aren't words in the English language to describe the way my heart breaks at his response. There aren't words because my heart has already been yanked out, torn, shredded, stomped on, beaten, slashed, lacerated, and drowned—both by my own hands and at the hands of others. What could possibly be left for this nearly dead heart of mine to endure? How could hearing the words I *knew* Nick would say make me feel as if my heart *may actually stop beating* this time?

And more importantly, what is wrong with me that I would ask him this question when I already knew his answer? Why did I need to hear, yet again, that this man is never going to choose me?

Am I some sort of masochist?

This deepest of wounds has roots somewhere else in my life, and as Nick continues explaining *why* he must give his all to his marriage, I barely hear him.

Instead, I am thirteen years old again, standing in my dad's apartment watching as he fights with my stepmother.

At this point in my life, I was making an effort to spend occasional weekends with my dad, even though I didn't enjoy going to his tiny country apartment where he barely asked me a single question about my life, my interests, or who I was becoming. Where he barely uttered a response to anything I shared with him, but instead stared straight ahead at the TV as if I hadn't even spoken. Where oftentimes, my stepmom wouldn't even say hi to me when I walked in the door.

When my dad did speak to me, he made jokes and talked to me as if I were still five years old, which only infuriated me. I was thirteen, and I had a brain! A really interesting, cool brain, and I had lots of interesting, cool things to talk about too, if only he would have seen me for who I truly was and stopped treating me like a baby.

I told myself that he simply didn't know how to handle a teenage girl, but that didn't make the way he treated me hurt any less.

On this particular weekend, my dad had decided that he was going to leave for the entire time I would be staying at his house. I was only there to spend time with him, and still, he was going to leave without any explanation.

As he was on his way out the door, my stepmom stopped him. "Why are you leaving? You never see your daughter, and she's only here for two days! Don't you want to spend time with her?"

My dad stared blankly at his wife, and then he grabbed his keys and walked out the door, letting it slam behind him.

He didn't look at me. He didn't apologize. He didn't say goodbye. He just left.

I went home the next day and announced to my mom, "I'm never spending the night at his house ever again."

Months went by with hardly a word from my father, even though he only lived fifteen minutes away. I heard through the family grapevine that my dad and stepmom were taking my two little cousins to Disney World, yet they hadn't called to invite me. In fact, they were always taking my cousins everywhere, treating *them* like their surrogate daughters, yet they steered clear of me.

I didn't understand. What had I ever done to them?

I was a kindhearted, calm, quiet, straight-A student. I was a disciplined ballerina. I was sweet and smart and creative, and I never mouthed off or said an unkind word to him or his wife, or to anyone.

More importantly, *I was his daughter.*

But he didn't treat me that way.

When my dad's birthday rolled around, my stepmom called to invite me to his party.

"No," I said firmly. "I haven't heard from you guys in months, so why would I want to celebrate his birthday?"

Then I hung up on her.

My hands shook, and my cheeks were flaming hot. I had never done anything like that in all my life. I had never defied them or said so much as a rude word.

After all the years of neglect, after all the years where he had made me feel like I didn't matter to him, it felt amazing. I felt strong, empowered, bold.

Finally, I was taking control of this horrible relationship. No longer would I be the passive, sweet little girl, letting my father and his wife treat me like an insignificant little bug that they could squash anytime they felt like it.

I was done with that.

Not more than a few minutes passed when the phone rang again.

This time it was my dad.

I thought that he was calling to apologize, but no. The first words out of his mouth were, "Well, *you* haven't called in a while."

My blood boiled over. My little heart screamed in my chest. *That's it.*

"I'm sorry, but you're forty-one years old and I'm *thirteen! You* are supposed to be the father here. The adult. The parent. Yet it is *my* responsibility to stay in touch with *you?*"

I continued yelling and crying and screaming at my father for over two hours. Once the floodgates had opened, years of pent-up grief poured out of me, and I didn't stop until I had said every last thing I'd ever wanted to say to him. I told him how neglectful he had always been and how insignificant and unloved he made me feel. I reminded him of how shitty it was that he barely ever came to any of my dance recitals, and even shittier when he would lie and say that he had been in the audience when I knew for a fact that he hadn't. I told him that I hated how he would barely be in touch for months and then shower me with gifts on Christmas as if that proved he was being a "good dad." I told him I didn't want his gifts.

I wanted his love. His attention. His affection.

That's all I had ever wanted.

He muttered a few excuses about work and being too busy to get together, but I told him that I didn't want to hear his poor, lame excuses. Finally, he apologized and said he'd never realized how much he'd hurt me. He promised he would come around more, that he would never neglect me again.

"I'll believe it when I see it," I said.

But when I got off the phone that day, I didn't believe him. And I made a choice.

I chose to be finished caring what that man did or did not do in my life. I chose to never again base my self-worth on his lack of love for me. I knew I was an awesome young woman, and it was his loss if he didn't want to be a part of my life. I chose to focus on the one solid parent I did have in my life—my mom, who, during my childhood and teenage years was my biggest cheerleader. Her unwavering love in those years canceled out my father's neglect and his lack of interest in my life.

Besides my mom, I had a stepdad who loved me like a daughter. I had the most wonderful friends. And I had ballet. My life was full without my dad, and he was only adding grief. Grief that I didn't need any longer.

Over the years, I held firm to this promise to myself to let go of my emotional connection to a man who seemed to be so emotionally stunted. And because I grew so detached from him and his choices, his patterns of coming and going throughout my

life—patterns that continue to this day—didn't bother me anymore, and they still don't.

In the times when my dad did show up more, I was kind and
loving and as supportive of our relationship as I could be. I did
my best to accept him for who he was, limitations and all, and to
appreciate the ways in which he grew into his own unique version of "Dad."

There is one moment that will always stand out in my mind
as the day my father showed me he could truly be a father.

It was early on a Saturday last August. I had woken up that
morning knowing that this would be the day I would tell my husband I wanted a divorce. My mom and dad didn't know that my
marriage was nearing the end, and they had no idea that I had
been struggling to survive a deep depression. I rarely shared the
intimate details of my life with either of my parents by this point
because their individual ways of not supporting me would only
add to my grief.

But that morning, I woke up in hysterics and I needed a
parent. I knew that if I called my mom in the state I was in, she
would plummet right into the hysterical loony bin with me. Yes,
this was mainly because she loved me so much and couldn't bear
to know I was hurting, but I needed someone who could listen
and be strong. I couldn't handle her tears when I couldn't even
handle my own.

So, even though I wasn't sure my dad could weather the
storm of grief I was about to hurl at him, I called him anyway.

As soon as he heard me crying, as soon as I told him how
terrified and devastated I was that I was going to end my marriage later that day, he shifted into Dad Mode. It wasn't a mode
I'd ever heard him operate in, but clearly it had been buried
inside him all along. Yes, it took the biggest crisis of my life to
pull it out, but it was there.

My dad showed up for me that day, on the day I most needed
him. He comforted me and listened to all the reasons why I felt I

needed to end the marriage. He validated my feelings and encouraged me to follow my heart.

He drew from the experiences of both of his failed marriages and gave me advice as someone who had been there and as someone who had survived.

But most importantly, he gave me advice as a father. *My* father.

After that day, our relationship didn't magically transform into the traditional father/daughter relationship I'd always wished for when I was a child. I'm an adult now, and I know that's not the way things work. In fact, we barely talk anymore—maybe once every few months—but that's okay. I will always hold on to that day when my dad was a dad. And I will always be thankful that he was there for me on a day when I had no one else to turn to, on the day when I most needed his love.

I've listened to my friends and therapists say countless times that we unconsciously attract relationships into our lives that mirror the ones we have with our parents, and more specifically, that as women, we attract men into our lives who are like our fathers. We do this so that we can work through all the unresolved baggage left over from our childhoods.

Up until this day, this moment, I'd never realized the ways in which Nick resembles my own father—not in their character traits per se, but in their actions, their choices, and their unavailability.

In so many ways, for so many years, my father didn't choose me. And Nick isn't choosing me, either.

I thought I'd already processed the grief left over from my father's neglect. But clearly, some of it remains to be worked through, and so I have sought out an unavailable man who has other priorities. Despite the outrageously strong bond of our love and the endless ways in which we are perfect for one another, this man can look me in the eye and tell me that he has made the right choice in not choosing me.

Of all the types of men I could have jumped into a relationship with during my first year as a single woman, I chose the man who would do to me what my father did so long ago.

At this moment as Nick talks at me over Skype, I'm too raw, too emotionally scorched by his words to process what all of this means, and more importantly, to grasp what I need to learn from it.

And so I let my pain speak.

"I wish I could erase you from my mind, from my memory, forever," I say through a shield of tears. "I wish this had never happened."

The next day, I send Nick the harshest e-mail I've ever sent him:

> *Nick,*
>
> *All I ask at this point is that you never do this to anyone else. Your affairs before me may have been more or less meaningless, but if even one affair has the potential to hurt someone this deeply, please think twice before carrying on with it. No one deserves to feel this way.*
>
> *If your marriage is as strong and has as much depth as you say, I wonder why you have had to sleep with other people for so many years, why she didn't want you to touch her for all this time, and why so much of your life with her is built on lies. But that is up to you to live with.*
>
> *I don't want to be in contact with you any longer, and I'm not going to sugarcoat this with optimism that maybe we can be friends someday. Please know that if you are in touch, I will not respond. I hold myself accountable for ever flirting with a married*

*man and for carrying on with it at all, but if any-
thing, at least I will be able to write about what this
feels like.*

*If you have the urge to cheat in the future, please do
the right thing and leave your wife, or leave the poor
girl alone. It's only destructive.*

Danielle

I am that poor girl and I am destroyed. Writing a hurtful
e-mail is the only way I know how to stab him back, straight in
the heart.

And it is the only way I know I will be able to move forward
without him.

Partie VI

Un Chemin Inattendu ~
An Unexpected Journey

"L'amour est l'emblème de
l'éternité; Il brouille toute notion
de temps; efface tout souvenir d'un
début, annule toute peur d'une fin."

"Love is the emblem of eternity;
it confounds all notion of time;
effaces all memory of a beginning,
all fear of an end."

~ Madame de Staël,
Corinne ou l'Italie

Chapitre 37

IF I were writing the story of my life as a novel, that last part—
the part where my heart broke more than I ever knew it could
break—would be called my *Big Black Moment*. It's the moment in
the story where our heroine loses everything that once defined
her. She is now lost, desolate, broken, and alone. She doesn't
know who she is anymore, where to turn, or how she will ever
turn the shit-show that has become her life into the fairy tale
she's always dreamt of.

It is only in her darkest hour that our leading lady will have
any chance at saving herself. It is only when she has been stripped
of all the things that once comforted her, all the things that gave
her a false sense of security, that she will be able to experience her
Aha Moment—that magical moment where she discovers who she
truly is and finds the courage to put on her big-girl panties, slay
the dragon, get the job, and ride off into the sunset on a white
horse with her Prince Charming before he gives her orgasm after
titillating orgasm in their Upper West Side penthouse overlooking Central Park.

Okay...perhaps I got a little carried away there, but you get the idea.

In my own novels, the Big Black Moment and the Aha Moment typically happen within the span of one or two chapters. So, with the turn of a few pages, my heroine's entire world comes crashing down *and* she finally learns whatever she needed to learn in order to embrace her true essence and build the life of her dreams.

Just a few page turns to enlightenment? Those bitches have it so easy.

If only real life were that simple.

My own journey has not been so concise, not in the least. The past year and a half has been riddled with Big Black Moments, each of them even more painful and world-shattering than the last. Rock Bottom is the place I call home now, and just when I think this place can't get any colder, darker, or more disheartening, it does.

What the hell?

Who is the demented author who came up with this ridiculous story?

Someone needs to give *her* a Xanax!

Okay...I'll stop bashing this fictitious author who I imagine to be calling the shots on my life from her vantage point on a white fluffy cloud in the sky where she's drinking lattes and eating cake and cackling each time I fall deeper and deeper down this dank rabbit hole.

Instead, I'll take responsibility for my own life.

I know that *I am* that crazy lady in the sky. I'm writing my own story, and I have willingly made all of the choices that have landed me exactly where I am today.

Yes, others' choices and actions have impacted my life in significant ways, but my reactions, actions, words, and choices are all my own.

I am a full believer in being one hundred percent accountable for one's own life, and so here I am, standing tall—well, more like slumped over and exhausted—knowing I am both the author and the heroine of my own life story and of all of the joys and catastrophes that I have experienced along this wild journey. I've been to the dark side and now I'm ready for my Aha moment. I'm ready for that glorious day when all of the heartache and pain I've endured as of late leads me to a magical, enlightening realization that will allow me to move toward brighter days. I'm ready for the clouds to part and for the heavens to open so that I can announce to the world, "*I have arrived in my enchanted forest! Now leave me the fuck alone!*"

And I would like for that moment to come within the next few pages of my story, not only because this book is now over three hundred pages long and it's time to wrap it up, but also so that I can leave all of this crap behind me and ride off into the sunset just like all the fabulous leading ladies in the stories I write.

Alas, the true journey of my own life has been far more intricate, complicated, and meaningful than anything I could write in a novel, which means there won't be *just one* shining Aha Moment. There will be many, and they will be spread out over the course of this long, winding journey. Some of my realizations will be big, some will be small, but ultimately each one is an essential step in moving me along my path.

After this latest heartbreak, after I have left my lover once and for all, I was hoping to experience my own glorious Aha moment, but I haven't. Instead, I am truly at a loss for what to do next. Ever since my first boyfriend in seventh grade, I have been jumping from boy to boy, from man to man, the way a monkey would swing from branch to branch. And I never let go of one branch until I have the next one firmly in hand.

I was able to let go of my husband's branch as soon as I had Nick's firmly in my grip.

But Nick's branch was a thin, weak branch to begin with—made even weaker by all of that forbidden fruit weighing it down. And now that I've gobbled up all the fruit and made myself sick in the process, his branch has broken.

And as for me, I have fallen.

My heart is bruised, my knees are skinned, and I'm still depressed.

But there are no more branches in reach from where I'm standing at this low elevation in the murky, dark forest of my life, and so I have no choice but to stand up, dust myself off, and walk alone.

I'm not sure where I'm going, but after only a few weeks of limping and hobbling along, of saying *yes* to life even when I feel like saying *no*, two new friends appear in my lonely forest.

Their names are Mike and Leah. They are a young married couple who share a passion and a zest for life like nothing I've seen before. Within only a few hours of meeting them, they share a most incredible story with me, a story that lets some light into this dark forest I now call home.

As the light seeps in, I remember that I'm not the *only* one writing my story. I remember that sometimes people sweep through our lives just at the right moment and change the way we see the world forever. These meetings are beautiful synchronicities. They are life's way of extending a branch to us when we most need it.

MIKE IS a twenty-eight-year-old engineer who is well spoken, handsome, and insightful. His wife, Leah, is a twenty-four-year-old beauty with brains, studying to become a Naturopath doctor. I meet this lovely couple at a brunch our mutual friend is hosting, and just after we've been introduced, Mike asks me what I do for a living.

"I'm a writer," I say.

"Oh really?" Mike leans forward in his seat, his interest piqued. "I want to write a book someday."

Being a writer, I hear this phrase almost daily. Everyone has a story to tell, and my unanimous response to all of these people with brilliant stories hiding deep within them is, "Write it!"

I'm sure I'll get to that point with Mike, but first I ask him, "What do you want to write about?"

"Reincarnation," he replies.

Now *my* interest is piqued. Even though I grew up attending Catholic mass where reincarnation is definitely *not* on the menu, the idea that perhaps our souls are traveling from body to body, soaking up all the joy and pain each of those individual lives has to offer and hopefully learning a thing or two before taking a much-needed break in heaven—this idea has always intrigued me. My strong connection to France and my insane, instant connection with Nick have only served to strengthen my belief in the possibility of past lives and reincarnation. Perhaps in a past life, I really was French, and perhaps in another, I loved Nick. It would certainly explain the familiarity I've felt with them both since the very beginning. I've pondered these ideas quite a bit in recent months, and now it seems I've met a new friend who has some light to shed on the topic.

"What has prompted you to want to write a book on reincarnation? Is it just something you're really interested in?" I ask Mike.

"No..." He hesitates, not looking all too enthused to share. But finally, he says, "I've had a personal experience."

Now I'm leaning forward in *my* seat. "What do you mean?"

"It's a looong story," he says.

"An incredible one," Leah adds.

"I'm a novelist. I *love* long stories," I say.

Mike hesitates. "Not many people in my life know this story, and it's not something I typically share with people I've just met."

"My third novel deals with reincarnation and past lives," I tell him. "I love this stuff. You have to tell me."

Finally, over mimosas and pancakes, Mike tells me the story of how he was born with vivid memories of his last life, his death, and his journey through the afterlife. He remembers being an old man in a rehabilitation center, paralyzed and depressed, living out his final days in a wheel chair. It was a tragic time in his life, and each of his memories is painful and heart-wrenching. That is until death finally whisked him away and he found himself in a new plane of existence where love is the only language.

Mike's journey into the afterlife is too grand and awesome to do it justice in only a few short paragraphs, but the part of the story that touches me the most is what he calls his *life review*.

Surrounded by several wise souls who were there to guide and support him through his transition, Mike watched the movie of his last life as the paralyzed old man in the rehabilitation center. He viewed the life he had just lived not through *human* eyes, though, but through the eyes of his soul—a very different thing altogether, he says.

As Mike explains to me, the soul is a pure entity overflowing with light and love, and this thing of beauty thankfully does not carry with it all of the wretched emotional baggage that our egos like to lug around during our time on earth.

And so it was with this pureness of heart that Mike reviewed scenes from his last life, the way one would watch a film. As he watched his interactions with loved ones, friends, and strangers, he realized that the only thing that matters while we are here, running around this chaotic earth, trying to do our best, is *love*.

In each moment where his soul crossed paths with another soul, he would watch the interaction and ask himself, "Did I leave that person—*that soul*—with love? Or did I leave them with pain?"

It didn't matter what they had done to him. All that mattered to Mike's soul was if *he* had chosen to give this person love...or not.

Love. That was all that mattered.

This is the message Mike has carried back with him after his extraordinary voyage, and this is the message I so desperately need to hear at this exact point in my life.

It's all about love.

It's *only* about love.

This was the same message I heard at Karen's service, of course, but after hearing it again through Mike's incredible story, this message of love is resonating with me more than ever.

Shortly after that fateful brunch, I meet Mike and Leah for dinner. Over nachos and margaritas, I agree to co-write Mike's book with him so that his beautiful story can touch more hearts, the way it has touched mine.

In the early weeks of our writing project, I spend hours interviewing Mike and his wife, and this gets me so excited about his story that I begin sharing it with everyone I know. Of course, some of my friends may not believe the full story, but I'm not telling them in the hope that they will suddenly believe in reincarnation or in the existence of an afterlife; I am sharing Mike's story to spread his simple but profound message, a message that is universal for everyone with a heart: *Love is the only thing that matters.*

One of the first people with whom I share his message is my mom. My mom grew up with Catholic nuns storming the halls of her all-girls high school, telling the young, impressionable teenagers that they would get pregnant if they so much as French-kissed a boy. Those nuns certainly did their duty in instilling the fear of God in my mom, but thankfully over the years, her views on God, heaven, and what happens when we die have softened and opened up a bit. After her own best friend passed away from cancer years ago, and after spending years as an RN, caring for the elderly in nursing homes, my mom has held the hands of more than a few souls as their bodies have given up. As a result, she has constantly longed to know more about what happens after we die. So, when I share Mike's story with her, especially the part about the afterlife and all of the lessons he learned there, she is deeply moved, and suddenly we have found a topic we can connect on. Something we can discuss for hours on end without stress or pressure or any of the more difficult aspects of our relationship coming into play. Our discussions on the possibilities that await after death and on the nature of love have begun to heal our relationship, and in this way, the beauty of Mike's message has already begun to transform my world.

After a few weeks of spreading the love and allowing my own heart to soften enough so that some of that love is coming back to me, I think back to the way I ended things with Nick, and I re-read the harsh e-mail I sent him—the e-mail I wrote with the express purpose of hurting him, as if hurting him would somehow make me hurt less.

It hasn't, of course. My pain over losing him is great, but that is only because I love him so much.

Now that Mike's story has opened my eyes and my heart, I know I cannot let my hurtful e-mail be the last letter I ever send to a man who has been, who is still, and who will always be so dear to me.

So, this is how I find myself back at my laptop, composing a new message to my former lover. This one is going to be all about love, of course, but not the passionate, lustful, can't-live-without-you kind of love. It's about a new kind of love, one that is timeless and unconditional. One that gives selflessly, no matter what wrongs have been done, no matter how many tears have been shed.

Dear Nick,

I want you to know that I am truly sorry for the hurtful things I have said and written, especially in my last e-mail to you. I am sorry that I let my pain and my ego get in the way of sharing the deep love I have for you, and will always have, no matter what our present circumstances are. I know you are doing the best you can, and I am doing the same. We are only human, but underneath that, we are two souls who have shared a beautiful connection, one I am truly grateful to have experienced. I know that there will always be a part of me that will wish we had made it together, that we had that island wedding we talked about over oysters (well, over your oysters) in New Orleans. But that's okay. We must have other purposes in this life, and maybe we'll meet in the next one, and it will all work out beautifully. All I know is that I do truly wish you only love, joy, and peace in your life, and I want you to know that I am always sending you that love.

I hope you can feel my sincerity, and that you can forgive me for hurting you.

Love,
Danielle

The very next day, Nick responds with his own e-mail of apologies, gratitude, and love. It is an absolutely beautiful, heartfelt message, written with the same sweet eloquence and perfect articulation with which he has been writing me for over a year.

In his message, he writes that *our romance was one for the ages.*

It certainly was.

After we have established a new kind of love between us, one that accepts and honors our present circumstances, Nick and I continue e-mailing each other about once a month—as friends who care about each other, yes, but mostly as two former lovers who feel that our connection was too strong and too important to never be in touch again.

WHILE MIKE'S story of past-life memories and traveling through the afterlife is certainly mind-blowing, perhaps the one detail that stopped me in my tracks more than all the others was when Mike and his wife, Leah, told me their middle names.

Leah's middle name is Danielle—*my first name.* And Mike's middle name is the same as *my ex-husband's first name.* This young, sweet couple already reminds me so much of me and my husband in our early years of marriage, but to learn that we share names with them? It's uncanny, especially considering neither of our first names make typical middle names, and it definitely feels like some sort of strange sign—a sign that I take to mean that my relationship with Nick isn't the *only* one I need to mend during this burst of love I am spreading throughout my little corner of the world.

Next up on the love list: my ex-husband.

When I envision watching my own life review, the day that burns most in my heart is the day I told my husband I wanted a divorce.

On that day, I said to him, "I don't love you in the same way I used to."

I did not say that I *didn't* love him anymore, because I did love him. What I meant by my statement is that my love for him had changed. At that point in time, after everything we had been through, I loved him, but I felt that I was no longer *in love* with him.

I may be wrong, but I believe that it was this statement that hurt him more than anything else I said on the day I left our marriage. Those are the kind of words that will leave a gash on someone's heart, a wound that may never be repaired.

I couldn't go the rest of my life knowing I had left my husband with the feeling that I didn't love him or that he wasn't good enough.

And so, I take to sharing my feelings the old-fashioned way, and I compose a handwritten letter. In my letter, I tell my former husband that no matter what becomes of us, I will always and forever love him unconditionally. I tell him that he is perfect just the way he is, and I apologize if my leaving our marriage made him feel that he wasn't loved or wasn't adequate. It is just the opposite.

While I don't pour my heart out in this letter to him with the intention of receiving a response, I would be lying if I say that I'm not hoping to hear from him.

But weeks pass, and my former husband never writes back.

Over the coming months, while I am writing the second draft of my screenplay and working on Mike's book, while I am continuing to share this most important lesson about love with everyone, including myself, I write my ex-husband more letters...letters I never send. I even choreograph dances I wish to perform for him when I realize that ballet was a part of me that I never truly shared with him when we were married. Sure, we met in a dance club and I spent years romping around our house dancing like a nut, but he has never seen me do ballet. He's never truly seen me dance.

And that wasn't his fault. Dancing was a part of my life that I shut down after we got married.

I never do perform those dances for him, though.

As Christmas nears, I am now writing an entirely new third draft of my screenplay, this time incorporating all of the recent notes I've received from the director. I'm hoping with every key stroke and with every dollar of debt I've accrued that this draft will be the one we sell. The one that digs me out of the financial mess I've gotten myself into. It is with this intense motivation that I am feverishly typing away inside a beachy Starbucks in the charming town where my husband and I lived when we were first married. I'm not there long when a familiar, handsome face pops in the door.

It's my ex-husband.

320 | JULIETTE SOBANET

I haven't seen or heard from him in months, but the minute he walks in, my heart flutters, and my cheeks flush. Even though I told him on that sad divorce day that I didn't love him in the same way any longer, I realize that something inside me has shifted, and there is still an immeasurable amount of love pouring through me simply at the sight of him.

Oh, how terribly inconvenient.

As soon as he spots me, we hug and he takes a seat next to me so we can catch up. By the way he's checking his watch, I can tell he's in a hurry. But this is probably because he ordered a Venti Coffee with sugar and cream—he *didn't* ask for a side of ex-wife.

Before I have a chance to process the whirlwind of emotions swirling inside me, he is gone.

That night, I text him, asking him to get together for a drink and talk.

He doesn't respond.

Later that night, as my desperation grows, I call and leave a voice-mail reiterating what I said in my text message.

Again, he doesn't respond.

And much later that night, after a few glasses of wine are consumed and many tears have been shed, I write him an e-mail telling him that leaving him was the gravest mistake of my life.

He doesn't respond to that either.

And rightfully so. *I divorced him*, after all. What do I expect?

It isn't until my depression lifts a few weeks later that I find out my ex has met someone else. It's serious, and he's happy. Which is, of course, what I want for him, even though it stings. That is unconditional love, after all.

And although our quick run-in sent me spiraling into the depths of depression, I do know, down to my core, that leaving him was *not* the gravest mistake of my life. In fact, it wasn't a mistake at all.

It was a choice.

A bold, powerful choice that has certainly had its consequences, but one I must embrace all the same.

Now that I have sent my ex my unconditional love letter, I know I must not contact him anymore. I must leave it at that. And I must avoid our old Starbucks like the plague.

Chapitre 38

WITH NO hope of reconnecting with my ex-husband even just to be friends, and with my former lover giving his all to his marriage, I am, for once in my life, left to my own devices. I know that this is *exactly* what I need after so many years spent pinning my happiness on my relationship status, but logically *knowing* something is good for me and *feeling it* in my heart are two separate things.

And what I am feeling in my heart these days is a whole lot of emptiness. Oh, and some grief and sorrow too. I do my best to stuff all of those icky feelings even deeper inside me, in a place where I cannot reach them, simply because I am *so* tired of feeling this way.

In the moments where I am able to pretend my heart isn't hanging on by an erratic, almost undetectable beat, I am writing. Writing, writing, and writing. Even though I'm not sure how I'll be able to pay my bills next month, I ignore practicality and I pour everything I have left into this screenplay.

The producers want it to be an R-rated comedy à la *Brides-maids*, and the director wants romance and depth of character à la *Crazy, Stupid Love*, so I'm doing my absolute best to throw it all in there. Raunchy humor, unforgettable characters, depth, romance, and of course, my favorite part—*Paris*!

The best part of all is that writing this story makes me so happy. Some of the scenes I am writing are so completely ridiculous that I find myself laughing out loud in cafés and making a total fool out of myself, but I don't care.

Between the divorce, the depression, and the affair, most of my writing mojo had been zapped. I haven't truly been in the flow with my writing since before I left my husband, and to find that spark within myself again is exhilarating. It's a huge relief, too, because there were many a day when I would stare blankly at my computer screen and feel a supreme heaviness settle into my chest when the only thing I had energy to do was to close my laptop and crawl back into bed.

I feared I had lost my writing mojo forever.

But with each new scene I complete, I realize that I didn't lose it. Not by a long shot.

Now I am filled with hope that I will once again make an incredible full-time living doing what I love. I am *also* filled with hope that this magical point where writing is paying all of my bills again arrives within the next month or two. Actually, this is not so much a hope as it is a *demand* I've placed on the Universe, God, or whoever may be listening.

I've been working on this script for a year and a half. I have written three entirely different drafts. I have put in my time to learn the craft of screenwriting and to write what I believe is a hilarious, sparkling, heartwarming screenplay adaptation of my very first novel, and now I want—*I need*—this baby to soar.

At the end of January, I send my golden-ticket script off to the producers. And again, I pray with all my might that the next call I receive from them is the call that will take me from

Depressed, Divorced Cat Lady with loads of debt to *Fabulous Up-and-Coming Screenwriter Cat Lady with hundreds of thousands of dollars in the bank!*

While I'm waiting for an answer on my fate, I know I need to be writing my next novel, but I'm at a loss for what that novel should be. Last fall, I still owed my publisher the option on my next romance novel, so I pitched a book that I had based rather loosely—or perhaps *not so loosely*—on my experiences of divorce and falling in love with a married man. Since my sales numbers for my first several books with this publisher were not nearly as extraordinary as those of my peer authors, I was fully expecting them to turn down my proposal. Even if they did make me an offer, I was fairly certain I would turn it down so that I could self-publish, as that had proved to be a more successful route for me in the past.

My publisher did as I expected and turned down my proposal, so now I am pouring through my inventory of partially written novels and my lists upon lists of story ideas, trying to decipher which of these stories is calling out to me the most.

The problem is, none of them feel right at the moment.

Fiction doesn't feel right at the moment.

The only thing I really want to write these days is the truth.

My truth. *My* story.

Over the past year and a half, in some of my most harrowing moments, the only thing I *could* write was the truth. My pen has filled up pages upon pages of journals detailing my star-crossed romance with Nick. Even more pages have been coated with the sorrow and doubt and grief I've experienced throughout my divorce. I've written poems to my lover and to my ex-husband. I've documented memories, poignant dialogues, and entire scenes that have taken place throughout this wild journey.

In writing the truth, I have begun to work through the jumbled mess that has been my life as of late. I've been able to take a closer look at the choices I made, *why* I made them, the feelings I felt as a result, and the way those choices have impacted others. This process is both exhausting and cathartic, and most of all, it is liberating.

But the idea of transforming these personal pages of truth into a book that others will read? Now, *that* is absolutely terrifying.

When I was completing my master's degree at NYU in Paris, I crafted my thesis around two female French writers from the eighteenth and nineteenth centuries who had written both fiction and memoirs—Madame de Genlis and George Sand. Both of these women wrote beautiful memoirs, but in those pages of truth, they *conveniently* left out all the juicy stuff—romance, love affairs, and how they truly felt about their husbands. Instead, they saved all of *that* for their fiction. I presume that they did this because their memoirs would be published while they were still alive, and if they included all of that scandalous material in the book, society would scoff, their husbands might leave them, and their lives would certainly take a fast and furious plummet into *les toilettes.*

But today, women are taking bolder strides in their writing, and this includes writing no-holds-barred memoirs. Elizabeth Gilbert, Cheryl Strayed, Jeannette Walls, Susanna Sonnenberg, and Jewel are just a few of the courageous women who have blazed the trail in writing honestly and beautifully on such sticky topics as divorce, drugs, depression, affairs, and destructive families.

I have all of their books on my bedside stand. I open them constantly. I read and I re-read their raw emotions laid bare on the page. Their stories let me know that my heart isn't the only one that is bleeding. That I'm not the only girl who has mourned a mother who is still alive or who has had to accept the reality that her father simply wasn't going to be there for her, without ever really understanding why.

Because of these daring women and their willingness to break their hearts open on the page, I know that I am not alone in choosing to leave a husband whom I still love. I am not alone in seeking pleasure outside of my marriage when I reached the end of my rope. I am not alone in needing antidepressants in order to survive the day.

I am not alone in hitting rock bottom, and hitting it over and over and over again.

And I am not alone in wanting to write about all of this—*needing* to write about all of this—in order to grow, heal, and move forward with my life.

But do I have it within me to be one of these trailblazers? To share my story with the world, knowing that there will be people—some of them my own friends and family—who will scoff, who will judge, who will realize I am not the woman they thought I was?

Do I have this kind of brazen courage?

I want to be brave. I want to write this story. I want my words, my truth, my journey to inspire others.

But at least for this day, this week, this month, while I am waiting to hear the news on my screenplay, I decide I will keep the idea of writing my memoir in my back pocket because I'm not quite ready yet.

IT IS late on a Tuesday in the end of February, and I am in the middle of a French tutoring session with one of my best students when I spot a missed call from the producer on my phone. As soon as I'm finished reviewing *le passé composé* with my student, I jet out to my car and listen to my voice-mail.

The producer has spoken with the director about my latest draft of *Sleeping with Paris,* and he has news to share. He doesn't say if this news is good or bad, although I sense from his tone that, whatever it is, it is definitive. A firm *yes* or a firm *no.*

Please, God, let it be a yes.

I swallow my nerves, and I dial the producer's number.

He doesn't hesitate to get right to the point. "The director decided to pull off the project," he says. "Unfortunately we only had a small window with him, and now that we've lost it, I think it's best for us to table the project for now. Without a well-known director or an A-list actress attached to the film, it wouldn't be fair to keep asking you to do revisions."

He goes on to explain that the director felt that the screenplay wasn't headed in the direction that he had envisioned, and that the R-rated comedy aspect was a little too much for him.

I am listening and nodding and pretending to keep my shit together, but my writer's heart is broken. I don't let him know this, though.

"I understand," I say, even though I don't totally get it, seeing as how they had all *insisted* so strongly on wanting an outrageous R-rated comedy, but perhaps the director just didn't get my sense of humor. Whatever it is, I can't fight it, and I have so enjoyed working with this producer, so I want to go out on a positive note.

"Thank you so much for giving me this opportunity," I tell him. "I've loved working with you, and if there is ever a chance for us to work together someday down the line, I would love that."

"Yes, the door is definitely open on my end," he says. "And I hope you keep writing screenplays. This was only your first one, and in this business, it can take a while before a writer produces the script that sells."

"Just like the publishing business," I say, although thanks to the advent of self-publishing on Kindle, I know that I will not work on a book for over a year and a half only to have it never see the light of day. I know that I can write books, and I know that I can sell books.

Screenwriting is a different beast altogether. This was only my first taste of it, and while the experience has been mostly exciting, fulfilling, and positive up to this point—with the exception of not being paid for all the work—tonight, it has left me deflated.

"You have had such a positive attitude throughout this entire process," the producer says to me. "That's rare to find in our business."

"Thank you," I say, not at all feeling positive about anything.

"There's always the chance that I'll come across another director or an actor who is looking for a story like *Sleeping with Paris,* and we could revisit the script if that happens. But in the meantime, you have a life to live and it wouldn't be fair to ask you to do another draft without a big name attached to the project."

Even if he did want me to write another draft, I would have to say no. Or at least, no for now. I have spent so much time on this screenplay that I haven't been working the way I've needed to in order to pay my bills, and it's gotten to the point where I am putting groceries on credit.

I need to do something, anything, to get my finances back on track, and I am beyond crushed knowing that all of the hours and love I've poured into this screenplay are amounting to...*nothing.*

The producer and I chat for another minute or two, and then we hang up.

I am zooming to another tutoring session, watching the oncoming headlights slice through the dark night ahead. I want to pull over and collapse on the steering wheel and cry.

But I have to teach two sweet little girls how to say *bonjour* and *ça va* and *je m'appelle.* I can't walk in there looking like a wreck. With their innocent giggles and their bouncy curls, these girls don't yet know that life can be so relentless, so harsh, so positively exhausting. They haven't tasted defeat and failure and loss yet—well, certainly not to the magnitude that I have, anyway. As I teach them my favorite language, I find myself wishing that they never have to know these things.

They are so bright and hopeful. They are shining stars for me on such a dark night, and they let me know that at least there is one thing I haven't lost—my passion for teaching French. Without the sale of the screenplay I was so thoroughly banking on, I may be doing quite a bit more teaching in the near future. And that's okay.

But as I get in my car and release the tears that have been bubbling just below the surface ever since I hung up with the producer, the voice of my heart isn't telling me to teach French or to write another screenplay or to allow myself to drown in despair after this disheartening news.

The voice of my heart is strong and bold and courageous. She is daring and inspiring, and she alone speaks my truth.

The voice of my heart knows what I really want to do.

"*Fuck it,*" she says. "*Write the memoir.*"

Chapitre 39

IF ANYONE knocks on my door this week, they will find a madwoman dressed in pajamas with messy bedhead wading in a sea of yellow, pink, and green post-its.

Yep, that's what telling the truth has done to me.

As soon as I gave myself permission to write the story in my heart, my creative genius reappeared after a long, lonely hiatus and said, *"Time to get to work, bitch!"*

So I'm outlining and I'm writing and I'm reliving my marriage, my divorce, my affair, and everything in between. It is intense. It is heartbreaking. It is maddening. But it is also empowering, thrilling, and healing.

For the first time in *years*, I am following my heart one hundred percent. I am facing the thing I have feared for so long— *the truth*—and I am diving right into her murky, stormy waters, swimming deeper and deeper and deeper still. I won't stop until I reach the point where the water becomes clear again, where its purity cleanses my tarnished heart and washes away all the debris so that I can emerge from this sea of truth as a new woman.

While I'm running around in pajamas with post-its blanketing my floor, swimming in my truth and embracing this new, brazen version of *me*, I remember that I also need to eat. And pay my bills. So, amid my creative storm, I apply to any and every job I can think of.

It's not long before I'm teaching yoga at three different studios, walking dogs five days a week, teaching kids and adults how to write, and tripling the number of French tutoring students I had, while raising my rates as well!

I'm waking up early every morning to write, and I'm writing on nights and weekends too. I'm spending my afternoons working all of my other jobs, and for the first time in a while, I'm paying all of my bills without having to put a dime on credit. What's even more fabulous is that I *love* everything I'm doing. I won't take on a new project now unless it brings me joy, and this method of following my heart so tirelessly only leads me to more fulfilling projects and more dedicated students each week.

Once this new work schedule of mine is in full swing and the memoir is pouring out of me the way my tears used to, I am sitting at my computer one day reflecting back on all of the choices and events that brought me to this new place in my life.

It is in this state of self-reflection that a few lost pieces of my puzzle finally click into place.

The screenplay didn't turn out to be my knight in shining armor as I'd hoped it would be. My lover didn't turn out to be my knight in shining armor as I'd hoped *he* would be. My husband wasn't my knight either—at least not the one I would stay with forever.

None of them saved me in the ways I wanted them to.

As I think back through all of the people and projects I have depended on throughout my life to *save me*, the idea of that monkey swinging from branch to branch comes to mind again. I realize that I haven't only been swinging from man to man for years—

there have been a few *other* branches mixed into my safety forest as well.

Again, I go back to that day on the phone with my dad when I decided I didn't need his love to be okay. I felt that I was able to let go of my dad *because* I had my mom. Her branch was strong and solid for most of my childhood and adolescence.

But when I got to college, my mom's love for me changed. She withdrew, she lashed out, and she blamed me for all of her sorrow. For years, I didn't understand what was happening, and I tried to fix her. I talked to her for endless hours on the phone, I assured her that I loved her more than anyone in the entire world, and I didn't understand why she didn't believe me. At one point, I even convinced her to move to San Diego to be near me, thinking that if only she lived close by, this madness would stop. But it didn't.

And so, at twenty-eight-years-old, after enduring ten years of intense emotional trauma in my relationship with my mother, I decided I had to let her go.

I felt that I *could* let go of her *because* I had my husband. He held me and loved me through that loss. He was my safety in the storm. My rock. My strength. My man.

Soon after, I decided it was time for us to focus on our own little family and create our own little baby.

But our baby never came. She didn't arrive to save the day.

Instead, my husband and I had to face the truth of our crumbling marriage.

And when *that* imploded, I *only* let go of my husband once I had my next branch, my next storm shelter in sight: *Nick*.

Nick never was a true storm shelter, though.

Instead, he was a mirror. He was a mirror into all the deepest, truest parts of my soul—the parts of my soul that my husband had a difficult time loving. The parts of my soul that *I* had been denying in order to stay in the marriage for so long.

Nick was not only the first man, but *the first person in my life* who finally understood *me*—the mess, the beauty, the dance, the art, the full-on wild creation of me—and who loved me for exactly who I am.

He didn't deny any of those sides of me the way my own father, mother, and husband had done.

He loved the whole me.

Of course I would never want to let him go. Who else would understand me the way he had? Who else would love all the bits and pieces of me? Who was I if I didn't have him reminding me that those parts existed and that they were beautiful?

I didn't have the answers to these questions when I let go of Nick, but I had to let him go all the same.

And without a man or a parent to save me, I turned to the screenplay. I pinned everything I had on that project. My hopes, dreams, financial woes, and career aspirations—they were all riding on the preferences of a few Hollywood film executives.

But then, those Hollywood film executives said *no*.

And I am so thankful they did.

Because for the first time in my life, I don't have a single branch to cling to. And it is here, in this lonely forest where I have met my true knight in shining armor. I have met the one who loves the deepest parts of my soul, who embraces all of my hidden dreams and desires, and who believes that each and every one of them can come true.

I have met the person who will save me.

As it turns out, she's been saving me all along; I just didn't realize it.

She is the same girl who had the courage to stand up to her father at the young age of thirteen and no longer accept his neglect in her life. She is the same woman who had the strength to walk away from her mother when she realized that she was not put on this earth to endure endless emotional abuse at the hands of anyone, let alone a parent. She is the same woman who has since found it in her heart to love both of her parents for exactly who they are, and instead of blaming them for the ways

334 | JULIETTE SOBANET

in which they hurt her, she seeks to grow and learn from the entire experience.

She is the same woman who was brave enough to walk away from her marriage when staying meant living an inauthentic life and denying her true self. She is the same woman who found her soul mate in a married man and had the strength to walk away from him anyway. She is the same woman who still sends unconditional love to both her former husband and her former lover, regardless of the ways in which they hurt her and she hurt them.

She is the same woman who believes that her story is extraordinary simply because it is hers. Simply because she has lived it. And she is the same woman who has rediscovered the courage within her—courage she has always had—to follow her heart, to live her truth, and to *write her story*.

In writing my story, in reliving all of the love, joy, sorrow, and heartbreak of my greatest loves, I have found the beauty in the pain, and my heart has begun to heal.

In writing my story, I have learned how to simply *be with myself*, to sit with my pain and my grief, and to honor that grief as an essential part of my growth.

In writing my story, I have learned to value the unending source of love within me, and to send that love to every single person who has crossed my path, and *especially* to those who have hurt me the most, for those are the ones I have loved the most.

Where there is great love, there is also potential for great pain.

Because I have hurt so deeply, I know that I have also loved deeply.

And since love is the bedrock of my journey—*of our journeys*—I know my particular journey has been worthwhile. Worth every tear I've shed, every meltdown I've had, and every dose of Wellbutrin I've taken.

Love is worth it.

I know that now, and so I don't curse the journey. Not a single moment of it.

Instead, I'm embracing the long, winding, wild road that has been my own, and I am so thankful to every single branch that has broken along the way, to every single person who has hurt me, because without them I wouldn't have learned how to love myself.

I've stopped swinging from branch to branch, expecting the next one to be the one that loves me the most. The one that pays my bills. The one that saves me from my fear of being on my own.

Instead I've rediscovered the unwavering strength within me, and I'm choosing to *love myself* the most. I've built an unconventional career doing all the things I love to do and I'm paying my own bills. I'm facing my fears every day, and I'm slaying my own dragons.

What I didn't realize until now is that I would continue to draw people and circumstances into my life that would ultimately deny me until I learned to stop denying myself. It is only when I am embracing every last part of me—from my greatest strengths to my most embarrassing weaknesses—and being *exactly who I am* that I will begin to attract people and circumstances in my life that will embrace me right back.

To celebrate this most monumental realization, I wake up one morning only a few days before my thirty-third birthday, and I use all the miles I have saved up to book a flight to Paris.

It is only fitting, I decide, for the story I am writing to end in the city I love so much.

How liberating it is that I don't have to fight with anyone to make this decision.

How beautiful it is that I don't need a man to meet me in Paris.

I am meeting myself in Paris.

I am a free woman now. Truly, wildly free.

Partie VII

PARIS, MON AMOUR ~ PARIS, MY LOVE

"My bounty is as
boundless as the sea,
My love as deep;
the more I give to thee,
The more I have,
for both are infinite."

~ William Shakespeare,
Romeo and Juliet

Chapitre 40

EVERY SINGLE time I've traveled to France since I was a teenager, I have packed the most massive, unreasonably heavy suitcase. Then I have to lug that damn thing through the airport, on and off trains, through metros, over cobblestone streets, and very often, up six or more flights of winding stairs when the apartment building I'm staying in is *sans ascenseur*.

And each time I carry one of these monstrosities to France, I say to myself, *I'm never packing this much again.* But somehow, when I'm in my bedroom back in the US, I convince myself that I *need* every pair of jeans, heels, and boots in my closet. I *need* every dress, top, and scarf. A girl has to have options, after all! And I *need* every single toiletry and medicinal item in my entire bathroom—as if Paris doesn't have all of those cute little pharmacies with their neon green crosses dotting the street corners.

Many of my friends who have traveled with me to France have had the misfortune of helping me drag these boulders through the country, and even *they* are exhausted by this extreme weight I have been lugging around for years.

As the French would say, *ça suffit.*

That's enough.

Well, this thirty-three-year-old woman has learned a thing or two. I've left my marriage. I've left my lover. I've faced the darkest days of depression and I've come out alive. Having a few extra shirts or scarves or books to read won't change any of that.

And so, for the first time in all the years I've been flying to Paris, I am zipping through the Charles de Gaulle Airport with only a small carry-on suitcase in hand and a breezy smile on my face.

There is no man by my side whipping me into a frenzy of emotions, and there is no fifty-pound piece of luggage making me sweat and giving me shoulder pain.

My load has lightened. *Significantly.*

I don't need all of those things to be happy. A marriage. A lover. A suitcase full of material items I once believed would keep me comfortable.

I only need one thing to be happy now, and thankfully I haven't left her behind, as I have so many times before. No, she's right here with me as I emerge from the metro at Place Saint-Michel and gaze around in awe at this hot, sparkling, spring day in Paris.

She is my heart, my soul, my dreams, my every desire.

She is the key that has unlocked my heart, cleared out the sorrow, and told me it's okay to let go and heal. It's okay to be happy again.

And I love her more than any man, any city, any glass of wine or antidepressant.

Funny how she's been in there all along, but it's only now, after a few trips to the dark side that she can shine her light just as bright as all the lights in Paris.

I'm so happy to have her back—my old friend, my long lost love, *myself.*

AFTER A brisk stroll down Boulevard Saint-Michel, past side-walk cafés brimming with tourists, Parisians, and early afternoon glasses of rosé, I wheel the smallest suitcase of my life over the creaky wooden floors in The Publisher's Left Bank apartment.

"*Bonjour, chérie.*" Stéphane's smile is soft and warm as he leans in to give me bisous on the cheeks. His little black cat, Ulfy, gives me a soft purr and a warm leg rub too.

"It's so good to be back," I say before dropping my bags in the bedroom and joining Stéphane in his small Parisian kitchen.

He is chopping carrots and onions and potatoes. There is a pot boiling on the stove. Stéphane, my French Casanova friend who wines and dines women like it's his job is...*cooking?*

"*Alors, tu fais la cuisine maintenant?*" *So, you're cooking now?* I ask him.

"Yes, I'm cooking now," he says with a grin. "A lot has changed since we last saw each other. I imagine you have a few stories to tell me, too."

"Oh, I sure do," I say.

After we catch each other up just a bit, Stéphane asks what I'm working on at the moment.

"I'm writing a memoir," I tell him. "A Paris memoir."

He stops chopping for a moment, his curious eyes meeting mine. "Oh really?"

"Yes, and it's going to be juicy."

We both giggle a little at this, before he asks, "Am I going to make an appearance?"

"*Mais, bien sûr,*" I say. "Well, if you're okay with it, that is. After all, you were the original catalyst who woke me up. You know how thankful I will always be to you for that. I think it would be remiss not to include our story in the book."

"I would be honored to be in the book," he says.

"Thank you," I say, loving how open-minded and honest Stéphane is. He is such a breath of fresh air. "The story will end with this trip to France," I say. "So, I don't actually know the ending yet...which I kind of love."

Stéphane turns to me and smiles. "You know, I have been working with authors for years, and I've never had the feeling I have now. That I'm actively creating a story with you. A story I will be in."

"I can't wait to find out what happens next," I say with a curve of my lips.

And really, I can't.

I ONLY slept for two hours on the plane, but I have a solid prescription for jet lag that always keeps me going through my first full day back in France when my body wants to crash.

Part I to my prescription: Don't stop walking. This is both easy and desirable when the magnificence of springtime has brought all of the trees into full bloom and laced the warm Paris air with the scents of fresh flowers, freshly baked baguettes, and strong coffee.

Part II: Don't stop eating. With crêpe stands and boulangeries speckling the street corners, this is a given, with or without jet lag.

Part III: Don't stop talking. Even though speech is limited and spacey when one has barely slept in over twenty-four hours and when one is consuming large quantities of French *patisseries,* it is imperative to at least make an effort to speak in between the consumption of said pastries.

My close friend Anne-Laure, the elegant French painter, has joined me in my quest to stay awake all afternoon. We are meandering through the Latin Quarter, eating *pains au chocolat* as we go, and catching each other up on our lives.

Anne-Laure is my friend who is married to a Frenchman but who has been in love with an Austrian violinist for the better part of a decade. Each time I've visited Paris in the past few years, Anne-Laure and I have sat in Café de Flore, discussing our marriages and our eternal debate of whether to stay or to go. Now, I am on the other side. I've done it. I've left.

Anne-Laure, however, is still in her marriage. She doesn't see her married Austrian lover any longer, but that doesn't mean she isn't still in love with him, and that doesn't mean her marriage has magically become a passionate, romantic, fulfilling relationship; it hasn't.

But, as Anne-Laure says, "It's comfortable. My husband and I are close friends, you know, and there is love between us...but still, there is something missing. I don't feel appreciated as a woman, and there is very little physical contact. There is no poetry in this life. No romance. At the same time, it's such a big decision to throw away the entire life we've built together. And then there is always the problem of being an artist—I'm painting, but I still don't earn enough money from my art to leave my marriage and live in Paris on my own. Not yet anyway. And my career is every-thing to me. How did you do it? Being a writer?"

"It hasn't been easy," I admit. I go on to tell Anne-Laure about the plethora of jobs I have worked to stay afloat since I lost my hus-band's stable income. "I've been cat-sitting, dog-walking, nannying, teaching yoga, *and* I'm teaching French again—I'll do anything *not* to get a soul-sucking desk job so that I can still have the time and energy to write. And I *am* writing—I'm writing early in the morning and late at night, and on weekends. Whenever I can."

Anne-Laure looks a bit overwhelmed as I am listing my ten thousand part-time jobs, and she should be. It has been over-whelming for me, and it would be for her too. That's just the nature of the beast.

"It's scary losing your husband's stable income," I admit. "But I've made it work. And you would too, if you decided to leave. My advice is to get everything in order—or as much as you can, any-way—*before* you go. Line up the jobs that will pay enough for you to live comfortably on your own before you leave."

As Anne-Laure and I continue our discussion on women with artistic professions who need their husband's stable income to continue practicing their art, I wonder, can we ever really have it all? Why is it that all too often, women find themselves financially tied to an unfulfilling marriage, and fears of what may be lurking on the other side—debt, financial instability, and not being able to continue their unstable artistic profession—are some of the strongest reasons keeping them in the marriage? I'm not sure if it's sad that women make the choice to stay, or if it's smart.

Sure, it would have been deemed financially smarter to stay in my marriage.

Sure, it would have been deemed "safe."

But I'm out here floating in my own little boat, and even though I've nearly drowned more than a few times, I'm in Paris now, and I'm alive and I'm happy and I'm writing. Most importantly, for the first time in so long, I'm embracing what it's like to be *me* with no apologies, no excuses, no exceptions.

From where Anne-Laure is standing, jumping into her own little boat may seem like the most dangerous decision of her life, and I would have to agree.

It is dangerous.

There is no guarantee of survival.

But until you jump, you don't know how glorious and messy and exhilarating life can be on the other side.

IT IS my first night back in the City of Light, and like the chivalrous host he is, Stéphane has asked me out to dinner. I am more than happy to hit the town with my favorite Parisian and continue our conversation from earlier. He leads me down the boulevard, only a block away from his apartment, to a charming little bistro called Au Phil...Du Vin. Right next door sits The Long Hop, a bumping English pub I used to frequent with friends and cute French boys when I was a student in Paris.

The owner of the bistro is a jolly older Frenchman who pats Stéphane on the back and welcomes him by name. After bisous are exchanged among us, he seats us at a table in the back corner of the restaurant. I am instantly in love with the intimate feel inside this oh-so-French restaurant—the checkered table cloths, the wall stacked with wine bottles, the chalkboard menu pinned to the wall, and to top it all off, there are live musicians playing guitar and violin as they sing traditional French songs right by our table.

I have to actually stop myself from standing up, wrapping my arms around Stéphane in pure joy and bellowing out, *I love France!*

Nothing would scream *l'américaine* more, so I keep my burst of joy to myself and instead tell Stéphane, "It's adorable. I love it."

"I'm so glad," he says.

We order three plates to share: *le gazpacho à l'asperge* (asparagus gazpacho), *le camembert gratinée au jambon* (a wheel of fried creamy camembert cheese with ham—*dear God*), and *le coquelet roti à l'estragon* (spring chicken seasoned with tarragon). Stéphane asks the server what he suggests as a good wine pairing, and a chilled bottle of rosé is the answer.

Yet isn't a chilled bottle of rosé *always* the answer on a warm Paris night when the sun doesn't set until almost 10:00 p.m.?

We've barely had a sip of our wine when Stéphane and I break into our easy conversation that is a mixture of both French and English. It's to the point with him where I don't even notice which language he is speaking or which language I am speaking because it is all just so natural. I know that I can tell him anything—*absolutely anything*—and this is a freedom I have never before experienced with a man. What a gift.

Stéphane gets things started with an update on what has happened in his world this past year.

"Almost one year ago, I was at my *maison à la campagne*—the country home that my parents left to me after they both passed—and I realized that after I die, I won't have anyone to leave this home to. And my apartment in Paris, who will I leave that to? It hit me then that I wanted a child. I wanted a child to pass along my legacy."

I nearly drop my wineglass at this.

Never in a million years could I have imagined hearing those words leave Stéphane's lips. The charming Frenchman I met almost three years ago at a romance writers conference, who told me over wine that he never wanted to be married or fall in love or *have his own children*, is now sitting before me telling me that he's changed his mind—well, at least on the topic of babies.

"Have I been transported to another universe?" I ask him, gripping the table. "Who are you?"

Stéphane laughs at my reaction and continues on with the story. "After this realization, I became obsessed with the idea of having my own child. So, I thought of all the women I've had relationships with who I would potentially want to have a child with, and I chose one. I called her and asked her if she would be interested in giving it a try. She said yes."

"Just like that? She agreed to be your baby mama?"

Stéphane grins. He's a man who's used to getting what he wants. Even a baby mama, apparently. "So we got together...but it just didn't work. There wasn't any chemistry. It wasn't her fault, but I didn't understand what happened. My therapist said that it was because I saw her as a mother, not a woman."

"Makes sense," I say. "Seeing a woman as the future mother of your child is entirely different from having that initial, sexy attraction that brings you together."

"Exactly."

"So what did you do? Did you have someone else in mind?"

I can't help but wonder if *I* was on the Baby Mama List. It's not likely, seeing as how Stéphane knew I was going through a divorce and sleeping with a married man when he had his child epiphany...but I'm still wondering.

"I decided not to have a child with her, or with anyone else. But I was still distressed about the decision, so I asked my therapist, 'What's wrong with me that I don't want a wife, a child, a home, and a family?' My conclusion is that this is just who I am, and I like my life. I have always had this impression that there is a path I *should* take, and that I've deviated from that path. That's wrong, though. There's only one life, one path, and it's the one I'm on. There are no shoulds in life."

Wow.

This Frenchman speaks the truth.

My own path has certainly been a weaving, winding, masterpiece of disaster at times, but just because it's been difficult and has tested the rules that society has set concerning marriage and fidelity, does that mean that the choices I've made and the path I've traveled along are *wrong*? Does that mean that my experience has been any less valuable than that of a woman who has taken a more traditional path by choosing marriage and having children and then staying in that marriage? I can guarantee that her path isn't any easier than mine has been, or any less valuable. And I can guarantee that in either path, the opportunity for growth is immense.

Now, after the dust has settled, I see the value in every single choice I have made, including the decisions that resulted in joy and happiness, and especially in the choices that have had catastrophic ends. Because it was *through* those dark times that I found my strength, that I became the woman I have always wanted to be.

A woman who is not afraid to be herself.

A woman who loves herself first, and who understands that only in doing this, can she love others.

A woman who speaks her truth and then *writes that truth.*

It is only from hitting rock bottom that I was able to shed all the parts of myself that were no longer serving me, and emerge to be the woman I am today.

Nothing about me is perfect. I may never make the choices that society or my family or friends think I should make.

But I believe that the beauty of an individual lies in her imperfections, her surprises, her unique way of being. And I no longer feel the need to stifle those lovely parts of myself. Instead, I'm revealing them, for all the world to see.

My hope is that readers will walk away with this one simple but strong message: *it's okay to be who you are.*

It's not only okay, it is imperative. What are we doing running around trying to be who our friends, family, and society think we *should* be? How is that in any way serving ourselves, our loved ones, or the world? Is the world not a better place when each individual is finding fulfillment by following her heart and being her true self?

Is there any other purpose to life if not to be who we are so that we may love and be loved?

We don't make our journeys any lighter or easier by ignoring and shutting down who we truly are. And we certainly don't invite love into our lives this way.

It is our duty, then, to be ourselves, no matter how much controversy it stirs up.

I realize that Stéphane and I aren't so different. Not at all. We've both chosen a "non-traditional path" of being marriage-free, child-free, and just free in general. And now, more than ever, I have a deeper understanding for why he said to me almost three years ago that he never wants to fall in love. With all of the intense heartbreaks I've accrued over the past few years, I now fully understand the desire to safeguard oneself against the possibility of that happening again. I understand the need for peace and stability, and as soon as love enters into the equation in a relationship, things get wild. And the potential for pain is great.

Although, despite the pain my lost loves have caused me, I am still open to love. And I believe that only in being my true self will I continue to discover and experience love, in all its gloriously mysterious facets.

Tonight, as Stéphane and I enjoy each other's company and all of this delicious French food—I could honestly die after eating this Camembert cheese—the potential for pain feels nonexistent. We are in Paris, eating, drinking, and talking about all of our common views on life, love, and relationships.

All is more than well in our Parisian corner of the world.

Stéphane holds my hand on the way home, and even though we're not *together* per se, and never will be in the traditional sense, I feel such a deep sense of contentment in his presence that I don't need to have a label on what this is.

This is his path. It is my path. And as Stéphane said earlier, this is the only path to take—the one we're on. There are no rules, no absolutes, no shoulds.

Only the pure bliss of not knowing what comes next in this intricate, weaving journey we call life.

AFTER NOT having slept for over twenty-four hours, what comes next in my journey is a deep, deep slumber. My all-consuming rest is interrupted early in the night, though, by a loud ding from my iPhone indicating that I've received a new e-mail. I wake with a start, knowing instantly who the message is from.

Nick.

Chapitre 41

THE BRIGHT light emanating from my phone screen burns my tired eyes, and Nick's words burn my heart. As they always do.

In our most recent e-mail exchange, just before I left for Paris, I dared ask the question:

"I wonder if we will really go our entire lives without being together again."

In his response, Nick wrote that he is haunted by this question every day.

And since I couldn't leave it there, I wrote Nick a long reply, which included these words:

> *I still love you. I love you in a different way than I loved you before. It's not desperate or needy. It's not "without you I don't know how I'll go on." It's the kind of love you have after something has happened, after the dust has settled, and I can look back on it now and fully appreciate the entire experience we had together—the beauty of it and the total mess*

of it—and love you for all of it. Now, after dating more and moving forward with my life, I can better appreciate the way you loved me and the fact that no one in my life has ever loved me the way you did. No one has ever seen me the way you did—you saw right to the heart of me, to my essence, and you loved even those deepest parts of me. The problem was that while we were together, you were the only one of the two of us who loved the full spectrum of me—which was why I clung to you so tightly. I was in such a dark place that I couldn't see it myself. But now, after all this time spent healing on my own, I've found the love inside of me, a love that doesn't need to come from someone else in order for me to feel fulfilled. But you showed me how to love myself again, and really, is there any greater gift in life?

Besides all of that, I love who you are. All the parts of you. Even, and especially, the part that decided to stay in your marriage and build a stronger relationship with your wife. That took courage, and in doing that you set me free to take an important, essential journey that I needed to take on my own.

So, here I am, and there you are. And I still love you, and I always will. A love like ours doesn't come around every day, or even every lifetime, and I'm so thankful that it happened to me, that you happened to me.

Which is what brings me to this moment on my first night back in Paris, where I am squinting to read Nick's latest response in the darkness of Stéphane's apartment.

In his e-mail, Nick confesses to still loving me, too, but he also reminds me of the pain we caused each other and reaffirms that he is staying put in his marriage.

I know! I want to yell at my phone. *I know you're never leaving your wife! No need to say it again!*

I feel like Meg Ryan's best friend in *When Harry Met Sally.* Marie, played by Carrie Fisher, is in love with a married man, and numerous times throughout the movie, she has the same conversation with Sally (Meg Ryan), where they reaffirm, for the hundredth time, that *he is never going to leave his wife.*

Of course he isn't!

Marie knows! Sally knows!

Meg Ryan knows! Carrie Fisher knows!

I know! We all know!

I wish Nick didn't feel the need to remind me of this fact over and over again. But I imagine my gushing, lovey e-mail has gotten him worried that I'm trying to suck him back into our star-crossed romance. And I'm not. I only wanted to tell him the truth about how I feel—that I still love him and always will, and that this love has evolved into something more whole and complete and mature than what we had before.

I turn my phone off and stare into the darkness of this bedroom in Paris. I know I won't be able to sleep after reading his e-mail. It wasn't that any part of it was meant to be hurtful; it's just that correspondence like this from my former lover makes me queasy and sweaty and anxious.

Yes, I'm a more enlightened woman now, but I'm still human.

I dig my old friend Xanax out of my purse and take half a pill. I refuse to stay up all night thinking about the not-so-happy ending of my own love story with Nick. I know it has all worked out for the best, but no matter how enlightened I may feel about the whole thing, loving someone who reaffirms time and time again that *he will never choose me,* still knocks the wind out of me.

WHEN I wake the next morning, I sit up all groggy and foggy and take a look around Stéphane's bedroom. All around me, the walls and dressers are decorated with paintings and pictures and mementos from my childhood home.

What are all of these things doing here? How did they get here? Am I dreaming?

This feels entirely too real to be a dream, though.

I stand and shuffle out of the room, wondering if I have woken up in some sort of alternate universe.

The hallway morphs into one that resembles my grandmother's old house in Ohio. In the bathroom, I find my mom. There is only love between us, even though she is the same and I am the same.

"How are you feeling?" I ask her, already knowing the answer.

"Not very good," she says.

She hasn't felt good for a long time, but here, wherever we are, I know that it's okay. I hug her, pulling her tight.

After our embrace, I notice two jars on the bathroom counter. One of the jars is labeled: *chemo,* and the other is labeled: *radiation.*

My mom had a skin cancer scare last year, but everything has been fine since she had it removed. She didn't need chemo or radiation.

So, why am I seeing this? Is this a premonition of things to come?

I know, for certain now, that I am in some sort of altered reality or dream state, but I sense that whatever I am doing here is very important and I must continue moving.

I leave the bathroom, and there, fixing the screen door in this replica of my grandmother's home is my husband. The minute I see him, I am overcome with joy. We are together. He smiles brightly in my direction, and I jump into his arms, beaming with love for him.

I am the only one of the two of us who knows I've somehow slipped into this alternate universe where we are still together. I am the only one who knows that in the *other* version of our life together, I left him. Here and now, as I wrap my arms around my husband, I can tell he doesn't know. And I am so genuinely happy that we are together.

After he sets me down, I turn and find four adorable little girls running into my arms.

They are *our girls. Our daughters.*

I wrap my arms around them, hugging and kissing them with the fervor of a woman who thought she could never have children. I have never been more in love with any other beings as I am with my four sweet girls.

It's a second chance at the marriage that I've lost, at raising the children we never had. And I'm beyond grateful. I'm delighted, I'm overjoyed, I'm radiating with love.

Next, I spot my husband's parents walking toward our house. I have the same experience as I just had with my own mother—any pain or hurt that we experienced in our relationship is gone. They are still the same people, and I am the same person, but we love each other, and everything is forgiven. Everything is okay.

Then, all of us—me, my husband, our four little girls, my mom, and my husband's parents—we all leave the house with our beach gear and walk through a neighborhood filled with palm trees and light breezes and sunshine. This place doesn't feel like any city I've ever been to—it too feels like a different universe, a place that doesn't exist on earth. But wherever we are, it is perfect.

We all walk to the beach together. I am holding my girls' hands. I'm smiling. I'm in love with my husband. I'm happy, and *this* is exactly where I want to be.

WHEN I wake from this vivid dream, I sit up, glancing around Stéphane's bedroom, hoping to find my childhood mementos, my husband, my mom, *my girls*, but there is only the sound of the

Paris metro rumbling beneath Stéphane's building and cuddly little Ulfy purring by my leg.

I am alone, but my husband, the man I have been split from for almost two years now, the man I should technically call my *ex-husband*, this man is still so obviously laced into my bones.

I feel hungover and terribly sad as I pad over the cold wooden floors in Stéphane's apartment. He is at work, and I need to shower and get out of this place to remember that I am in Paris. But this glimpse of what could have been is haunting me with each breath I take.

Could there be an alternate universe in which I *didn't* leave my husband? In which we didn't only have the two children we'd always talked about, but where we had *four* lovely girls? In this space, could everything be forgiven with our parents?

In this moment, I feel that I would do anything to taste even for one more day, one more hour, one more minute, the glimpse I had of the "us" that never split.

I am gripping the bathroom sink now, having a hard time breathing as my grief threatens to ruin my second day in Paris. God, I thought these feelings had subsided. I want so badly for them to go away. I want so badly to never again feel an ounce of regret over what I have done.

But the grief of leaving my marriage isn't going anywhere. And the regret isn't either.

As soon as I catch my breath, my shaky hands reach for my toiletries. I may have packed the lightest bag ever for this trip, but thank God I didn't forget my antidepressants.

I throw one back, willing it to kick in and make me forget the dream I just had. I don't want to think about what could have been when I am supposed to be running around Paris being happy and *fabulous!* and filled with self-love.

I *have* found that love within myself that I spoke of in my e-mail to Nick. The love that has given me the courage to stand strong in who I am and own my choices. But that doesn't change the fact that I still miss my husband and that there are days when just the thought of him brings me to my knees.

I suspect with a loss this great, I will always miss him. And part of me will always wish we could have made it work.

Leaving him was both the best decision and the most tragic decision of my life, and there are still days when it is difficult for me to reconcile those two polarities.

Today is starting off as one of those days.

Since I know the drill by now, I step in the shower and let my old friend Grief kick me in the gut. I am better at riding her waves now, though. Letting her pass through me when she needs to.

After Grief has said her piece, I drink a cold glass of water, put on some makeup, and I open the door to Paris, trusting that this city will warm my sad heart, as she always does.

Chapitre 42

NEVER UNDERESTIMATE the power of French cuisine to take away all of your pain. I know about this exquisite power of French food, of course, as I have experienced it firsthand for years now—*dear God*, the chocolate here has actually given me food-gasms!—but it seems this afternoon I have forgotten all about the magical properties of French food.

I'm at Chez Gladines, a very unassuming bistro just down the street from Stéphane's apartment on Boulevard Saint-Germain, chatting with my former NYU professor about books and writing and marriage and divorce when I innocently order *la salade parisienne*, having no idea that this salad—*a freaking salad!*—of tomatoes, potatoes, emmental cheese, ham, and egg will have the power to make me forget all about my lost loves, my agonizing regrets, and my late-night dreams of the children I never had.

As our chipper French waiter places this thing of beauty before me, I am once again reminded of the magic of eating in Paris. (Yes, you read that correctly—I said *chipper* French waiter. Contrary to the rumors that fly about rude Parisian waiters, I

358 | JULIETTE SOBANET

have found most of the waiters in this city to be kind, friendly, and even chipper!)

Overflowing from a large metal mixing bowl, my *salade parisienne* is a masterpiece unto its own, a culinary work of art. A colorful array of *tomates, patates, emmental,* and *jambon* lie on a full bed of lettuce with *un oeuf sur le plat* garnishing the top.

One bite of the greasy potatoes and that delicious mustard dressing that flavors all salads in France, and I'm transported to another world. The world where I remember why I love France so much. The world where pleasure is found in something as simple as a salad.

The ravenous energy with which I am devouring every bite must be giving my professor the impression that I am starving myself in California. And when I think about my daily diet back home of kale smoothies and hard-boiled eggs and crunchy protein bars, I realize that I *am* starving there! I'm starving in a land of wheatgrass guzzling, paddle-boarding, meditating happy people! Granted, I drink the smoothies, I teach yoga, and I meditate. There is nothing wrong with all of this, of course.

But the obsession with superficiality that often comes with life in Southern California, the obsession with body image and being *perfect* is exhausting to me.

I'm tired of turning down my friends' requests to go hiking or paddle boarding or surfing. No, no, and *no.* I want to eat mouthwatering salads and decadent chocolate desserts and drink wine at sidewalk cafés and travel through the countryside on a high-speed train and have conversations in French with all of my international friends about literature and film and art and dance and love.

I don't care about having six-pack abs or about looking like an emaciated model or injecting toxic chemicals into my face so that I can never truly smile again.

I'm not knocking the people who *do* care about those things. I'm simply saying that it's not for me.

I love my California friends dearly—after all, they are the ones who have kept me laughing on some of the worst days of my divorce—but over the years, I have had the distinct feeling that I don't belong there. And as I am eating this Parisian salad with the fervor of a woman who has been starving for far too long, I realize that is precisely because I don't belong in California, not forever anyway.

I belong here, in France. A wonderful, magical place that has fit me like a glove ever since I set foot on its cobblestone streets as a fifteen-year-old girl.

My next two days of gorgeous springtime in Paris only serve as confirmation of this truth—that I belong here and always have.

I meet with girlfriends at quaint neighborhood cafés like Le Petit Cardinal in the Latin Quarter and at posh restaurants like Café Ruc near Palais Royal. We talk about being married and taking lovers, getting divorced and taking more lovers. We talk about how important our art is to all of us—whether it be writing, dancing, acting, or singing, there is always creation and imagination involved in everything my Parisian friends devote their time to. These are the women with whom I connect, the women who stimulate and challenge me, the women who understand my heart, my essence. And I understand theirs.

I do love drinking my kale smoothie every morning in San Diego. I do. But I can buy a damn blender in France and pair that smoothie with a chocolate croissant and be all the better for it.

On my last night in Paris before I hop on a train to Lyon, I am meandering down the quay of the Seine by myself, marveling at the golden hues of sunshine that are peeking through the trees and glistening on the water as the sun just begins to set at the late hour of 9:00 p.m.

My heart is full here, and when I return back to a candlelit dinner at Stéphane's apartment, my wheels are turning.

I'm finally—*finally*—beginning to appreciate the freedom I have created for myself in leaving my marriage and leaving my lover. I'm not *only* appreciating it, though. I can *see* it now. *I can feel it.*

I am free to choose where I live. Free to choose how I spend my time and with whom I spend it.

I am free to take lovers and have undefined relationships and close friendships with men whose company I adore, like Stéphane.

I am free to be me.

I am free to live in France.

WHEN THE train pulls into Lyon, I notice that the usual outrageous euphoria I feel upon arrival in this city hasn't hit yet.

Interesting.

I take the metro and emerge in *Vieux Lyon*, or *Old Lyon,* where I'll be staying. As I roll my tiny suitcase over the bumpy cobblestones of rue Saint-Jean, past cafés and crêperies and pubs I have visited a million times, the euphoria *still* doesn't come.

There is something else going on inside me, though. Something that has replaced the drug-like high I usually experience when I take my first steps back in Lyon.

It is the feeling that you get when you come home to a place you've lived before, a place you love and appreciate, a place where you feel comfortable and safe.

It's a feeling of knowing, of acceptance, of peace deep down in my heart, and I realize that even though I'm not doing somersaults down the lovely streets of Lyon, that perhaps, this new feeling of calm contentment is even better.

Soon, I spot Mark, my tall, handsome British friend who makes me laugh more than anyone in the entire universe, and his sweet replica of a son, Alfie. They have just ridden their bikes across the city, so they are both tired and sweaty, but Mark doesn't hesitate to grab my (tiny) suitcase and haul it up the six flights of winding stairs in his ancient apartment building.

Mark and his sweet Italian fiancée, Camilla, have been kind enough to offer me their spare bedroom for the duration of my stay. I'm not sure what to expect when we arrive at the monstrous wooden door, but on the other side, Camilla is waiting with her genuinely warm smile and a quiche in the oven.

Their apartment is fantastic—a large three bed, two and a half bath flat on the top floor with picturesque views of the rooftops, the brick chimneys, and the weathered old buildings that line the famous rue Saint-Jean. Even from way up here, we can hear the chatter of all of the tourists meandering through Vieux Lyon down below, but it only adds to the charm of their home.

"You guys, this place is amazing!" I say as Mark and Camilla give me a tour. "And it's clean! And organized!" Camilla gives me a knowing nod—she certainly remembers the state of affairs in Mark's old bachelor pad, and it's clear that she's helped him make the transition from messy bachelor to grown-up couple.

More than that, though, they've created a home together. A real home.

"I'm so glad you have Camilla," I say to Mark as we sit down at the kitchen table to eat.

"Yeah, me too," he says. "Not many women would have patience with me like she does. I don't know what I would do without her."

Later that same day, at a café down the street, Camilla would turn to me when Mark wasn't listening and say, "I don't know what he would do without me."

Priceless.

But on my first afternoon back in Lyon, before I see the full spectrum of just how perfectly these two are suited for each other, Camilla joins us at the kitchen table and presents the lovely quiche she just whipped up.

"Camilla, this is delicious!" I say, devouring every bite, so happy to not be eating a smoothie and hard-boiled eggs and a bland protein bar.

Camilla waves her hand. "Oh, it's nothing," she says in her cute Italian accent.

"So, how are the wedding plans coming along?" I ask. Mark and Camilla had only just gotten engaged the last time I was in Lyon, which was over a year and a half ago now, but the couple still hasn't tied the knot.

"We have to meet with Don Giuseppe first," Mark says all matter-of-fact before taking a big bite of quiche.

"Who's Don Giuseppe?" I ask with a giggle, already knowing that whatever story Mark is about to tell is going to have me rolling.

"He's the priest, over in Italy where my parents live," Camilla says.

"He's a cool dude, that Don Giuseppe," Mark chimes in, "but we have to have a few more meetings with him, and for the Catholic wedding in France, we have to do all of this preparation—classes, counseling, and these insanely long questionnaires."

"Oh, the questionnaires!" Camilla moans.

"What's on them?" I ask.

"The best question—rate your sex life from one to five," Mark says.

"Are you kidding me? Is that actually on there?" I say.

"It is," Camilla says.

"Honestly, what are you going to do?" Mark says, moving on from quiche to a cigarette. "Circle a two?"

"Then you'd have to discuss your sex life with Don Giuseppe," I say, leaning down to pet Ringo the cat. "That could be awkward."

As Mark and Camilla continue filling me in on the hilarity of preparing for their wedding, I realize that this is the first time in the last two years where I am actually, truly, genuinely happy for my friends who are in couples with no underlying feelings of jealousy or emptiness. It's such a relief to be able to feel joy for the people I love most and not envy them or wish I had what they had.

I am thrilled that Mark has met his match in Camilla. Even though I was skeptical when Mark first told me he was getting married, I realize now as I watch the way they interact so easily in this comfortable home they've built together, that marriage is a good idea—*a great idea*—for these two partners. They may have to meet with Don Giuseppe in Italy and cross all sorts of red Catholic tape in France to make it happen, but none of that matters, really. It's clear that they are happy together, that they fit so nicely into each other's lives, and that they are in love.

And for the first time since the years when *I* was happily in a couple, I feel faith that it will be possible, one day, for me to have what Mark and Camilla have.

The cool part, though, is that I'm content being exactly where I am, without even the slightest craving for a man to complete me.

THE NEXT day, I am sipping a vanilla tea at Diplomatico, a chic brasserie situated right on the Saône River, when my friend Dimitri rolls up. Dimitri is the one who writes about the splendor of Spain, its raging bulls, and its beautiful women and who loves fondant au chocolat as much as I do.

Yeah, he's pretty awesome.

While Dimitri drinks his espresso, he sheds light on my lack of Lyon euphoria.

"It is because your life is more even now," he says. "Things are better for you at home, and you're a happier person. You're not *escaping* to France any longer. You don't have anything to escape from."

"You're right," I say. "The last few times I came here I was running. Running from my marriage, from my divorce, always running from some impossible situation. So when I arrived here, I was always beside myself with joy. It was such a contrast to whatever was going on at home."

"Exactly," he says. "And now that things are more stable, you arrive in Lyon, and it's calm. It's happy. It's good."

"It is good," I say. "And it's always so good to see you."

Dimitri smiles at me, such a sweetheart. "You too, Juliette."

"So, how are things with your girlfriend?" I ask. "Are you guys talking about marriage?" Dimitri is living with his latest girlfriend, and they are in love.

"*Oui*...yes, we have talked about it."

"Wow. What do you think? Do you want to get married?"

"You know how it is...I want both. The wife and the children, but I also want freedom. I know I can't have them both at the same time, though. It is always this same problem with me."

"It's our eternal debate," I say.

"Indeed."

"If you love her, then you have some serious thinking to do," I say.

"I do love her," he says. "So much."

"Well, whatever path you choose, I'm happy for you that you've found love."

And just like with Mark and Camilla, I mean it. I want Dimitri to be happy and if love with a significant other is part of that equation, all the better!

As for me, I'm not worried about when I'll find love again. I'm just thinking about where to get my next croissant.

"Want to meet at the Boulangerie de la Martinière tomorrow morning for a pain au chocolat?" I ask. La Martinière is Dimitri's favorite boulangerie in all of Lyon, and after he first took me and Hannah there for a delightful pastry picnic a couple years ago, it's mine too.

"I would love to, but la Martinière is closed tomorrow," Dimitri says with more than a hint of agitation in his voice.

"Tomorrow is Saturday," I point out. "Aren't the boulangeries only closed on Sundays, along with everything else in France?"

"This used to be the case, yes, but ever since the economy in France went down, people in Lyon have been eating much less frequently at nice restaurants and instead stopping at the boulangerie for a quick sandwich. So, the boulangeries are making more money now, and many of them are closing for the whole weekend because they don't need the business." Dimitri shakes his head at this abomination. "Where are we supposed to get our pastries and baguettes on the weekend? It's horrible."

I am so in love with the fact that the biggest problem in Lyon right now is where to find fresh bread and buttery croissants on the weekends. I also love that this dilemma seems just as important to Dimitri as the eternal question of whether to commit to a relationship or commit to a life of freedom.

"I would love nothing more than to live in Lyon and drink my vanilla tea and talk about the problem of the pastries as each weekend approaches," I say to Dimitri with a grin.

"*C'est vraiment un grand problème!*" he insists.

"I know it's a big problem, which is why I love this country so damn much."

AFTER A lengthy search, I do find one open boulangerie the next day on my walk to the park, so I order not one but *two pains au chocolat* (well, if most of the boulangeries are closed on *both* Saturday and Sunday, I must have two chocolate croissants in order to survive the weekend, obviously).

The serenity inside the expansive Parc de la Tête d'Or surrounds me like a soft, sweet embrace. I have loved this park since the moment I first discovered it as a twenty-year-old student in Lyon. That was thirteen years ago now, and the tree-lined pathways and flower gardens haven't lost an ounce of their charm or beauty. As I stroll along the quiet path, I take photographs of the gorgeous apartments and houses that circle the park, wondering what it would be like to live in one of them. I can see myself sitting in one of the big windows that faces the park, writing my next book, eating a pain au chocolat, and feeling the same deep sense of contentment that I'm feeling right now. My cats Bella and Charlie are there too, purring by my side, and perhaps there will be a man in this picture...but perhaps not.

Either way, in this vision, I am living and enjoying life in a place that makes my heart sing. A man would simply be the cherry on top of this already fulfilling experience.

I spend the afternoon sitting on a park bench, close to one of those outstanding mansions, feeling like one day, a home bordering this tranquil haven in Lyon really could be mine. An apartment overlooking the park would be just fine, too, but I figure if I'm going to visualize this dream, I may as well be living in the mansion.

It's a quiet afternoon. Peaceful. Calm. And as I eat my pain au chocolat and read a most enlightening book titled *The Untethered Soul,* written by Michael Singer, a sense of acceptance washes over me. Acceptance for all that I've experienced. For the extreme highs and the extreme lows. Without them, I may not have made it exactly where I am today, breathing in the scent of flowers and trees and grass in a city that makes my soul dance.

And I am thankful.

TRUE ENLIGHTENMENT comes the next day, as I am sitting in Le Nord, eating a spoonful of decadent *fondant au chocolat.*

Well, if enlightenment can come from a bite of chocolate lava cake on an unassuming Sunday afternoon, then I've found it.

The topic on today's menu, besides chocolate of course, is babies.

And the couple with whom I'm discussing the issue of babies is Isabella and her latest Frenchman—yes, you guessed it, *another Jean!*

To recap, the Jean trajectory has gone like this:

First there was Jean-Michel the architect.

Then Jean-François the forty-nine-year-old sex god.

Next up, Jean-Sébastien the restaurant owner.

And finally we arrive at the newest Jean on Isabella's Jean Menu: Jean-Pierre.

Confused yet?

Yeah, I thought so.

Anyway, Isabella and Jean-Pierre have been together for over a year now. Jean-Pierre is in his mid-forties, Isabella in her mid-twenties, and as I've discussed at length with Isabella, this is the age difference that works for her. She is a very mature twenty-six, and she needs a man who can meet her there. The twenty-year age gap fits perfectly for this lovely woman of the world.

The main problem with these older men is the problem of babies. If Isabella wants to have one, it's likely that the baby ship has sailed for a childless man in his mid-to-late forties.

Since all of my friends in France are so transparent with their love lives, I decide to broach the topic over lunch. Well, *after* I've had my food-gasm from the fondant. Obviously I couldn't even try to have a coherent conversation while *that* was going on.

"So, do you want children?" I ask Jean-Pierre. I already know Isabella's answer to this question—that she is open to having children and definitely doesn't want to be with someone who closes off that possibility for her.

Jean-Pierre doesn't hesitate in his response. "Yes, I would love to have a child."

"With Isabella?" I probe.

"Of course. Why not?" he says, and I can see by his nonchalant attitude that he is totally non-fussed by this idea of procreating with the beautiful Isabella.

Later that afternoon, Isabella and I are alone at Diplomatico, enjoying our cafés on the outdoor terrace in the sun when she admits to me that she and Jean-Pierre haven't been using any form of birth control for close to a year now.

"Whoa, so you could be pregnant right now," I say.

"We're not trying or anything," she says. "But we're not stopping it either. If we had a baby together, I think Jean-Pierre would make a wonderful father."

"And you would be an amazing mother," I say.

"Thank you," she says before taking a sip of her coffee. "But do you think it's odd that nothing's happened yet? That it's been a whole year and I haven't gotten pregnant?"

I can tell Isabella isn't too bent out of shape about this, but being a woman, there is always a concern that someday, when you really want that baby you've been using birth control your whole life to prevent, you won't be able to have one.

Isabella knows that this is exactly what happened to me, but I don't want her to fret for a second that my fate will be hers.

"I wouldn't worry," I tell her. "If it's meant to happen, it will."

"That's what I think," she says.

"If you're not in a rush to get pregnant, and you're just enjoying your relationship, then just keep enjoying it," I say. "You're so young and you have time."

As we continue chatting about relationships and babies and love, I realize that nowhere in this conversation has Isabella mentioned marriage. While a baby may be on her radar—even if it is only on a passive level—marriage isn't even a slight concern. She loves Jean-Pierre, he loves her, and if they get pregnant, cool. Maybe they'll marry one day, maybe they won't, but neither of them seems the least bit anxious about an issue that seems to be on the forefront of most of my friends' minds back in the States.

Where's the ring? Why is he taking so long to propose? If he loves me, why doesn't he want to commit to me for life?

To the contrary, Isabella doesn't care about a ring or a lifetime commitment.

What matters to her is that she is enjoying her time with Jean-Pierre.

And isn't that all that ever really matters when you're in a relationship?

Again, I find myself asking the question: why the obsession with marriage? Why must we lock it down by signing a legal certificate? Why can't we just love the people we love and if there comes a time when that love has overstayed its welcome, we can let each other go, without the hassle and the heartache that divorce adds to the breakup?

I'm not sure if I'll ever reconcile my feelings toward marriage after having to say goodbye to my husband in a court room, but I know that I'm open. I'm open to finding love again, I'm open to the idea that marriage may one day be in the cards for me, but I'm also open to the idea that I may never want to marry again.

Soon, Dimitri, Mark, and Camilla join us for a café at Diplomatico. As I gaze around at their friendly faces, I realize that I don't need to wonder if I'll ever find another soul mate or if I'll marry him one day or not, because today, I am surrounded by soul mates. Isabella, Mark, Camilla, Dimitri, and, of course, my dear city of Lyon—they are some of the greatest loves of my life.

I've already found them, so I can just sit back, relax, and enjoy this spectacular view.

Chapitre 43

A QUICK train ride later, and I am back in the South of France, surrounded by bamboo trees in Marie So and Chris's backyard. We are sipping red wine and celebrating the release of the album we all collaborated on, *City Of Lights.*

When I woke up one morning in San Diego and decided to book a flight to France, I had no idea that my trip would coincide perfectly with Marie So's album release. But as it has been with so many of my experiences in France, this one, too, is perfectly timed.

"I have a proposal for you," Chris says to me.

Marie lets out a laugh before taking a long sip of her wine. "Get ready for this."

I'm intrigued. "What's your proposal?"

"We know that your dream is to live in France one day," Chris starts, "and my dream is to live in California, so will you marry me?"

Marie So is laughing so hard she can barely breathe, and I'm giggling now too, even though I don't quite understand where Chris is going with this.

"Let me explain," Chris says. "I will divorce Marie—"

"He's already talked about this with you, Marie So?"

"Oh yes," she says with a big grin.

"After I divorce Marie, you and I will get married," Chris says to me. "This way you will get the French visa, and I will get an American visa. We will only stay married as long as we need to to be able to keep the visas. Then we will divorce, and you can stay in France, and we can stay in California. What do you think?"

"Awww, it's my first marriage proposal post-divorce!" I say through my laughter. This guy is too much, but I love him.

"So romantic, Chris," Marie says.

"No, no, I'm serious!" Chris says. He keeps outlining the marriage plan, and I can see by the way he has thought this out so intricately that he *is* serious. He's the kind of guy who would really do something this crazy. And like every other risk he has taken in his life, just because it's Chris, it would probably work out beautifully.

"Chris, I love you, but I *really* don't want to get married again," I joke. But they know I'm serious too. While his proposal is enticing—a French visa that would allow me to live in France for the rest of my days, yes please!—it is too risky for my taste. And too ridiculous.

But I understand why Chris is proposing marriage to me in front of his wife. It's because he feels about the California coast the way I feel about France. Ever since he and Marie spent a year in the lovely town of Cardiff-by-the-Sea, his heart has been in California, and he simply *must* go back and retrieve it.

"There are a few other visa options I might try *before* marrying my friend's French husband," I tell the couple, "but if those don't work, I'm all yours."

To this, we clink our glasses and spend the afternoon listening to Marie So's brilliant new album, and to the songs we co-created as this lovely spring day dances on.

MARRIAGE IS the topic of the evening, too, as Marie So cooks dinner for the family in her quaint little La Ciotat home.

"Did you know that the feminine word for spouse in French, épouse, means 'to mold'?" Marie says to me as she breaks a bunch of capellini into a pot of boiling water. "This is so telling, don't you think? So often, it is the woman who molds to the man's life, to the way he prefers to do things, and not the other way around."

I think about my own marriage, and the myriad of times when I did just this. It was precisely when I *stopped* molding to who my husband was and instead stood firmly in who *I* was that our marriage began to fall apart.

"Men are who they are. No apologies," I say. "Women tend to make more adjustments and compromises to keep everyone happy. But in doing so, they end up losing parts of themselves."

"You know what I think is the saddest thing?" Marie continues. "When women stay in a marriage for money. They are afraid to leave and to have to support themselves."

"I was afraid," I say. "And it's been messy, but I'm okay. I survived."

"I've never been afraid of this," Marie says. "My marriage with Chris is wonderful, but if things ever fall apart someday, I would never stay and be miserable just for money. I would go. I would figure it out. I've always known this about myself. My happiness is more important than depending on a man for money."

Marie affirms this with such confidence, that even though I have actually left my marriage and faced the financial unknown, I find myself admiring her courage and strength. She is an artist, just like me, yet she harbors no fear about finding her way, with or without a man. The fact that she is a mother makes her statement all the more courageous.

Perhaps this is one of the reasons why her marriage works so well. Because it is more of a conscious partnership than a marriage. They are not together because they decided to sign a marriage certificate in Vegas on a whim. They are together because they choose to be.

It's liberating to see such a couple in action.

When Marie hands me a plate of pasta and asks if I would like some more wine, I smile, thinking the exact same thing I thought the last time I was here—*yes, I'll have more of what you're having.*

THE NEXT day, my future French husband, his wife, and their two kids whisk me away on a whirlwind day-tour of Marseille. After illegally parking their massive van on the crowded city streets—traffic and parking rules in France are irrelevant—we eat a delicious meal of couscous and sweet tea. Then we hop back in the van and circle the Vieux Port, while I aim my iPhone out the car window and snap photos of the Ferris wheel and the sailboats like the happy tourist I am.

The skies are a bold shade of blue, and the wind is fierce as we arrive on a hilltop that houses the Notre-Dame de la Garde Basilica along with a most spectacular view of the city and the Mediterranean Sea. The first photo that Chris takes of me and Marie So and this beautiful vista has all of us doubling over in laughter. The wind has blown whole sections of our long brown hair straight up into the air, so in addition to our jubilant smiles, we now have wild hair antennae sticking straight up into the sky.

Marie and I are laughing for a good fifteen minutes at this photo, and it is in my teary laughter that I realize how lucky I am to have a French family who calls me their own. A girlfriend with whom I can laugh until I cry.

How lucky I am to be gazing out over a new French city which I have only just begun to explore.

How lucky I am to be standing on the roof of the world, on a majestic hilltop as my hair blows like a wild woman and my laughter echoes through the skies.

The darkness is behind me. I know that now.
And all I can think is:
How beautiful is this life.

WHEN I arrive back at Stéphane's apartment in Paris a few days later, my bag seems to have gotten even lighter. I don't know how, but it is.

And as for me, I'm certainly a few pounds heavier with all of the croissants and chocolate and butter and cheese I have consumed, but I feel more like myself than ever before.

I am in the perfect state to welcome my close friend James—the hard-hitting Manhattan attorney who grilled Nick over dinner—and his amazing partner, Shawn, for one last jaunt around Paris.

Shawn is sleeping off the jet lag in their fancy hotel room at the Hôtel San Regis while James and I set off down the Champs-Élysées in search of lunch. This is James's first trip to Paris, and he's barely walked a block, but I can see that he's already in heaven. That may have something to do with the pain au chocolat I have just handed him—the pain au chocolat that he is devouring and moaning over—but I think it has a little bit to do with Paris, too.

We find a chic little bistro just off the Champs on rue Marbeuf. It's called Le Cosy Paris, and after we order our magical spring salads along with some *frites*, we get cozy and get down to gossip.

"So, I want to move to France," I announce to my friend.

James is totally nonplussed; he's heard me say this before. In fact, everyone I know has heard me say this before.

"What are you running from this time?" James is, of course, referring to all of my obvious "escape trips" to France where I was fleeing my marital problems, my divorce, and everything in between.

"That's the thing," I say. "I'm not escaping anything this time. I'm not running from anyone or any horrible life situation. My life at home is good now. It's stable. I'm happy in San Diego, and I know I could be happy here too, but the key is that I don't *need* to move to France to be happy."

"Even still, do you think you have unrealistic expectations of how perfect it will be here?"

I have to think on this a moment, but I know my answer. "No, it's like this. My relationship with France has evolved in the same way that my relationship with men and sex has—I don't have unrealistic expectations that any of them will keep me happy and fulfilled. That's on *me* to do."

"Life is *so* much better when you're getting laid, though," James chimes in.

"Agreed," I say, and to this, we clink our wineglasses.

"This is the first time, ever, that you've been totally and completely single," James points out. "You've always been running from or to *someone*."

"I know," I say. "And this would be the first time I'm going somewhere just for me."

"Well, obviously Shawn and I will get a Paris apartment if you move here."

"Obviously," I say, loving how quickly James has jumped on board to my new life plan.

Later that evening, after I've introduced James and Shawn to the café scene in Paris, and we have sufficiently stuffed ourselves full of wine, bread, and cheese, we are strolling down the Seine at sunset, laughing and taking photographs, when I realize that if I move here, I won't only have all of my fabulous France friends to keep me company, I'll have nonstop visitors from the States, too.

Because honestly, who doesn't want to come to Paris?

IT'S MY last day in Paris, and I have decided to take my friends on a walking tour of Montmartre. I haven't visited these winding hilltops since I was last here with Nick, and despite the fact that my friends and I walk almost the exact same path as those two lovers long ago—strolling up rue Lepic; meandering past Café Montmartre and Le Consulat, La Maison Rose and Au Lapin Agile; and even stopping in a boulangerie for *pains au chocolat* and *croissants aux amandes*—I find that I am not longing to have Nick by my side.

I am amazed that it can be so, but these cobblestone streets aren't haunted with our tragic love story the way I thought they would be. Yes, I can still feel Nick here. I can still see us holding hands, stealing kisses in secret courtyards, and whispering sweet and dirty somethings in each other's ears. But I'm not haunted by him, by us, by the way we were.

Soon, I find myself gazing up at a tall red brick house with bunches of red flowers spilling over its charming black balconies, and I remember.

This was the house.

The house Nick said would be ours, if we ever lived in Paris together.

In our most recent e-mail exchange, Nick and I were discussing whether or not we would honor our promise to meet again in Paris during the promised five years. Finally, Nick affirmed that yes, we absolutely *must* wander the streets of Paris again.

I agreed that it would be lovely to spend more time in Paris together.

But today, as I am admiring the home that we once chose to be our own, the home that will never be our own, I realize that perhaps it would be even lovelier to let the memory of us live on in these cobblestone streets. To let the magic of us swirl through the trees with the hot wind that blows on this magnificent spring day. And to let the romance of us pave the way for new pairs of lovers to set fire to the streets of Paris, the way we did so well.

I don't know if I will meet Nick again in Paris, or if I will ever see him again at all.

And I don't know if I will ever stop missing the closeness, the comfort, and the beautiful friendship I shared with my husband.

What I do know is that the love I feel for both of these men doesn't obey the confines of marriage or divorce. It doesn't fit neatly into any of the relationship boxes that society has labeled as the norm.

My love for them is boundless, limitless, and it exists outside of the labels we place on each other—husband and wife, ex-husband and ex-wife, married lover and mistress.

The titles don't matter to me.

All that matters to me is that love was shared, and that love will continue to live on.

Because love, as I've learned, will never die.

Perhaps this is the perfect ending to my fairy tale—the realization that there is no perfect ending. The boy doesn't always get the girl, and the girl doesn't always get the boy.

Instead the boy misses the girl, and the girl misses the boy. They will miss each other forever.

But the girl is stronger because of it, and she no longer needs the boy to survive.

She has Paris, she has her friends, but most of all, she has the love within herself.

And this is the greatest ending I ever could have hoped for.

L'Épilogue

THREE MONTHS LATER

IT IS a hot summer morning in San Diego, and I am sitting at my desk, hands poised over my laptop, about to buy the most important plane ticket of my life: a one-way flight to Paris.

Before I hit the *Confirm* button, I must be sure that everything is in order:

Sufficient funds in the bank to purchase plane ticket: *Check.*

Appointment with the French Consulate in Los Angeles to apply for my Visa: *Check.*

Diet plan for my giant cat Bella so that I can bring her on the plane with me: *Check.*

Anxiety medication for my cat Charlie so that he will survive our eleven-hour flight to Paris: *Check.*

Gift bags filled with ear-plugs, chocolate, and Xanax for all of the unsuspecting passengers who will have the misfortune of sitting near me and my giant, howling cats on the flight: *Check.*

Gratitude for everything in my life that has led me to this moment, this moment where I am finally going to take the leap I have wanted to take for years: *Check.*

Faith that even though I don't know exactly *how* everything will work out, I still know that it *will* work out: *Check.*

And finally, the moment comes when I know there is nothing left for me to do but trust in the inherent wisdom of my heart that is not whispering, but shouting: *You left your husband, you left your lover, what the hell are you waiting for, girl?*

It's time to jump!

And so, with a simple click of my mouse, I do.

I jump.

I'm nervous and elated and tears are rolling down my cheeks. But these are joyful tears, the kind that come when you've embraced who you are and you decide, once and for all, to follow your heart.

And so it is, that in the quiet of my little bedroom in San Diego, with only my massive, purring cats to hear the news, I make the official announcement:

I'm moving to France.

La Fin
—
The End

My Wish for You, Dear Reader

May you love truly so that you may know true loss
May you lose so that you break open
May you be broken so that your light seeps in

May your light shatter the darkness

And in its place, may you rediscover
The unending source of love
That has always existed within you

May you blossom in this love
In your own unique way

And trust, in your heart
That where there is love,
Wounds are healed
The lost are found
And dreams—even your wildest—come true

May you not fear loss, dear reader

For within that loss,
Lies your greatest power
Your greatest strength

Your source
Your love
Your light
Your truth

Within that loss
Lies the greatest gift
This Universe has ever known:

You

READ ON FOR A SPECIAL PREVIEW

CONFESSIONS
OF A CITY GIRL

LOS ANGELES

BY  JULIETTE Sobanet

PROLOGUE

"NATASHA, *DARLING,*" my mother coos softly, her voluptuous pile of platinum blonde curls sprawling over the crisp white hospital pillow.

"Yes, Ava." I take her clammy palm in mine, trying not to notice the silver roots lining her weathered forehead or the way her chest rattles every time she tries to speak.

Even from this sterile Los Angeles hospital room, I can still hear my mother's young, devastatingly glamorous voice belting out tunes in our Hollywood Hills home, see her prancing around in a scarlet negligée, breasts spilling over lace, smudged mascara rolling down rouged cheeks, messy curls tumbling over bare shoulders...and *always* a man waiting in the bedroom.

That ever-present image of the infamous Ava Taylor—who will forever be adored by the film-going masses for her scandalous, dazzling beauty on the silver screen—will haunt my dreams long after we say goodbye.

"The envelope," she whispers, losing strength. "In my purse."

With trembling fingers, I reach for her pink Dior bag, rifle through the makeup, the pill bottles, and finally emerge with a manila envelope.

"Open it," she urges, choking on her words, the glamour being sucked straight out of her with each beep of the machines at her bedside.

I pull a packet of papers from the envelope, combing the first page quickly as I find myself praying she'll hang on just a little longer. For as much pain as this woman has caused me, I'm amazed at how deeply I still love her, at how much I am hanging on to her every word, every breath.

"Downtown DC photography gallery sold to Ava Taylor," I read out loud, instantly recognizing the address as that of a popular gallery I've visited, and adored, many times. "Named *The Natasha Taylor Photography Gallery…*" I trail off, lifting a shocked gaze to my mother. "Ava, what is this?"

"Your photographs, Natasha—it's time for you to release them to the world." The cancer in her lungs has made her voice barely recognizable, but it hasn't stolen that mischievous twinkle in her eyes. "In your very own gallery."

"But you know I take family portraits—wholesome photos of glowing pregnant women and husbands kissing their wives' bellies. Not exactly the kind of photos you'd feature in a prominent DC photography gallery."

The twinkle dissipates as my mother levels a serious gaze at me. "Natasha, *dear*, don't get me started on the misery that is your life." She stops to clear her throat, the way she always does when she's about to judge me. "I simply cannot bear the thought of it— you photographing all of those happy families, shoving it in your face day in and day out that you can't get pregnant with that stuffy professor husband of yours who was *never* suited for you."

"Oh, and you know me so well, do you?" I snap. This isn't the time to let out the years of pent-up anger toward the woman who was supposed to be a mother to me, but after that comment, I can't help myself.

"Better than you might think...and that man—well, he doesn't deserve you, Natasha. He doesn't see the beautiful dancer I once knew." My mother's emerald gaze cuts right through me, and I can't handle it. I never could.

"Well, I'm sorry my life, my choice in a husband, and my body's inability to make a baby have been such a disappointment to you. And we both know that I am not the *only* one to blame for the demise of my dance career."

A maddening grin spreads across her full lips. "Oh, let's not be so dramatic," she taunts. "*I'm* the actress here, after all. Yes, the end of your dance career was...*tragic*...but let's not go there today." With a trembling hand, she points to the cup of water on her bedside tray. I swallow my anger as I press the cup to her mouth. She is only able to take the tiniest of sips—what irony after all those years spent guzzling straight from the bottle.

"Back to the photographs—I'm not referring to your family photography, darling. While beautiful, we both know that *those* aren't the photographs that will draw in the masses and make you a huge success."

Dread coats my stomach as I realize where she is going with this.

"It's time to reveal all of the photographs you've taken *of me* over the years. The good and the bad, my darling. It's time for the public to see the real Ava Taylor. The one only *you* knew."

"But you've seen those photos. They're...they're..." I trail off, a slideshow of images flashing through my mind.

Ava in the glamorous emerald evening gown she wore to the Oscars, sobbing and slumped on the kitchen floor, a cigarette pressed between her lips, a bottle of whiskey in hand; Ava lounging naked on the back deck, legs spread for the world to see, downing a martini; Ava in a jealous rage, hurling a black vase at one of her lovers.

Ever since I was a little girl, I've been photographing every disastrous, glitzy, humiliating moment of growing up with my troubled Hollywood mother. It was my way of dealing with her, with my lack of a childhood—documenting the mess instead of partaking in it.

"They're raw," she says, interrupting my stream of memories. "They're me. And I'm not giving you this gallery unless you agree to feature them in your opening exhibit."

I sigh, exhausted by her, by years of her unreasonable demands. "You've got to be kidding me."

"The stipulations are all there in my will. The date for the exhibit has already been set. Six weeks from today."

"Six weeks? But you know I'm in the middle of my third round of IVF, and I have shoots scheduled every single weekend for months...shoots that I can't cancel or we'll lose the house in Georgetown. I don't have the time or the energy to put this together right now. And besides, you *don't* want me to release those photographs to the public."

She snatches the papers from my hands and gives me a slight scratch with her long red nails in the process. "Do you hear yourself? Don't you see the train wreck that has become your life?" Her voice wavers, swallowed up by her raspy lungs. "It's too late for me, darling...my train has already wrecked and burned. But it's not too late for you." She sucks in a loud, wheezing breath before continuing on her final diatribe.

"I know I wasn't always there for you, not in the way you needed me, but just this once, let me try. I'm giving you a chance to change your life, make your career dreams come true. Screw IVF, screw that dreadfully boring husband of yours, and screw that godforsaken house that you've never been able to afford. This obsession you have with creating a *normal* family...it's time to let it go, Natasha." She coughs deeply, her sick, withering body shuddering underneath the sheets.

"You came from *my* womb, and you will forever be unique because of that. Normal just isn't in our genes, darling." A nauseating shade of gray spreads down her face as she shakes the papers at me. "*This* is your story, Natasha. And it's time for you to tell it."

I take the papers from my mother, nodding numbly, realizing that even on her deathbed, even as she is giving me the first true gift she has ever given me, she has still found a way to make this all about her.

But then another thought—one that I do not want to give any credit to—pops into my mind. I wonder if somewhere, deep down, she does have a maternal instinct, after all.

Ava glances around the bleak white hospital room, down at the tubes in her arms, and finally to the machines at her bedside, and there it is. That impenetrable sadness, spilling down her porcelain skin. I am so used to seeing this look of desperation in her eyes—the look she has only ever shown to me—and yet every time, it pains me. Rips my heart to shreds.

I both hate her and love her immensely.

But above all, I cannot bear to see her suffer a moment longer.

"Promise me, Natasha. Promise me you'll do it," she begs softly.

Her outburst has taken every last ounce of energy she had left. Tears cloud her beautiful green eyes, and I know I must give her what she wants.

I squeeze her hands in mine and lean over to kiss her forehead. "I promise, Mom. I promise."

Her breathing slows, and just when I think she's leaving me forever, a whisper escapes her lips. "It's *Ava*, darling," she corrects. "You know the 'M' word makes me feel old."

With a dramatic bat of her eyelashes and one sharp inhale, *those* are my mother's last words.

ACKNOWLEDGMENTS

I am humbled when I think of all of the beautiful souls who have crossed paths with mine along this journey. To all who have helped me become the woman I am today, whether it was through loving me or challenging me, or a combination of both, my gratitude for you is immeasurable.

I would like to send a heartfelt thank you to my amazingly talented editor, Andrea Hurst. Your insight and guidance helped me take my story to a depth I didn't think I was ready for, which was exactly why I needed to go there, both in my writing and in my personal journey. Thank you, thank you, thank you.

My sincerest thanks goes to my incredible design team, Blue Harvest Creative, for honoring my love of the color pink and for giving me the Paris cover of my dreams.

To my awesome agent, Kevan Lyon. I will always be so grateful to you for signing me on as a bright-eyed first-time novelist, and for believing in me all the way. I would also like to thank my fabulous foreign rights agent, Taryn Fagerness, for bringing my stories to new landscapes.

It is with my deepest gratitude that I thank all of my lovely friends in France who have so graciously shared their homes, their lives, and their stories with me. I am especially grateful to Sylvia, Anne-Laure, Stéphane, Valérie, Michelle, Roniece, Isabella, Dimitri, Mark, Camilla, Benoît, Marie So, Christophe, Mary Kay, and Lisa. The times I have spent with all of you in the past several years have quite simply been some of the most magical, beautiful days of my life. *Merci.*

I am incredibly blessed to have the love and support of a most amazing team of friends, whom I consider family. There are too many of you to name, but I would specifically like to thank the following friends for helping me to survive my divorce and for encouraging me to write this book: Angie, Amanda, Kelly K., Liz, James, Shawn, Deirdre, Bridget, Christine, Sophie, Jimena, Sebastian, Sarah T., Alejandra, Kelly B., Dan, Carl, Micah, Coby, Ryan, Jan, and Belinda.

Thank you to my beautiful friend Katie for traveling to France with me, for being there for me during some of the most trying times of my divorce, and for just being you. You're fabulous.

I would also like to thank my dear friends Mike and Leah for making the decision to come to brunch on that random Sunday. Your story has changed my life in so many beautiful ways and has opened me up to a spiritual journey that I never anticipated. What a gift you have given me.

I am forever indebted to my very first critique partners and writing teachers: Karen, Sharon, and Mary. I wouldn't be here without your wisdom and love.

I have been fortunate enough to cross paths with a few healers along my journey, and I would like to send them my warmest thanks for all they have done to help me heal, grow, and thrive. Thank you to Ananda, Lorraine, Shawna, Leslie, Brent, and Joe for being these angels for me.

My immense love and gratitude goes to a special baby girl named Kaia who helped bring me back to life. Your light, even as an infant, was so bright that I couldn't help but smile every day in your presence. Thank you.

I am deeply grateful to my mom and dad for bringing me into this world, for encouraging my creative streak, and for loving me.

To my big beautiful cats, Bella and Charlie. This may be the first time a writer has thanked her pets in the acknowledgments, and although I am crossing dangerously into *Crazy Cat Lady Territory*, I don't care. Your purring and your love have saved me and healed me in so many ways. Thank you.

From the bottom of my heart, I would like to thank all of the writers who have blazed the trail in writing their truth. I am especially grateful to these brilliant authors: Elizabeth Gilbert, Cheryl Strayed, Jewel, Jeannette Walls, Susanna Sonnenberg, and Anaïs Nin. Your words have lifted me up in some of my darkest times, and your bravery has inspired me to embrace my truth and to write that truth. Thank you for your courage.

My most heartfelt thanks goes out to all of my lovely, loyal readers. Your continued support for my writing amazes me every day, and I am beyond thankful for each and every one of you. I hope my story has helped you to recognize that hidden within each loss you experience, there is an immense opportunity for growth, and that no matter how alone you may feel, *you are loved.*

And finally, to the three greatest loves of my life. You know who you are.

Thank you.

ABOUT THE AUTHOR

JULIETTE SOBANET is the award-winning author of five Paris-based romance and mystery novels and four short stories. Her books have hit the Top 100 Bestseller Lists on Amazon US, UK, Germany, and France, and her work has been published in Italian and Romanian, with more on the way. A former French professor, Juliette holds a B.A. from Georgetown University and an M.A. from New York University in Paris. She is a blogger for *The Huffington Post*, and she writes about her personal experience with divorce on her blog, *Confessions of a Romance Novelist*. Juliette is currently planning her move to France, where she will fulfill her dream of writing full-time while devouring chocolate croissants every morning and sipping wine at sidewalk cafés every evening. *Meet Me in Paris* is her first work of nonfiction.

Visit Juliette's website at
www.juliettesobanet.com.